The Blaxploitation Horror Film

ADAPTATION, APPROPRIATION AND THE GOTHIC

HORROR STUDIES

Series Editor
Xavier Aldana Reyes, Manchester Metropolitan University

Editorial Board
Stacey Abbott, Roehampton University
Linnie Blake, Manchester Metropolitan University
Harry M. Benshoff, University of North Texas
Fred Botting, Kingston University
Steven Bruhm, Western University
Steffen Hantke, Sogang University
Joan Hawkins, Indiana University
Alexandra Heller-Nicholas, Deakin University
Agnieszka Soltysik Monnet, University of Lausanne
Bernice M. Murphy, Trinity College Dublin
Johnny Walker, Northumbria University
Maisha Wester, Indiana University Bloomington

Preface

Horror Studies is the first book series exclusively dedicated to the study of the genre in its various manifestations – from fiction to cinema and television, magazines to comics, and extending to other forms of narrative texts such as video games and music. Horror Studies aims to raise the profile of Horror and to further its academic institutionalisation by providing a publishing home for cutting-edge research. As an exciting new venture within the established Cultural Studies and Literary Criticism programme, Horror Studies will expand the field in innovative and student-friendly ways.

The Blaxploitation Horror Film

ADAPTATION, APPROPRIATION AND THE GOTHIC

JAMIL MUSTAFA

UNIVERSITY OF WALES PRESS
2023

For Dennis

© Jamil Mustafa, 2023

All rights reserved. No part of this book may be reproduced in any material form (including photocopying or storing it in any medium by electronic means and whether or not transiently or incidentally to some other use of this publication) without the written permission of the copyright owner except in accordance with the provisions of the Copyright, Designs and Patents Act. Applications for the copyright owner's written permission to reproduce any part of this publication should be addressed to the University of Wales Press, University Registry, King Edward VII Avenue, Cardiff, CF10 3NS.

www.uwp.co.uk

British Library Cataloguing-in-Publication Data

A catalogue record for this book is available from the British Library.

ISBN   978-1-78683-997-8
eISBN 978-1-78683-998-5

The right of Jamil Mustafa to be identified as author of this work has been asserted in accordance with sections 77 and 79 of the Copyright, Designs and Patents Act 1988.

Typeset by Chris Bell, cbdesign
Printed on demand by CPI Group (UK) Ltd, Croydon, CR0 4YY

Contents

Acknowledgements	ix
List of illustrations	xi

Introduction
Blaxploitation, Adaptation/Appropriation
and the (Black) Gothic 1

1. **Queer Bloodlines**
   The Vampire 15

2. **Making Monsters**
   Frankenstein's Creature 63

3. **Beyond 'the animal within'**
   Jekyll/Hyde and the Werewolf 91

4. **Body and Soul**
   The Zombie and the Evil Spirit 125

Conclusion
The Legacy of the Blaxploitation Horror Film 165

Notes	175
Bibliography	209
Filmography	227
Index	233

Acknowledgements

I AM GRATEFUL TO Sarah Lewis, Head of Commissioning at the University of Wales Press, for moving this book forward and for keeping it (and me) on track. I would also like to thank Xavier Aldana Reyes for the advice that he offered when we initially discussed this project. Finishing it in three years would not have been possible without the support of those at Lewis University who awarded me a very timely and valuable sabbatical. I am also deeply indebted to the readers whose constructive commentary on the first draft of the manuscript greatly improved the final version. Finally, my heartfelt thanks are due to colleagues, friends and family members who were brave enough to ask, 'What's the book about?', and patient enough to listen to my answer. Writing can be an isolated and isolating experience, but their interest and encouragement kept me connected.

List of Illustrations

Figure 1. Blacula (William Marshall) attacks Billy Schaffer (Rick Metzler) in *Blacula* (1972). AIP/Photofest   40

Figure 2. Blacula (William Marshall) attacks Willis Daniels (Richard Lawson) in *Scream Blacula Scream* (1973). AIP/Photofest   53

Figure 3. Jack Moss (Rosey Grier) is conjoined with Dr Maxwell Kirshner (Ray Milland) in *The Thing with Two Heads* (1972). AIP/Photofest   78

Figure 4. Eddie Turner (Joe DeSue) degenerates into a monster in *Blackenstein* (1972). Exclusive International/Photofest   85

Figure 5. Dr Henry Pride (Bernie Casey) transforms into his alter ego in *Dr. Black, Mr. Hyde* (1976). Dimension Pictures/Photofest   101

Figure 6. Tom Newcliffe (Calvin Lockhart) targets the werewolf in *The Beast Must Die* (1974). Cinerama Releasing Corporation/Photofest   119

Figure 7. Bishop Garnet Williams (William Marshall) employs syncretic clothing and objects in *Abby* (1974). AIP/Photofest   145

Figure 8. Memphis (Wally Taylor) and Jenny (Marlene Clark) watch Billie (Avis McCarther) in *Lord Shango* (1975). Bryanston Pictures/Photofest — 147

Figure 9. Petey (Rudy Ray Moore) holds the Devil's cane in *Petey Wheatstraw* (1977). Generation International Pictures/Photofest — 161

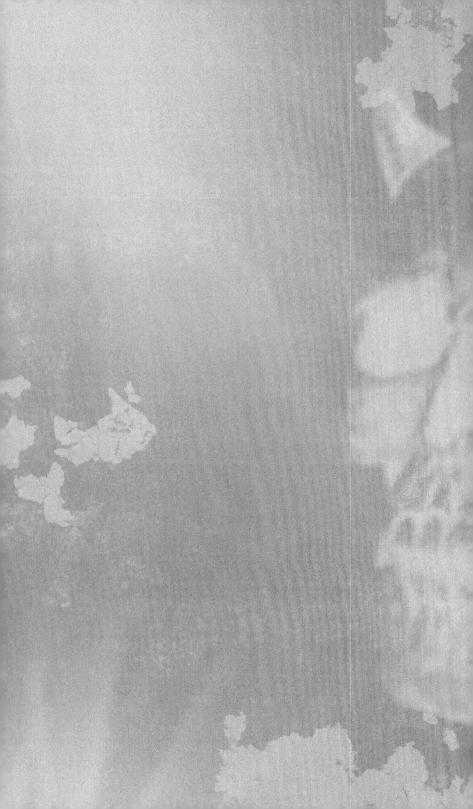

Introduction

Blaxploitation, Adaptation/Appropriation and the (Black) Gothic

WITH THE RELEASE of films including *Cotton Comes to Harlem* (Ossie Davis, 1970), *Sweet Sweetback's Baadasssss Song* (Melvin Van Peebles, 1971), *Shaft* (Gordon Parks, 1971) and *Super Fly* (Gordon Parks Jr, 1972), a genre emerged that came to be known as 'Blaxploitation'.[1] This pejorative portmanteau word for what Novotny Lawrence characterises as 'the flood of black-oriented films depicting sex, violence, vigilantes, pimps, and drug dealers'[2] racialised 'exploitation' cinema, an industry term used since the 1950s to describe films that had 'low, substandard budgets', capitalised on 'topical issues and controversial trends, thus enabling sensational promotion', and 'included explicit and stimulating subject matter'.[3] 'Blaxploitation' was coined by Junius Griffin, once the president of the Beverly Hills-Hollywood branch of the National Association for the Advancement of Colored People (NAACP).[4] Throughout the 1970s, Griffin and others working for civil rights protested against what they viewed as the white film industry's distortion of Black lives, and its exploitation of the intense desire of African American audience members to see themselves represented on screen. As Jesse Algeron Rhines explains, 'These films were released during the height of the civil rights/Black liberation movement, yet their subject matter of sex, violence and "super-cool" individualism was the antithesis of what contemporaneous [B]lack political organisations . . . supported for Black people'.[5] These groups advocated for racial self-determination, empowerment, pride and solidarity – values that, while hardly absent from Blaxploitation films, were generally obscured by their luridness. In 1972, the NAACP, the Southern Christian Leadership Conference and the Urban League formed the Coalition Against Blaxploitation, which sought to establish a ratings system for Black films ranging from 'superior' to 'thoroughly objectionable'.[6] This proposal 'sparked a public debate that included a host of actors, producers, directors, writers, and intellectuals', some of whom argued that audiences were the best judges of content, and that Blaxploitation films not only provided the representation that viewers craved, but also created opportunities for African Americans within the film industry.[7]

A neutral characterisation of Blaxploitation would note that the genre's protagonists are strong African American men, and sometimes women, who live and work within Black urban spaces such as Harlem in New York City and Watts in Los Angeles, and who fight against the injustices of white hegemony on (n)either side of the law. John Shaft of *Shaft* is a detective, as are 'Gravedigger' Jones and 'Coffin Ed' Johnson in *Cotton Comes to Harlem*. Youngblood Priest of *Super Fly* is a drug dealer. Sweet Sweetback, the eponymous protagonist of *Sweet Sweetback's Baadasssss Song*, is a sex worker turned rebel. All these diverse figures 'are strong because they possess the ability to survive in and navigate the [white] establishment while maintaining their blackness', Lawrence writes. They 'may work for or within the system; however, they do so on their own terms and for the betterment of the black community'.[8] These empowered and empowering characters featured in a wide range of narratives, since 'Blaxploitation incorporated elements of many other genres' and included comedies, westerns, melodramas, contemporary dramas and horror films.[9]

The appeal that Blaxploitation held for African American filmgoers was crucial to the business of cinema. 'By the late 1960s, Hollywood, in the midst of a financial collapse, was desperate for an influx of cash', Paula J. Massood explains. 'It began to target an African American audience, in part because it was estimated that the black box office generated somewhere between 30 and 40 percent of the total American box office.'[10] Indeed, according to Donald Bogle, 'the black audience's support of the new black films may well have saved the commercial film industry at a time when general ticket sales were in a slump'.[11] Bogle goes on to claim that Blaxploitation is important in cinematic history not only because it was so lucrative, but also because 'the success of the black-oriented films helped change the look and feel of the American feature', influencing works including Martin Scorsese's *Mean Streets* (1973) and *Taxi Driver* (1976), together with Sidney Lumet's *Dog Day Afternoon* (1975) and John G. Avildsen's *Rocky* (1976).[12]

Although these profitable and culturally significant films featured Black performers and were marketed to and viewed by Black audiences, the extent to which they represented the creative vision of African Americans is debatable. All four of the films that initiated the Blaxploitation genre had Black directors, as did a number of other notable works in the category. Yet the majority 'were written, directed, and produced by whites'.[13] In fact, 'fewer than one-fifth were under African American control. Even fewer came from Black-owned production houses, and fewer still were financed and/or distributed by African Americans'.[14] Thus, in a *New York Times* article, 'Black Movie Boom – Good or Bad?', Griffin begins his attack on Blaxploitation by claiming, 'At present, black movies are a "rip-off" enriching major white film producers and a very few black people. These films are taking our money while feeding us a forced diet of violence, murder, drugs and rape. Such films are the cancer of "Blaxploitation" gnawing away at the moral fiber of our community.'[15]

While useful, Griffin's term of opprobrium is problematic, since drawing a clear line between exploitation and representation can be difficult. Although Blaxploitation films are by no means accurate depictions of everyday life or people, they do, as Lawrence points out, present African Americans 'in a variety of three-dimensional roles' and focus on 'a black hero or heroine who is both socially and politically conscious', a protagonist who is 'surrounded by other black characters who are integral to the plot', not 'a token character'.[16] Furthermore, in their era these films engaged with issues of deep concern to their audiences, including not only racism and the Black Power movement, but also women's and gay rights, the status of the African American family, the role of religion, and relations between the community and the police. Bogle contends that Blaxploitation films 'played on the needs of black audiences for heroic figures without answering those needs in realistic terms', but he concedes that 'many films from this period today retain a certain edge' and that their 'political and social messages' provided 'insights and comments on the quality of life in America'.[17] As Mikel J. Koven has observed, Blaxploitation films also spoke to 'contemporary fears and anxieties' that had 'direct relevance for black communities'.[18] Such fears were addressed directly in Blaxploitation horror films.

The first of these was *Blacula* (William Crain, 1972), which was also the first horror film to feature a Black vampire and the first to include contemporary music, both of which were innovations designed to appeal to a Black audience.[19] *Blacula* was directed by an African American, William Crain, one of the earliest graduates of the renowned University of California Los Angeles (UCLA) film school. In the late 1960s, Crain attended UCLA together with Charles Burnett, Larry Clark, Haile Gerima and Jamaa Fanaka, all Black directors who pursued distinguished careers.[20] These and other filmmakers formed what was known as the 'Black Independent Movement' or the 'LA Rebellion', whose goal was to offer an alternative to 'the dominant American mode of cinema', which 'routinely displayed insensitivity, ignorance, and defamation in its onscreen depictions of people of color'.[21] While Crain's films are arguably more mainstream and less groundbreaking than those of his colleagues, he nevertheless resisted the executives at American International Pictures to bring his own ideas to *Blacula*, '[seeking] to make not just a good blaxploitation film but a good horror film, one that would reach beyond its target black audience'.[22] After the success of *Blacula*, Crain enjoyed greater latitude in directing *Dr. Black, Mr. Hyde* (1976), his version of the story of Jekyll and Hyde.[23]

Like Crain, Bill Gunn, an African American playwright, novelist and director, overcame obstacles while making his own vampire film, *Ganja & Hess* (1973). To realise his vision, Gunn, who wrote, directed and acted in the film, had to circumvent Kelly-Jordan Enterprises, the production and distribution company that had commissioned his work. As Christopher Sieving explains, 'To make the movie he really wanted to make, Gunn deemed it was necessary to employ deception. The initial draft he submitted was, therefore, structured much like a conventional genre narrative in order to receive Kelly-Jordan's blessing'.[24] When the studio executives read an updated version of the screenplay, though they were alarmed by the extent to which it departed from standard horror-film fare, they refrained from interfering with Gunn during casting and filming.[25] The director was somewhat less successful in achieving his goals for staffing *Ganja & Hess*. Although he had hoped to hire an all-Black crew, the film's production team was predominantly white, but people of colour did comprise most of the technical crew.[26]

Following Crain and Gunn, a third African American director, the playwright and producer Cliff Roquemore, created *Petey Wheatstraw* (1977), a horror-comedy about a murdered comedian who is resurrected by the Devil and seeks vengeance on his killers. With the significant exceptions of Crain, Gunn and Roquemore, white men directed most Blaxploitation horror films. These include *The Thing with Two Heads* (Lee Frost, 1972), *Scream Blacula Scream* (Bob Kelljan, 1973), *Blackenstein* (William A. Levey, 1973), *Sugar Hill* (Paul Maslansky, 1974), *The Beast Must Die* (Paul Annett, 1974), *The House on Skull Mountain* (Ron Honthaner, 1974), *Abby* (William Girdler, 1974), *Lord Shango* (Ray Marsh, 1975) and *J. D.'s Revenge* (Arthur Marks, 1976).

Scholarship on these films is valuable but limited in scope. Most critics examine what are considered the two best works in the genre, *Blacula* and *Ganja & Hess*.[27] While other films have received far less attention, there are a small number of journal articles and book chapters that consider *Blackenstein*, *The Thing with Two Heads*, *The House on Skull Mountain*, *Sugar Hill* and *Abby*.[28] To the best of my knowledge, only four scholars have taken a broad approach to Blaxploitation horror films. Lawrence devotes one chapter of *Blaxploitation Films of the 1970s: Blackness and Genre* (2008) to horror, though almost all his analysis focuses on *Blacula*.[29] In contrast, Harry M. Benshoff's groundbreaking 'Blaxploitation Horror Films: Generic Reappropriation or Reinscription?' (2000) discusses a number of films, as does Steven Jay Schneider's 'Possessed By Soul: Generic (Dis)Continuity in the Blaxploitation Horror Film' (2002).[30]

The only other critic to consider more than one or two films is Robin R. Means Coleman, who spends a chapter of *Horror Noire: Blacks in American Horror Films from the 1890s to Present* (2011) discussing Blaxploitation horror.[31] She faults the genre for its lack of originality, writing that 'though there were many horror films featuring Blackness, often they are derivative' and '[borrow] from *Dracula*, *Frankenstein*, and *Dr. Jekyll and Mr. Hyde* films'.[32] Since these works are themselves adaptations of literature, her critique of Blaxploitation horror films could go even further by characterising them as degraded copies of copies. Yet what Means Coleman sees as a shortcoming is, in my view, a strength. At once drawing and innovating on not only their cinematic but also their literary precursors, Blaxploitation horror films render well-established characters, plots and themes freshly relevant. When we study how these texts address one another across time periods and cultures, we discover developments and lines of influence that are illuminating and sometimes unexpected. For instance, by following the depiction of law enforcement from Robert Louis Stevenson's *Strange Case of Dr Jekyll and Mr Hyde* (1886) through film adaptations by John S. Robertson, Rouben Mamoulian and Victor Fleming to *Dr. Black, Mr. Hyde*, we realise not only that the police play an ever-larger role in the story, but also that an African American director portrays them more sympathetically than his white counterparts do, and that Crain's understanding of the often shifting line between the legal and the criminal aligns quite well with Stevenson's own nuanced representation of this boundary. Insights such as these emerge naturally when we approach Blaxploitation horror films not as inferior, imitative versions of their antecedents, but rather as important participants in the long-standing conversation between Gothic fiction and film.

Although white authors and filmmakers began this dialogue in the nineteenth and early twentieth centuries, they do not have the last word in it. Neither does the Blaxploitation horror film's ostensible and questionable status as an adaptation of an adaptation, even if accepted, render it somehow subordinate to its precursors. As Linda Hutcheon astutely observes, because adaptation is 'a creative *and* an interpretive act', and 'an extended intertextual engagement with the adapted work', an 'adaptation is a derivation that is not derivative – a work that is second without being secondary. It is its own palimpsestic thing'.[33] Originality, particularly when understood as being first in a potentially endless series, is no longer the hallmark it once was. Adaptation studies has progressed far beyond its initial focus on fidelity to the source text, according to which 'literary cinema [represented] a falling off from the book, an inferior reproduction of a superior original'.[34] As Simone Murray explains, from the 1950s to the present, the field has moved through three phases: fidelity criticism, narratological criticism and current practice.[35] This last, informed by 'post-structuralism, post-colonialism, feminism and cultural studies', seeks to examine how 'adaptations [interrogate] the political and ideological underpinnings of their source texts, translating works across cultural, gender, racial and sexual boundaries to secure cultural space for marginalised discourses'.[36] Translation and space-making of this sort are central to my own project, which I hope will help to situate Blaxploitation horror films within the Gothic ideological and aesthetic traditions, and to shift them and their enduring concerns from the margins towards the centre of literary, film and cultural criticism. Moreover, I hope to elucidate not only how Blaxploitation horror films relate to other cinematic adaptations of canonical Gothic texts, but also how they engage such texts directly. I trace these intermedial, intercultural and interracial relations from Britain to the United States, and from the 1800s to the 1970s. In keeping with the ethos of contemporary adaptation studies, this chronological approach is designed not to privilege literary sources or earlier adaptations, but to offer readers, in particular those unfamiliar with the texts under consideration, a logical and legible account of how Blaxploitation horror films develop from and speak to their forerunners.

This book is the first to concentrate on these films, and the first to connect them with both nineteenth-century Gothic narratives and other twentieth-century cinematic adaptations. Yet my project develops the insights of critics who have recognised that Blaxploitation horror films do something radically new with old cinematic materials. Lawrence calls *Blacula* 'an important revision to the horror genre',[37] and Leerom Medovoi characterises it as 'an intervention within the historical operations of the vampire narrative'.[38] More broadly, Benshoff contends that *Blacula* and similar films 'attempted to reappropriate the [horror] genre for racial advancement'.[39] I concur with their opinions and argue in the following chapters that Blaxploitation horror films appropriated rather than adapted their precursors. As Julie Sanders explains, adaptations are 'reinterpretations of established texts in new generic contexts or perhaps with relocations of an "original" or sourcetext's cultural and/or temporal setting, which may or may not involve a generic shift'.[40] Whereas 'adaptation signals a relationship with an informing sourcetext or original', appropriation involves 'a more decisive journey away from the informing source into a wholly new cultural product and domain'.[41] Like adaptation, appropriation 'may still require the intellectual juxtaposition of (at least) one text against another', but 'the appropriated text or texts are not always as clearly signalled or acknowledged as in the adaptive process'.[42] This understanding of appropriation is clarified by Timothy Corrigan, who explains that 'appropriations are transformative adaptations that remove parts of one form or text (or even the whole) from their original context and insert them in a different context that dramatically reshapes their meaning'.[43] Adaptation and appropriation are therefore different in kind rather than degree, for the latter involves fundamental and profound change.

What film theorists classify as adaptation and appropriation parallels what Henry Louis Gates calls unmotivated and motivated signifying. In *The Signifying Monkey: A Theory of African-American Literary Criticism* (1988), Gates contends that 'repetition and revision are fundamental to black artistic forms', and he sees unmotivated and motivated signifying embedded in linguistic practices ranging from 'the black vernacular tradition to the Afro-American literary tradition'.[44] Unmotivated signifying demonstrates 'not the absence of a profound intention but the absence of a negative critique', while motivated signifying is akin to 'the vernacular ritual of "close reading"' and entails, among other methods, 'critiques of language use, of rhetorical strategy'.[45] Unmotivated signifying involves repetition and alteration; motivated signifying, revision and resistance. As might be expected, the theory of signifying developed by Gates has been applied to films about African Americans by critics including Gladstone Yearwood and Keith Harris.[46] Indeed, Jonathan Munby has employed it to analyse Blaxploitation films, arguing that these works '"signify" on mainstream [i.e., white] film and the expectations that come with it'.[47]

Whereas horror films created by studios such as Universal Pictures and Hammer Film Productions adapt Gothic texts, Blaxploitation horror films appropriate both these texts and their mainstream adaptations, signifying on them not to exploit but to meet the needs of their audiences, and doing so in ways that some might find surprisingly complex, given the multiply marginalised status of these films as occupying a subgenre of two often devalued genres, Blaxploitation and horror. Deploying appropriation and motivated signifying, Blaxploitation horror films revise and resist the notion coded into both Gothic fictions and mainstream horror films that Blackness is invisible or horrible, and that African Americans are monsters. Moreover, in moving Blackness from the periphery to the core of representation, Blaxploitation horror films signify not only on their filmic and literary predecessors, but also on the Freudian notion of the return of the repressed. This concept, as Robin Wood has stressed, is essential to horror, since 'the true subject of the horror genre is the struggle for recognition of all that our civilization represses or oppresses, its re-emergence dramatized, as in our nightmares, as an object of horror, a matter for terror, and the happy ending (when it exists) typically signifying the restoration of repression'.[48] In many mainstream horror films, even before repression is ultimately restored it persists, its return incomplete, since Blackness remains repressed and finds expression only allegorically, as when Mr Hyde or Frankenstein's Creature figures the African American Other. Blaxploitation horror films are therefore arguably purer works of horror than their mainstream counterparts, and certainly more liberal and liberatory ones, though the degree of their progressiveness remains a matter of debate.

These films at least appear to perform the distinctive cultural and ideological work of the Black Gothic, which likewise uses appropriation and motivated signifying to deconstruct and reconstruct the white Gothic. From its inception, the Black Gothic has offset its counterpart. Dating the 'emergence of a black Gothic' to the antebellum period, Charles L. Crow contends that the 'dialogue of black and white is one of the distinguishing facts of American literature', and notes that 'for both black and white writers, the Gothic was a natural form for this discourse'.[49] María M. García Lorenzo discerns within nineteenth-century 'white gothic' the tendency to 'demonize racial otherness', which during its earliest iteration 'black gothic' countered by '[appropriating] gothic imagery or settings in order to portray the cruelty and violence of enslavement'.[50] More generally, Corinna Lenhardt contends that the Gothic is 'an ultra-adaptable, discursively active writing strategy whose racialized (and racializing) quality can also be employed creatively and critically by historically and culturally marginalized groups and individuals'.[51] Maisha Wester draws on the language of deconstruction to explain how the Black Gothic functions to 'both dismantle and dismiss racial constructions at play in dominant Western society and within the Gothic itself',[52] and how it '[goes] beyond merely inverting the color scheme of the gothic trope – blackened evil that torments and is defeated by good whiteness – to destabilizing the entire notion of categories and boundaries'.[53] I would underscore how such radical destabilisation, together with the liberation of the repressed noted above, amplifies and enriches the Black Gothic, for violating boundaries is at the heart of the Gothic in all its myriad forms.[54] Defined not only by its focus on the experiences, agency and subjectivity of African Americans, but also and especially by its transcendence of the racial limits that have circumscribed even a fundamentally transgressive mode, the Black Gothic represents a significant evolution in the Gothic as a whole.

Some scholars have questioned the degree to which Blaxploitation horror films advanced or even participated in the Black Gothic's project of deconstructing boundaries, particularly those related to race, gender and sexuality. Beginning with the notion that the (racial) Other is typically construed as monstrous, and wondering whether this dynamic is still at work when such monsters are 'viewed through the lens of a marginalized racial collective', Benshoff concludes that 'by embracing the racialized monster and turning him or her into an agent of black pride and power, Blaxploitation horror films created sympathetic monsters who helped shift audience identification away from the status quo "normality" of bourgeois white society', though 'female gender and sexuality were still often figured as central conceits of monstrous Otherness'.[55] Citing and magnifying Benshoff's reservations, Wester argues that 'though the monsters were sympathetic, there was no question about their monstrosity', even though it resulted from 'a heinous social system'.[56] In her view, Blaxploitation horror films 'reinforced problematic racial and sexual ideologies, deeply embedding Black sexuality and identity as monstrous even as they appealed to the fantasies of Black audiences'.[57] Moreover, while Black monsters 'fought against antagonists who metaphorised racist oppression', they failed to challenge 'the larger systems of oppression' and their fight died with them, 'suggesting that change was ultimately limited and fleeting'.[58] After critiquing Blaxploitation horror films and before analysing *Ganja & Hess*, Wester separates the latter from the former, asserting that though the film was commissioned by 'a studio hoping to replicate the success of *Blacula*', its writer and director Bill Gunn 'refused to pander to the studio's exploitative desire'.[59] She then claims that 'Gothic tropes allow Gunn to do what Horror tropes could not for other Blaxploitation films: avoid replicating ideologies of Black monstrosity and of aberrant Black sexuality'.[60] While *Ganja & Hess* is located within the privileged category of the Black Gothic, *Blacula* and similar films are relegated to the inferior one of Blaxploitation horror.

Complicating questions of definition still further, Schneider classifies both *Ganja & Hess* and the werewolf film *The Beast Must Die* as 'quasi-blaxploitation horror films' because while 'each of them presents viewers with an ostensible monster, however sympathetic', when considered 'from the standpoint of cinematic-narrative discourse neither film can be said to target a specifically African American commercial audience'.[61] *The Thing with Two Heads*, in which a white man's head is grafted onto a Black man's body, Schneider categorises as 'proto-blaxploitation horror', since its eponymous character is a monster only in 'an ironic sense of the term', which 'merely serves to expose that insidious strain of social prejudice which remains more or less concealed so long as everything – and everyone – remains in its proper place/body'.[62] While interesting, such categorical refinements are less significant than Schneider's taking issue with claims that Blaxploitation horror films by turns resist and reinforce the notion of Blackness-as-monstrosity. On the one hand, he cites instances of Black monsters who are 'none too interested in combatting racial prejudice'.[63] On the other hand, he argues that Black monsters of the 1970s are neither more nor less monstrous, sympathetic or bestial than white ones, and that their monstrosity is not a function of their race.[64] Schneider also notes that while Black female sexuality may be monstrous in some Blaxploitation horror films, it is closely associated with empowerment.[65] His ultimate goal, however, is to move the discussion of these films away from monsters, who 'form far too heterogeneous and racially ambiguous a lot to justify any general claims concerning their allegorical import', and towards 'those central themes and issues which turn up again and again in a wide selection of blaxploitation horror films'.[66] These include interracial relationships, the depiction of African religions as compatible with rather than opposed to Christian worship, and the racist fear that Black 'primitivism' will overtake white 'civilisation'.[67]

Taking a circumspect approach to how African Americans are represented in (Blaxploitation) horror cinema, Peter Hutchings acknowledges that 'blaxploitation horror is an important reference point for later horror films', but also notes that 'the transition it seems to mark from the subjection of black characters in horror films from the 1930s–1960s period to the more active and independent black characters that start showing up in horror from the late 1960s onwards is far from straightforward'.[68] He counsels critics to 'attend to the complexities and nuances of individual films' treatment of blackness and be aware of the ambiguities that often gather around black characters in horror films', which enable them 'to be interpreted in a range of different ways'.[69] This range is certainly evident in the analyses of Benshoff, Wester and Schneider.

In my own view, Blaxploitation horror films, though problematic, constitute an important part of the Black Gothic. Some are less progressive than they could be, but more so than we might expect. Although *Blackenstein* depicts the eponymous monster's attack on a nearly topless Black woman who appears in posters advertising the film, it also features among its leads an accomplished African American woman scientist. *Dr. Black, Mr. Hyde* and *Blacula* likewise showcase Black women scientists at a time when such characters were essentially invisible in films, decades before *Hidden Figures* (Theodore Melfi, 2016) and *Black Panther* (Ryan Coogler, 2018). However incompletely and imperfectly, Blaxploitation horror films resist and revise the racist codes of the white Gothic. For example, *Dr. Black, Mr. Hyde* and *The Beast Must Die* first invert and then destabilise the pernicious white/Black binary opposition, just as *Blacula* and *Scream Blacula Scream* deconstruct that of heteronormative/queer. Yet the relationship between these films and the white Gothic, particularly its original nineteenth-century iterations, is far from entirely adversarial. In fact, even as they appropriate rather than adapt the characters, storylines and themes of their literary antecedents, Blaxploitation horror films retain the essential concerns of these texts, sometimes demonstrating more fidelity to them than is evident in conventional adaptations.

In the chapters that follow, I explore the overdetermined relations among Blaxploitation horror films, their mainstream predecessors, the Gothic texts that inspired both, and issues of concern to Americans in the 1970s. In so doing, while working within a general framework of adaptation theory, I also draw on historicist and psychoanalytic approaches. Moreover, by bringing Gothic texts into conversation with the films they engendered and taking into account the fact that, as Ewan Kirkland points out, 'the history of Gothic fiction is one of adaptation, translation and appropriation',[70] I pose questions about how the Gothic mode shifts across media and cultures. How, and to what purposes, do Blaxploitation horror films appropriate the formal, figurative and thematic features of the Gothic – for example, complex narrative structures, tropes such as the beast within, and themes such as the relationship between the orthodox and the aberrant? Given that adaptation and appropriation involve not only spectrality but also doppelgängers and repetition with a difference, are these practices fundamentally uncanny? To what extent are Blaxploitation horror films inspired by mainstream horror films, themselves inspired by Gothic novels and stories, not only intermedial but also intercultural phenomena? In seeking to answer these questions, I employ Gothic ways of thinking about adaptation and appropriation, construing them as closely bound up with vampirism, monster-making, the uncanny and diabolical possession.

This book explores how mainstream horror films adapt and Blaxploitation horror films appropriate some of the most prominent archetypes in Gothic fiction: the vampire, Frankenstein's Creature, Jekyll/Hyde and the werewolf, the zombie and the evil spirit. Each chapter identifies the social, political, cultural and psychological work that these canonical Gothic figures perform across media, beginning with fiction and moving from mainstream adaptations to Blaxploitation appropriations. Chapter 1, 'Queer Bloodlines: The Vampire', contends that Blaxploitation horror films draw on Black Power and the intersection of civil rights and gay rights to forge strong links among lineage, vampirism and queerness. Chapter 2, 'Making Monsters: Frankenstein's Creature', demonstrates how *Blackenstein* and *The Thing with Two Heads* determine whether monsters are born or made, and how making monsters involves collage and (in)justice. Chapter 3, 'Beyond "the animal within": Jekyll/Hyde and the Werewolf', argues that *Dr. Black, Mr. Hyde* depicts not only division and opposition but also multiplicity and hybridity, particularly with respect to race. Chapter 4, 'Body and Soul: The Zombie and the Evil Spirit', shows how uncanny doubling is vital to stories about zombies and the possessed, as are the (dis)empowerment of women and conflicts between and about religions. The Conclusion, 'The Legacy of the Blaxploitation Horror Film', describes how thematic concerns established in the 1970s remain relevant today and outlines directions for future research.

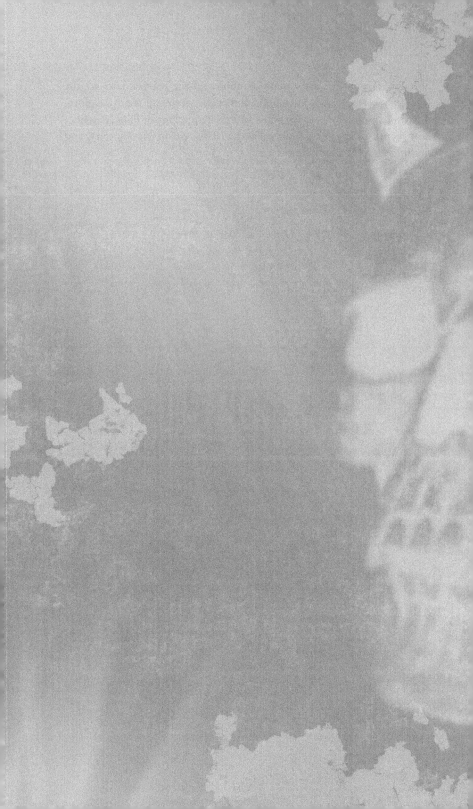

1

Queer Bloodlines

The Vampire

BLACULA IS NOT ONLY the first Blaxploitation horror film, but also the only one to include the Gothic figure who inspired it, and from whom its eponymous title derives. It opens in eighteenth-century Transylvania, where Dracula vampirises an African prince, Mamuwalde, who emerges from his coffin nearly two centuries later to terrorise Los Angeles. The distinctive frame narrative of *Blacula* reinforces the film's association with Gothic fiction in general and Bram Stoker's *Dracula* (1897) in particular. The 'frame function' is 'to guide and even to enable interpretation',[1] and Gothic frames serve their function by authenticating and buffering the potentially unreliable and typically outré materials they enclose. They thereby facilitate the willing suspension of disbelief and ease readers into and out of extraordinary tales. The Gothic frame often resembles the transgressive text(s) that it encompasses by performing its functions imperfectly, leaving readers in doubt over the verisimilitude and reliability of framed and framing materials alike. A case in point is *Dracula*, which is framed by contrasting opening and closing statements about its contents. Stoker's novel begins with a claim that in the documents comprising its narrative, 'a history almost at variance with the possibilities of later-day belief [stands] forth as simple fact'.[2] This claim's authentication and buffering functions are problematised by the 'Note' at the end the novel, which concedes that the vampire hunters 'could hardly ask anyone . . . to accept these [accounts] as proofs of so wild a story'.[3]

The frame of *Blacula*, together with the film's relationship to *Dracula* and mainstream adaptations of Stoker's novel, invites a reading informed by narratology and intertextuality. Such an interpretive approach is also in keeping with the multipart structure of *Dracula*, which features interrelated texts produced by several narrators. Employing this method and Gérard Genette's terms for original and adapted texts, 'hypotexts' and 'hypertexts',[4] we might note that Stoker's *Dracula*, the hypotext, sits like one of Renfield's spiders at the centre of an ever-expanding web of hypertexts, including *Blacula*. The aptness of this simile becomes apparent when we recognise that intertextuality is akin to vampirism, for, as Julia Kristeva observes, 'any text is the absorption and transformation of another'.[5] Vampires reproduce geometrically. Likewise, the intertextual web of *Dracula* has extended so widely that Stoker's vampire is featured in over two hundred films, to say nothing of his appearances in other media.[6] Intertextuality-as-vampirism appears not only as a web, but also as a series. Kristeva's insight that the genotext produces the phenotext[7] enables us to appreciate how the genotext, *Dracula*, is encrypted within and continually re-emerges along the line of phenotexts it has spawned. Thus, the chain of signifiers parallels the sequence of vampiric assimilation. *Blacula* vampirises prior adaptations, which vampirise Stoker's *Dracula*, which itself vampirises Sheridan Le Fanu's *Carmilla* (1872) and John Polidori's *The Vampyre* (1819), and so on. Readers act as vampire hunters, tracing textual bloodlines to their source in order to understand rather than destroy the elusive master vampire/narrative.

A linear view of intertextuality-as-vampirism is useful in terms of both theory and praxis when analysing relations among *Blacula* and the texts with which it is associated. Understanding these relations means decrypting vampiric narratives – both decoding and disinterring them – in order to appreciate how intertextual traces manifest themselves across narratives and time periods. One of Dracula's defining characteristics is his ability to resurrect in various incarnations, each of which works its ill will when it appears, before being destroyed and leaving a remnant (a ring, a skeleton, a pile of dust) by means of which the vampire is eventually reconstituted or his evil influence persists into another era. Like Dracula himself, the series of stories about the vampire is recurrent and unending. Moreover, each iteration in the series engages what Mikhail Bakhtin calls its ideologeme, the ideological milieu within which the text operates when it is produced.[8] The ideologeme is necessary to understand the typological as opposed to the referential aspect of intertextuality: how texts share thematic patterns and linguistic structures, rather than how they incorporate fragments of other texts. As Kristeva explains, semiotics aims to create '*a typology of texts*; that is, to define the specificity of different textual arrangements by placing them within the general text (culture)' and employing the 'ideologeme', which 'stretches along the entire length of [a text's] trajectory, giving it its historical and social coordinates'.[9] Thinking of intertextuality-as-vampirism in sequential terms not only calls attention to the ideologeme, but also highlights the typological link between vampirism and lineage (both ancestry and aristocracy) that is vital to *Blacula* and related narratives. This connection involves a third constituent that is just as significant as the other two: queerness. The lineage-vampirism-queerness nexus develops from *The Vampyre* and *Carmilla* to *Dracula*, and from Stoker's novel to both its canonical film adaptations and Blaxploitation appropriations: *Nosferatu* (F. W. Murnau, 1922), *Dracula* (Tod Browning, 1931), *Dracula* (released as *Horror of Dracula* in the United States) (Terence Fisher, 1958), *Blacula*, *Scream Blacula Scream* and *Ganja & Hess*. While each text represents these connections differently, all focus and depend on them. The typological trajectory is remarkable, particularly with respect to how queerness is by turns implicit, explicit and repressed. Energised by Black Power, and by the intersection of civil rights and gay rights in their ideologeme, the Blaxploitation films forge links among lineage, vampirism and queerness in the most compelling fashion.

Queer Originals: *The Vampyre, Carmilla* and *Dracula*

These interrelated elements are first articulated in *The Vampyre* and *Carmilla*, before reappearing in *Dracula*. Polidori's tale begins with a frame explaining the history and nature of vampirism, which is followed by the story of the relationship between Aubrey, a wealthy young man, and the suave and mysterious Lord Ruthven. Aubrey meets Ruthven at a London party, travels with him through Europe, and leaves him after learning of his plan to seduce an innocent woman in Rome. In Greece, Aubrey falls in love with Ianthe, a beautiful young woman whose murder is attributed by locals to a vampire. He then reunites with Ruthven, who is killed after the two are attacked by bandits. On his deathbed, Ruthven persuades Aubrey to swear to remain silent about his death for a year and a day. Aubrey comes to suspect Ruthven as the murderer of both Ianthe and the woman he seduced. After returning to London, Aubrey is shocked to find Ruthven there, living under a new identity. Ruthven becomes engaged to Aubrey's sister. On his own deathbed, Aubrey is finally released from his oath and tells Ruthven's story in an attempt to stop the wedding. He is too late, for 'lord Ruthven [has] disappeared, and Aubrey's sister [has] glutted the thirst of a VAMPYRE!'.[10]

Lord Ruthven is at the head of a long line of high-born vampires that includes Countess Karnstein (Carmilla), Count Dracula and Prince Mamuwalde. Discussing these figures in nineteenth-century Gothic fiction, Carol A. Senf explains, 'Polidori, Le Fanu, and Stoker link the aristocrat's hereditary power over others and the vampire's supernatural power over human beings'.[11] Both vampires and aristocrats not only dominate but also drain the lower orders. In an interview with Michel Foucault, when Guy Le Gaufey observes that 'the vampire is always an aristocrat, and the saviour a bourgeois', Foucault points out that 'in the eighteenth century, rumours were already circulating that debauched aristocrats abducted little children to slaughter them and regenerate themselves by bathing in their blood'.[12] Such upper-class depravity was beyond even the notorious Lord Byron, Polidori's patient and travelling companion, and the model for Lord Ruthven.[13] That Byron was bisexual is but one way in which Polidori's alignment of vampire and aristocrat involves queerness.[14] Speaking generally, George Haggerty observes that 'aristocratic privilege' in the eighteenth century included 'the "luxury" of male-male desire'.[15] Eve Kosofsky Sedgwick traces relations among aristocracy, queerness and the Gothic in the eighteenth century, and considers how Gothic fiction 'came in the nineteenth century to seem a crystallization of the aristocratic homosexual role'.[16] Discussing *The Vampyre* in particular, Max Fincher contends, 'The underlining of class is based on how homophobia in the eighteenth century is partially inscribed in the tensions between evolving middle-class values in opposition to an aristocratic *vampire regime* denigrated through its association with tabooed sexual desires', including homosexuality.[17]

In *The Vampyre*, vampirism figures both aristocratic predation and queerness, which are correlated. Aubrey, like Ruthven's female victims, is doomed to ruin at his hands, for he has 'that high romantic feeling of honour and candour, which daily ruins so many milliners' apprentices'.[18] This comparison points to the queerness of the relationship between the two men. In the play *Tunbridge Walks* (1703), the 'Effeminate Coxcomb' called Maiden explains, 'I was put Prentice to a Milliner once, only a Gentleman took a fancy to me, and left me an Estate'.[19] The unsparing entry for *milliner* in G. P. Putnam's *Hand-book of Chronology and History* (1852) likewise associates the occupation with queerness, noting that 'in 1810, men-milliners and other classes of an epicene character were very strongly censured in the Society of Arts' and describing the male milliner as a 'perfumed coxcomb' who 'lisps . . . in lady phrases'.[20] While the comparison between Aubrey and a milliner's apprentice certainly suggests that he and Ruthven are, respectively, queer victim and victimiser, it seems outweighed by the fact that Ruthven vampirises Aubrey's sister rather than Aubrey himself, and that both he and Aubrey pursue Ianthe. Yet the manner in which these men compete for women reinforces rather than vitiates their desire for each other.

The relationships among the main characters in *The Vampyre* involve the concept of erotic triangles as developed by René Girard and refined by Sedgwick, who notes that 'Girard seems to see the bond between rivals in an erotic triangle as being even stronger, more heavily determinant of actions and choices, than anything in the bond between either of the lovers and the beloved'.[21] That Aubrey's sister is referred to only as 'Miss Aubrey'[22] indicates her function as Ruthven's substitute for her brother. Conversely, Aubrey substitutes for Ianthe. When Ruthven attacks Ianthe and Aubrey comes between them, he takes her place beneath the vampire, who '[throws] himself upon him'[23] in the dark. The most logical explanation for Ruthven's selecting Ianthe for his victim is that he sees women as interchangeable. Aubrey has deprived him of a woman; thus, he will deprive Aubrey of a woman. When the two men return to London, the object of their rivalry shifts from Ianthe to Miss Aubrey. In draining her, Ruthven indirectly drains Aubrey. Infuriated by Ruthven but unable to reveal the monster's true nature, Aubrey '[breaks] a blood-vessel' and dies as a result of 'the effusion of blood'.[24] Ruthven then gluts his thirst for blood with Miss Aubrey. If the mores of Polidori's world had not obliged the author to triangulate Ruthven and Aubrey's mutual desire, then they might have consummated it vampirically. Hence *The Vampyre* might have reproduced the story of its frame narrative, in which 'Arnold Paul', having 'been tormented by a [male] vampire', himself '[becomes] a vampire' and victimises others.[25] The homoerotic displacement suggested by this queer transformation and transmission is at once elucidated and repressed by a note accompanying the frame: 'The universal belief is, that a person sucked by a vampire becomes a vampire himself, and sucks in his turn'.[26]

In *Carmilla*, the association of lineage, vampirism and queerness is even more pronounced than in *The Vampyre*. The frame narrative informs readers that the story within it is transcribed from a manuscript found among the papers of the late Dr Hesselius. The tale is told by Laura, who lives in a castle in Styria with her widowed English father and two governesses, Madame Perrodon and Mademoiselle De Lafontaine. Through her deceased mother, she is a descendant of 'the proud family of Karnstein, now extinct'.[27] At six years old, Laura recalls being joined in bed by an unfamiliar woman who seems to have punctured her breast, though no mark is discovered. Twelve years later, Laura learns from her father that Bertha Rheinfeldt, the niece of his friend General Spielsdorf, has died suddenly and mysteriously. Shortly thereafter, a carriage overturns outside the castle and a young woman within it, Carmilla, is entrusted by her mother to Laura and her father. Laura and Carmilla recognise each other from what the latter describes as a shared dream. As they become close friends, girls and women in the area begin dying of an unidentified illness. Eventually, Laura's own health begins to decline, and she dreams of being bitten in bed by a cat-like creature that transforms into Carmilla. En route to the nearby ruined castle and village of Karnstein, Laura and her father meet Spielsdorf. He tells them how he and Bertha met at a masquerade ball a young woman named Millarca, whom he ultimately realised was a vampire preying on his niece. In Karnstein, Carmilla appears and Spielsdorf attacks her, but she easily escapes him. He explains to Laura that Carmilla and Millarca are both anagrams for Mircalla, the entombed and undead Countess Karnstein. With the aid of Baron Vordenburg, the descendant of a Moravian nobleman who drove vampires out of the region in years past, Spielsdorf finds Mircalla's hidden tomb. She is exhumed and destroyed.

Carmilla construes vampirism as aristocratic, matrilineal and queer. Carmilla is actually Countess Karnstein, and the woman identified as her mother is called 'Madame the Countess' and even 'the princess'.[28] Carmilla drains to death those below her: the 'peasants'[29] of the region and Bertha, a member of the bourgeoisie. In contrast, she intends for Laura, who is within her own noble bloodline, to join her as a vampire. Their symbolic mother-daughter relationship is reversible, for after Laura's father asks Carmilla's putative mother to 'entrust her child to the care of [his] daughter', Laura mothers Carmilla by figuratively breastfeeding her when the vampire sinks her teeth 'deep into [Laura's] breast'.[30] That Laura and Carmilla are not mother and infant but two adult women renders their bedroom activities very queer,[31] and their queerness is inextricable from their aristocratic and vampiric bloodline. Carmilla is drawn to Laura not only because she is a beautiful young woman, but also because she is a Karnstein, in blood if not in name. Their union, in which the roles of mother and daughter alternate and blur, just as do those of milk and blood and life and death, enables Laura to resurrect and reconnect with her deceased mother. 'My mother, a Styrian lady, died in my infancy',[32] Laura explains, linking aristocracy, birth and death – and, implicitly, vampirism. All these elements combine in Carmilla, the Karnstein materfamilias, who is at once the beginning and the end of the family line. Laura's yielding to Carmilla's seduction enables this line to continue through its women, not conventionally but vampirically. After Carmilla '[draws] near' to Laura, she 'in [her] turn, will draw near to others',[33] perhaps including other female relations.

Such a queer, aristocratic, Gothically incestuous form of reproduction must be stopped by those it would exclude, including Laura's father. In the conflict between the bourgeois, heteronormative patriarchy and the aristocratic, queer matriarchy, Laura seems aligned with her mother and surrogate mother against her father. 'Your mother warns you to beware of the assassin', she hears in her dream, before she sees Carmilla covered 'in one great stain of blood'.[34] Although the assassin could be Carmilla herself, bathed in the blood of those she has killed, Laura awakens 'possessed with the one idea that Carmilla [is] being murdered'[35] – as indeed she will be, while submerged in blood, by Laura's father, Spielsdorf and other male vampire hunters. Thus, the assassin against whom Laura's mother warns her may well be not her friend but her father, whose helping to destroy Carmilla ends his campaign against the Karnstein matriarchal nobility. He has already in effect displaced the Styrian aristocracy by moving into one of its castles, which he bought by drawing on the resources of the patriarchy: his military 'pension and his patrimony'.[36] Moreover, in an example of what Freud refers to as 'tendentious jokes' that are 'highly suitable for attacks on the great',[37] Laura's father reveals his unconscious hostility and aggression towards the aristocracy in general and the Karnsteins in particular. 'I hope you are thinking of claiming the title and estates?',[38] he quips after hearing that Spielsdorf wants to go to the castle and village of Karnstein. His friend declares, 'I mean to unearth some of those fine people'.[39] Spielsdorf's tone is ironic, but his tenor is literal: he intends to remove the Karnsteins from their land. Like Laura's father, who '[inhabits] a castle' though he is 'by no means magnificent', Spielsdorf is a bourgeois, castle-owning patriarchal soldier who portrays himself, in contrast with the aristocracy, as a 'nobody' who intends to bring an end to a noble family line.[40] The success of his anti-aristocratic campaign depends, paradoxically, on a member of the nobility, Baron Vordenburg, who knows the location of Mircalla's hidden tomb.

Like Countess Mircalla, Count Dracula is the last of his aristocratic lineage and involved in a life-or-death struggle with members of the bourgeoisie who are aided by a nobleman. In *Dracula*, the solicitor Jonathan Harker describes in his journal his visit to Castle Dracula in the Carpathian Mountains to help the Count buy Carfax, a medieval abbey near London. Harker, who soon realises that his host is a vampire and himself a prisoner, is menaced by three vampire women. After Dracula leaves his castle for England, Harker escapes from it to Budapest. Meanwhile, letters between Lucy Westenra and her best friend, Harker's fiancée Mina Murray, describe proposals of marriage to Lucy from Dr John Seward, who manages a lunatic asylum; Quincey Morris, an adventurous Texan; and Arthur Holmwood, who becomes Lord Godalming on the death of his father. Lucy accepts her third suitor and joins Mina in Whitby, where the ship that Dracula has taken from Transylvania runs aground after a storm. Dracula begins vampirising Lucy, who sickens as Mina marries Harker in Budapest. Although Seward's mentor, Prof. Abraham Van Helsing, treats Lucy, she dies and becomes a vampire. Van Helsing, Seward, Morris and Godalming confront her, and her fiancé kills her. Harker and Mina return and join the others in Seward's asylum to plot against Dracula, who gains access to the asylum through Renfield, a patient, and vampirises Mina. The men hunt Dracula in London and force him to return to Transylvania, where the group follows him. Mina and Van Helsing go to Castle Dracula, and he kills the vampire women. The men attack Dracula, who is destroyed by Harker and Morris. A note written seven years later by Harker closes the novel by mentioning that he and Mina have a son named Quincey.

In *Dracula*, as in *The Vampyre* and *Carmilla*, aristocracy and vampirism are closely linked. The landed noble and the vampire alike are defined by blood, land and mastery, which are themselves intertwined. Dracula's power stems from blood – his own, and that of his ancestors, adversaries and victims. The centuries-old vampire 'of the Dracula blood'[41] is at once the conclusion and the concentration of a long and potent bloodline. As such, he is also the ultimate embodiment of his venerable family. Harker notes that 'whenever he [speaks] of his house he always [says] "we," and [speaks] almost in the plural, like a king speaking'.[42] This form of speech is appropriate for 'the King-Vampire', in whose 'veins flows the blood of many brave races who fought as the lion fights, for lordship'.[43] Over years of fighting, their shed blood and that of their enemies seeped into Dracula's long-embattled land. It therefore comes as no surprise that the regal vampire is rooted in the blood-soaked soil of his homeland, and that when he leaves Transylvania for England, he must bring with him 'fifty boxes of earth'[44] in which to rest. Absent blood and land, the aristocrat loses both the foundations and the tokens of his power. Declaring that 'your peasant is at heart a coward and a fool', Dracula scorns those below him for fearing to pursue the weird blue flames that '[show] where gold was hidden'[45] in Transylvanian soil over the ages to frustrate foreign invaders. In discussing this buried gold, Dracula naturally conflates it with blood, another vital substance that he must draw on to thrive. He explains to Harker that 'there is hardly a foot of soil in all this region that has not been enriched by the blood of men, patriots or invaders'.[46] This interchangeability of blood, gold and soil is essential not only to how *Dracula* associates vampirism and aristocracy, but also to how this association involves queerness.

To appreciate these connections, we must turn to Freud's 'Character and Anal Erotism' (1908), where he contends that while heterosexual adults who retain yet repress an infantile anal erotic fixation tend to be 'orderly, parsimonious and obstinate', there is 'no very marked degree of "anal character" in people who have retained the anal zone's erotogenic character in adult life, as happens, for instance, with certain homosexuals'.[47] In the normal course of psychosexual development, those who move beyond the anal stage sometimes transfer their psychic attachment from defecation to money; thus, faeces and money, especially gold, become interchangeable. Freud's thinking developed in part from comments made by his patient Oscar Fellner, who associated money and excrement 'by way of Cagliostro – alchemist'[48] and the alchemical process of transmuting base metals into gold. Discussing how 'money is brought into the most intimate relationship with dirt' in 'superstitions, in unconscious thinking, in dreams and in neuroses', Freud cites the belief that 'the gold which the devil gives his paramours turns into excrement after his departure', and the ancient dictum that 'gold is "the feces of Hell"'.[49]

These allusions to the infernal indicate how, in a scatological twist on the alchemical goal of transmutation, *Dracula* figuratively turns gold into dirt/excrement and vice versa, while associating the eponymous vampire with the unrepressed anal erotism that Freud claims characterises some homosexuals. Dracula is a 'devil' whose dirt-filled boxes, 'his earth-home', are also 'his hell-home'.⁵⁰ The Transylvanian earth inside these boxes, which once held buried gold, has itself become precious to the vampire who depends on it to survive. This transmutation is in keeping with Dracula's status as an 'alchemist'⁵¹ who has completed, albeit in a perverse fashion, at least half of the alchemical Great Work by discovering a means of achieving immortality. The other half, transmuting base metals into gold, is unnecessary given his willingness to unearth the buried treasure of his homeland, which piles up like excrement in his castle. In entering the Count's room, Harker discovers 'a great heap of gold . . . covered with a film of dust', which doubles the 'wealth of dust' elsewhere in the castle.⁵² Dracula's house in Piccadilly is in 'orderly disorder',⁵³ an oxymoron suggesting the tension between retention and expulsion key to the anal phase. In addition to being dependent on and closely associated with dirt, Dracula produces a terrible smell. Struggling to describe this awful odour, Harker reaches for abject imagery of the sort that Kristeva associates with both excrement and death.⁵⁴ He writes, 'It was not alone that it was composed of all the ills of mortality and with the pungent, acrid smell of blood, but it seemed as though corruption had become itself corrupt'.⁵⁵ Dracula's reek of abjection, overpoweringly present even in his absence, is a physical manifestation and remnant of his aristocratic will to power, the 'instinct for mastery' that Freud ascribes to the 'sadistic-anal' stage of development.⁵⁶ This instinct is complemented by one for submission and passivity, since anal erotism is defined by retention/expulsion, activity/passivity and dominance/submission.⁵⁷

These instincts are split between Dracula and those he subjugates, particularly Harker and Renfield, with whom his sadomasochistic relations are decidedly queer. Dracula derives enormous sadistic-anal pleasure from retaining and controlling Harker, who is 'absolutely in his power',⁵⁸ within a castle that Ellis Hanson describes as figuring the male body and evincing 'a certain anal-retentive exoticism'.⁵⁹ Unable and perhaps unconsciously unwilling to leave the castle, Harker describes himself as '[behaving] much as a rat does in a trap',⁶⁰ drawing an analogy that further empowers Dracula, a Mephisto-like 'lord of rats',⁶¹ and foreshadows Freud's Rat Man, who feared and fixated on a punishment whereby rats trapped in a pot attached to a criminal's buttocks would burrow into the victim's anus.⁶² Like these rats, Harker, unable to escape Dracula's castle-as-body, goes more deeply into it, thereby becoming even more passive and feminised. Acknowledging that he can 'do nothing', he '[sits] down and simply [cries]'.⁶³ When Harker decides to sleep, fittingly, 'where of old ladies . . . lived sweet lives', Dracula's warning against falling asleep in that section of the castle '[comes] into [his] mind, but [he] [takes] a pleasure in disobeying it'.[64] His childish pleasure in defying Dracula indicates not only his regression, which is symbolised by his moving into an older part of the castle, but also his regressive anal erotism. As Harker tries to cope with an all-powerful father surrogate, he exercises what little control he does possess, that over his own body, thereby evoking Freud's description of the gratification children take in disobeying their parents and refusing to defecate. As Freud explains, 'The contents of the bowels' are 'treated as a part of the infant's own body and represent his first "gift": by producing them he can express his active compliance with his environment and, by withholding them, his disobedience'.[65] Ultimately concluding that only by risking his life to leave the castle can he live or die 'as a man',[66] Harker demonstrates both his masculinity and his maturity by escaping Dracula's symbolic body through an opening with neither oral nor anal associations: a window.

Whereas Harker gets out of Castle Dracula only with great difficulty and danger, Renfield leaves Seward's asylum with relative ease. Both men exit through anatomically ambiguous windows and pass through sphincter-like doors. While Harker is 'led through a stone passage' to Dracula and his boxes of earth, Renfield '[flies] down the passage' outside his room to rendezvous with the vampire and his dirty coffins.[67] The frequency of Renfield's explosive escapes, together with his volubility, render obvious the pleasures of unrepressed anal erotism that remain fairly subtle in Harker's case. Exhibiting and enjoying the 'ambivalence'[68] that Freud discerns in the anal stage, Renfield oscillates between expulsion and retention, between bursting out of the madhouse and allowing himself to be held within it. Even more passive than Harker, who seeks the keys to doors or pushes against them until they yield, Renfield is content to '[press] close against the old iron-bound oak door of the chapel'[69] where Dracula lies, without seeking to open it. The lunatic is likewise more submissive than the solicitor, behaving in a 'servile' and 'cringing' manner towards Seward and the asylum attendants.[70] Renfield's submission is complemented and intensified by Dracula's dominance, as the activity and passivity of the anal stage develop into sadomasochism. When the vampire demands that Renfield 'fall down and worship [him],' the madman declares, 'I am here to do Your bidding, Master. I am Your slave'.[71] Their relationship reaches its logical climax when Renfield ecstatically admits Dracula into his room, crying, 'Come in, Lord and Master!'.[72] The fact that the vampire enters via a small orifice, '[sliding] into the room through the sash, though it [is] only open an inch wide',[73] indicates his symbolic penetration of Renfield's body. In accordance with the novel's repression of intimate contact between men,[74] Dracula neither bites nor exchanges blood with the lunatic; thus, he fails to honour his promise to transform him into a vampire.

Indeed, Dracula is highly selective about those he turns into vampires, choosing only the women in his castle, Lucy and Mina – all of whom are aristocratic, queer, or both. The three female vampires, apparently related to Dracula by blood or marriage,[75] share not only his aristocratic lineage but also his exaggerated masculinity. He practically bristles with phallic symbols: 'peculiarly sharp white teeth', ears whose 'tops [are] extremely pointed', and nails 'cut to a sharp point'.[76] The vampire who '[arches] her neck' while her 'red tongue' laps 'sharp teeth' as she prepares to penetrate Harker's limp, feminised body is similarly phallic.[77] Also closely affiliated with the aristocracy and queerly masculine is Lucy, the would-be Lady Godalming, whose desire to 'marry three men'[78] aligns her with Dracula and his three vampire women, and who, with teeth that have grown progressively 'longer and sharper',[79] seeks to penetrate her noble fiancé. The elevated status of Lucy and the vampire women is at once reflected and intensified by their vampirism, as is the case in *The Vampyre* and *Carmilla*. By contrast, Mina is merely 'an assistant schoolmistress' who must content herself with 'castles in the air'.[80] Her appeal to Dracula is a function not of her class, but of her figurative hermaphroditism. As Van Helsing observes, Mina 'has man's brain . . . and woman's heart'.[81] For the alchemist Dracula, this 'so good combination'[82] would call to mind the rebis or double being, a metaphorical union of masculine and feminine qualities that personifies the philosopher's stone and represents the alchemical process. Kathleen P. Long explains that the rebis 'could be read *in bono* or *in malo*, either as a symbol of the divine or of the diabolical'.[83] The conventional ending of *Dracula* seems to highlight the diabolical rather than the divine potential of the rebis, and to stress that vampirism, decadent aristocracy and monstrous queerness are to be extirpated. Accordingly, when Harker visits Transylvania seven years after Dracula has been destroyed, he claims that 'every trace of all that had been [is] blotted out'.[84] Yet in the next sentence he admits, 'The castle stood as before'.[85] Likewise, Harker celebrates the birth of his and Mina's son, Quincey, while eliding the fact that some portion of Dracula's blood flows through the boy's veins. Just as 'the old centuries had, and have, powers of their own which mere "modernity" cannot kill',[86] queer bloodlines are not so easily ended.

Shadows of the Vampire: *Nosferatu, Dracula* and *Horror of Dracula*

Murnau's *Nosferatu*, Browning's *Dracula* and Fisher's *Horror of Dracula* follow their fictional precursors by interrelating vampirism, lineage and queerness. Browning's *Dracula* is thematically similar to the adaptations that precede and come after it, but much less formally sophisticated. Whereas Murnau and Fisher modify the complex narrative structure of their source material, Browning dismantles it. *Dracula* begins in *medias res*, as Renfield, replacing Harker, travels via carriage to Castle Dracula. This action is framed only by references in the opening credits to the film's proximate source, the play *Dracula* (1924) by Hamilton Deane and John L. Balderston, and to Stoker's novel, which is established as at once the foundation and the outermost frame for the other two films as well. Murnau's film adapts Stoker's novel by depicting how Hutter (Gustav von Wangenheim) sells Count Orlok (Max Schreck) an empty house facing his own home in Wisborg, a fictional German town. After journeying to Orlok's castle in Transylvania, Hutter is attacked by the vampire but manages to return home to his wife, Ellen (Greta Schröder), just before Orlok arrives and sets off a mysterious plague. Ellen sacrifices herself to kill Orlok, who is destroyed by the light of the rising sun.

As *Nosferatu* begins, it moves from its extradiegetic framing credits to a second, diegetic frame, *An Account of the Great Death in Wisborg, Anno Domini 1838*. This anonymous narrative's seemingly objective point of view is problematised by its enigmatic exposition, which directly questions the audience: '*Nosferatu*. Does this word not sound like the deathbird calling your name at midnight?' Despite its apparent *non sequitur*, this opening develops the Gothic frame's authenticating function by circling back to Stoker's novel, since *nosferatu* is the author's neologism for *undead*.[87] The text returns to form in the next sentences: 'I have reflected at length on the origin and passing of the Great Death in my hometown of Wisborg. Here is its story.' The film then begins to substitute for this written account, though excerpts from the latter occasionally appear to comment on the action of the former. Embedded within these two narratives is a third, *Of Vampyres, Terrible Phantomes, and the Seven Deadly Sins*, which Hutter discovers at his bedside in the inn where he spends the night before meeting Orlok, and which provides Ellen with the means of destroying the monster: 'an innocent maiden maketh the vampire heed not the first crowing of the cock, this done by the sacrifice of her own bloode.' That this book of the occult is positioned inside written and filmed accounts of a plague is in keeping with the Gothic frame's buffering function. These distinctions collapse and the concentric narratives conflate, however, when all of them turn out to be versions of the same bizarre tale.

A similarly complex storytelling structure is at work in *Horror of Dracula*. In this adaptation, Harker (John Van Eyssen) is vampirised in Castle Dracula and staked by Van Helsing (Peter Cushing), who follows him there. Meanwhile, Dracula (Christopher Lee) travels from his lair outside Klausenburg to Karlstadt, where he menaces Arthur Holmwood (Michael Gough), his wife Mina (Melissa Stribling) and his sister Lucy (Carol Marsh). Dracula vampirises Lucy, whom Van Helsing kills, then seduces Mina. Holmwood and Van Helsing follow Dracula back to his castle, where the professor destroys the vampire. The film's opening sequence authenticates Fisher's adaptation of Stoker's novel by situating it within an established fictional and cinematic lineage. Accompanied by James Bernard's unnerving score, blood-red Fraktur opening credits appear over an imposing low-angle shot of a massive statue of a predatory bird that evokes 'the deathbird' of *Nosferatu*. The camera pulls back from the statue, which is positioned in the courtyard of a castle, before tracking across stone walls and massive wooden doors topped by an escutcheon symbolising Dracula's family line. The camera moves towards a cellar door, then through it via a fade. The scene is dominated by an enormous tomb whose name plate reads DRACULA. The weird means by which the camera passes through the cellar door alludes to how doors open themselves in *Nosferatu* and Browning's *Dracula*, and to how vampires move past closed doors in Stoker's novel. The tomb itself is drawn from Van Helsing's description of a 'great tomb' on which '[is] but one word, DRACULA'.[88] The camera moves towards the tomb and closes in on this word, which comes to occupy the entire frame. Blood begins to spatter on the name, the music ends and the scene fades to black. The close-up of the tomb's blood-spattered nameplate is then replaced by another close-up of the blood-red cover of a book featuring the entwined initials JH. This book is opened by a man's hand to its first page, on which is written, 'The Diary of Jonathan Harker'. After these consecutive shots indicate that both Harker's book and Dracula's tomb contain horrors, the shot of the diary dissolves into one of a coach, and the action proper begins.

Horror of Dracula and *Nosferatu* share not only an intricate framing structure, but also a fixation on queer relationships. Long before Orlok moves into Ellen's neighbourhood, he seems telepathically linked with her. Their connection is shown in an astonishingly transgressive scene that reveals the strong undercurrent of queer desire running through *Nosferatu*. Before this scene takes place, just after the stroke of midnight Hutter cuts his thumb while slicing bread, and Orlok attempts to take his hand and suck the blood from the wound. Hutter retreats from him, gripped by what Sedgwick terms the 'homosexual panic'[89] that often mars relations between men in Gothic fiction. Nevertheless, Hutter agrees to sit with Orlok, and eventually falls asleep in a chair. When he awakens after sunrise, he discovers two puncture marks on his throat. Hutter experiences what appears to be a second minor accident the next night, when he drops a locket containing Ellen's picture on a table before Orlok, who snatches it up, leers at it and remarks, 'Your wife has a lovely neck'. After Hutter returns to his bedroom and the clock strikes midnight, he opens the door to find Orlok standing outside. Terrified, he shuts the door and runs to the window, beyond which a precipitous drop leads to a rushing river. He climbs into bed and turns his face away from the door, which opens on its own to admit the vampire who stands within its arch. As Orlok's eyes move towards Hutter in bed, a crosscut shows Ellen awaken and leave her own bed, before being returned to it. Crosscuts then show the vampire's shadow covering Hutter, who lies still and passive, as Ellen again rises and cries his name. Orlok stops moving towards Hutter and turns to the right as if acknowledging Ellen's call, while she stretches her arms to the left as if beckoning him away from her husband. He slowly leaves the room, the door closes behind him, and Ellen lies back, exhausted but satisfied.

This scene at once repeats and reconfigures the erotic triangle of *The Vampyre* and Stoker's *Dracula* whereby two men compete for a woman, though their bond with each other is stronger than their attraction to her. What distinguishes relations among this trio from those in other iterations of *Dracula* is the reversal of Hutter and Ellen's stereotypical gender roles, the ways in which the androgynous Hutter doubles both Orlok and Ellen, and the explicitness of Hutter and Orlok's mutual desire. When Hutter first appears onscreen in *Nosferatu*, his face visible in a mirror before which he adjusts his cravat while pursing his lips and smiling in a self-satisfied fashion, his effeminacy, vanity and narcissism are established. These traits are re-emphasised when he extricates himself from an embrace initiated by Ellen, who worries about his impending departure, so that he can use her to help him arrange his clothing and prepare for his trip. That Ellen is playing with a cat when she is introduced to the audience suggests her attraction to predators, including both Orlok and Hutter, whose affinity as destroyers of beautiful things is signified when Hutter picks a bouquet of flowers for Ellen and she asks, despondently, 'Why did you kill them?'. She trades one vampire for another when she gallantly sacrifices herself to Orlok in order to protect her feckless husband, since Hutter disregards how the prospect of his journey energises himself but exhausts his wife. Husband and vampire are likewise connected insofar as Hutter's enthusiastic eating and drinking evoke Orlok's own voraciousness, and the link between their respective means of sustenance is made explicit when Hutter cuts his thumb and bleeds onto the loaf of bread he is consuming, thereby triggering Orlok's sanguinary and erotic appetites.

Hutter's ostensible accident also illustrates how he mirrors his wife as well as his host, for what seems to be a mishap may instead be an enticement that duplicates Ellen's inviting Orlok into her bedroom during the film's climax. Similarly, Hutter's dropping Ellen's locket before Orlok may be interpreted not as an accident, but as his unconscious attempt to deflect the vampire's attention from himself to his wife. In this effort Ellen succeeds where Hutter fails, telepathically drawing Orlok away from her husband and towards herself. Although Ellen is a more conventionally appropriate object for Orlok's lust, his focusing on her phallic neck and overlooking her feminine features underscores the queerness of his desire. The nature of her own longing is more ambiguous, though certainly her wish to be penetrated and drained by the vampire is conscious, expressed and premeditated, whereas Hutter's is unconscious, repressed and opportunistic. Accordingly, while Ellen deliberately unlatches and opens the windows for Orlok, Hutter waits in bed while the door opens by itself. This door, like those in Stoker's novel, serves as an overdetermined metaphor for the mind, mouth and anus alike, and it opens to enable characters to violate boundaries, cross thresholds and satisfy illicit lusts. It opens at midnight, the liminal moment when Hutter cut himself the night before. The arch framing it replicates the one framing Hutter's bed at the inn, connecting the door with the bed and Hutter with Orlok. The stage is set for a second erotic encounter between the two men, for the vampire has penetrated his guest once before. This initial experience seems to have satisfied Hutter. A full shot shows him casting a shadow on a fireplace while looking into a small mirror that he has, of course, brought with him to Orlok's castle. The camera cuts to a close-up of the mirror, which he angles downward while opening his cravat in order to examine the punctures in his neck. He then moves the mirror so that it reflects his mouth, and smiles. Focusing on Hutter's mouth and the holes in his neck, the scene aligns the oral, anal and phallic. It also associates shadow and mirror, projection and reflection, thus drawing yet another link between Hutter and Orlok – the latter of whom not only casts cinema's most famous shadow but also, contrary to vampire lore, appears in the mirror of Ellen's bedroom as he 'suckles himself' on the blood from her neck, not her breast, recalling how *Carmilla* and *Dracula* likewise conflate body parts and bodily fluids.

The erotic triangles of *Nosferatu* also structure *Horror of Dracula*, which features three of them. The first involves Harker, Dracula and an unnamed vampire woman who claims she is being held prisoner in the castle and asks for Harker's help. In their initial scene together, she approaches him in the library but draws back after seeing Dracula. In their next shared scene, Harker again encounters her in the library, where she sinks her fangs into his neck before Dracula roughly pulls her away from him. At this point, the dynamics of the triangle shift: Harker, not the woman, becomes the focus of contention and longing. Homoerotic desire is, however, still displaced. Although Harker writes in his diary, 'I have become a victim of Dracula and the woman in his power', he has been victimised by the male vampire only indirectly, through the female. This situation changes after he meets the vampire woman one last time, in the crypt she shares with Dracula. In voiceover, Harker has revealed himself as a vampire hunter travelling to Castle Dracula to destroy its owner. In his new role, he tracks Dracula and the vampire woman to their tomb and prepares to kill the latter. His staking her is shown not directly, but via a shadow projected on the wall. Unfortunately for Harker, this shadow is cast by the setting sun, which drops moments after the woman is slain and enables Dracula to escape. The vampire then appears at the top of the stairs, a low-angle shot emphasising his ascendency, while a complementary high-angle shot of Harker shows how helpless he has become. Harker drops the hammer and stake he is holding, his emasculation complete, and backs against a wall. When Dracula shuts the door behind him, the physicality of his action enhances his menace and suggests the assault to come. Before it does, the scene discreetly fades to black. Viewers are left to imagine the ensuing queer penetration, though its transformative results are apparent when Van Helsing, searching for Harker, discovers him occupying Dracula's sarcophagus, fangs protruding from his mouth. Harker's phallic empowerment is, however, only temporary. Van Helsing finds the hammer and stake that Harker dropped, and a low-angle shot shows him carrying them to his friend's body, which is concealed below the frame. The scene fades to black, and Harker is once again impaled by another man off-screen.

The second and third queer, triangular relationships in *Horror of Dracula* involve Dracula and Arthur Holmwood, whose sister Lucy and wife Mina fall under the vampire's influence. When Holmwood is finally convinced that Lucy has become a vampire and must be killed, rather than release her himself he watches Van Helsing do so. As the stake is driven into her heart, he clutches his own heart and writhes together with his sister. In Stoker's novel, Arthur demonstrates his manly fortitude by staking Lucy. In Fisher's adaptation, Holmwood not only declines to do so, but also identifies with Lucy to a degree that calls attention to what the film construes as his feminine passivity. Holmwood's effeminacy is likewise highlighted in his relations with Mina and Dracula. After vampirising Mina, Dracula makes himself at home in her cellar, a location signifying both the erotic and the repressed nature of their relationship. Having spent the night with Dracula, Mina tells Holmwood that she rose early and walked in the garden, a story belied not only by her knowing smile, but also by the sexually suggestive way in which she buries her fingers in the fur that lines the collar of her coat.[90] That evening, while patrolling in a futile attempt to keep Dracula out of the house that he has already moved into, to keep warm Holmwood holds a fur-lined collar to his throat. By reproducing Mina's post-coital gesture, he indicates his potential interchangeability with her. Unaware that his wife has invited Dracula into their home, Holmwood insists to Van Helsing, who debunks the 'common fantasy' that vampires can transform into bats or wolves, that 'he *can* change into something else. He *must* be able to. How else could he have got in?'. Dracula gets into Mina's bedroom and body alike not by taking a different form, but by taking the place of her emasculated husband.

The vampire can, however, transform into an animal in Browning's *Dracula*, which follows its source in connecting animality, aristocracy and queerness by drawing on late-Victorian notions of degeneration, according to which people might descend the evolutionary scale towards the levels of lower animals.[91] As William M. Greenslade observes, the concept of degeneration threatened 'mankind's separateness from the beast' by making the public aware of how 'lower-order species' were contiguous with 'the civilisation which had assumed an unquestioning "natural" hegemony over them'.[92] The influence of degeneration theory on Stoker's novel appears in Mina's observation that 'the Count is a criminal and of criminal type. Nordau and Lombroso would so would so classify him, and *qua* criminal he is of imperfectly formed mind'.[93] She cites Cesare Lombroso, who believed that lawbreakers were born with 'physical and psychological abnormalities' similar to those of 'primitive peoples, animals, and even plants', and who argued that 'the most dangerous criminals were atavistic throwbacks on the evolutionary scale'.[94] Mina also refers to Max Nordau, who shifted the focus of degeneration discourse from crime to culture, contending in *Degeneration* (1895) that 'rich educated people' are contributing to a '*fin-de-siècle* disposition' in contemporary art and literature that he associates with 'degeneration (degeneracy) and hysteria'.[95] Inflected by middle-class antipathy to the upper and lower orders, degeneration theory was 'at once a branch of biology and a form of cultural criticism undertaken by a beleaguered bourgeoisie',[96] who transmuted their 'class fear into a biological fact'.[97] Figures such as the scientist and eugenicist Francis Galton 'perceived a real decline at the upper end of the social scale, especially though not exclusively within the ranks of the aristocracy'.[98] Both as a concomitant of decay among the elite and an atavistic phenomenon in its own right, homosexuality was included among the manifestations of degeneration. Lombroso, for instance, initially traced male homosexuality, which he referred to as 'pederasty', to degeneration, though he later came to believe that mental illness might combine with atavism to cause pederasty.[99]

Repeatedly connecting vampires with animals of various sorts, the opening scenes of *Dracula* depict queerness as bestial, aristocratic predation. Attempting to dissuade Renfield (Dwight Frye) from travelling to Castle Dracula, an innkeeper (Michael Visaroff) declares that 'at the castle there are vampires' who 'take the form of wolves and bats'. While Renfield is en route to the Borgo Pass, a scene in the castle's crypt cuts between shots of vampires who emerge from their coffins and those of opossums moving around and within caskets, and one of an insect that leaves its own tiny coffin. After Renfield boards Dracula's carriage, the vampire (Bela Lugosi) transforms from a coachman into a bat and flies over the horses. When Renfield enters the castle, bats hover and wolves howl outside, while armadillos roam within. Once inside the vast interior of this quintessential symbol of Gothic nobility, the middle-class Renfield is so reduced as to be almost imperceptible. The oversized castle swallows him, as Dracula threatens to do. The Count appears on an enormous stone staircase, flanked to the right by a huge pillar and a gigantic spider's web. Walking past the column, which connotes both phallic power and aristocratic privilege, the vampire descends to meet the bourgeois. Low-angle shots render Dracula more imposing, while high-angle shots disempower Renfield. Passing through the web, the vampire intones, 'A spider spinning his web for the unwary fly'. As Renfield struggles within this web and activates the spider that spun it, the implication is clear: the vampiric aristocrat has entrapped the ambitious lawyer and will soon drink his blood. That Renfield cuts himself with a paperclip underscores how his bureaucratic function is to serve and feed Dracula.

The queer nature of this service and sustenance is only thinly veiled. 'I trust you have kept your coming here a secret', Dracula tells Renfield after ushering him into his bedroom. While indicating that their meeting is not to be spoken of, thereby evoking the love that dare not speak its name, he suggestively holds a wine bottle by its neck. As the solicitor sits at the food-laden table, the vampire moves towards the bed. 'I hope you will find this comfortable', Dracula says. 'It looks very inviting', Renfield responds, a moment before cutting himself. The camera zooms to the vampire, whose predatory nature has been aroused. A close-up then shows Renfield pressing his finger as blood oozes from its tip. With the bed in focus behind him, Dracula creeps towards the man, ready to suck on his member, until the crucifix given to Renfield at the inn drops in front of his hands and the vampire recoils. In what amounts to a symbolic act of self-fellatio, Renfield sucks the blood from his own finger while Dracula watches avidly. He then pours his guest a glass of wine from the bottle that he held earlier, but declines to join him in imbibing, famously quipping, 'I never drink . . . wine'. The sequence aligns the table with the bed and food with sex, while conflating wine, blood and semen. Given the homoerotically charged *mise en scène*, it comes as no surprise when Renfield, overcome by the heady wine, faints and is at last penetrated by Dracula. What follows begins as a heteronormative scene, in which the three vampire women approach the prone Renfield. It is queered when Dracula changes from bat to man, drives them away, and bends over the solicitor to bite him as the scene fades to black. When Renfield next appears, he has been reduced to a servile creature whose first word is 'Master'. He has given himself entirely to Dracula, only to be rejected when the Count vampirises Lucy and Mina.[100]

Vampirism, Black Power and Gay Rights: *Blacula*

In Blaxploitation vampire films, as in canonical adaptations of *Dracula*, queerness, lineage and vampirism are closely interrelated, though queer elements and characters are less coded and more explicit. The depictions of lineage and queerness in these films also engage contemporary Black

Power and gay rights movements, which gained momentum in the late 1960s and early 1970s. Black Power emerged after the assassination of Malcolm X in 1965 and uprisings in cities across the country in 1964 and 1965. As Jeffrey O. G. Ogbar explains, the movement 'demanded inclusion while advocating autonomy and self-determination. It asserted black access to full citizenship rights while conspicuously cultivating pride in much that was not American' – that is, in 'African names, clothes, rituals, and "sensibilities"'.[101] Tom Adam Davies notes that the 'fixed core values and goals' of Black Power included 'pursuing self-determination through black political and economic empowerment, the redefinition of black identity, greater racial pride and solidarity, and a critical emphasis on a shared African heritage and history of racial oppression'.[102]

Lineage was also valued by the gay rights movement, for the notion of gay pride '[served] a special role in uniting LGBT people around a common history and identity'.[103] As Simon Dickel observes, marginalised groups 'often try to legitimize themselves by emphasizing the trans-historical validity of a collective identity'.[104] Advocates for gay rights, like those for Black Power, stressed not only pride but also equality and resistance to oppression. David Carter points out that 'at the end of the 1960s, homosexual sex was illegal in every state but Illinois. Not one law – federal, state, or local – protected gay men or women from being fired or denied housing', and 'police aggressively patrolled the few places where homosexuals could mingle'.[105] In 1969, during a raid on the Stonewall Inn, a gay bar in New York City, members of the queer community resisted the police and began protests that catalysed activism for gay rights. In 1970 the first gay pride parades took place, and 'by the early 1970s, it began to seem . . . that the law was not always hostile, that those in power might listen, that demands might be granted'.[106]

During this period of activism within the Black and gay communities, 'groups and activists of all types were in communication with one another about the unfolding and manifold requirements of liberation',[107] and contemporary observers recognised links between the Black Power and gay rights movements. 'We all figured that the Black Panthers were going to start the revolution', Danny Garvin, a gay man, recalls. While witnessing the Stonewall raid and riot, he concluded, 'The revolution had started!'.[108] Thinking along similar lines, Leo Laurence, a reporter for San Francisco's KGO radio and the founder of the Committee for Homosexual Freedom, declared, 'The social revolution that is sweeping the country has given new pride to the Blacks and is now giving fire to the homosexuals'.[109]

Although co-operation between those advocating for Black Power and those seeking gay rights was hampered to some extent by racism within the white gay community[110] and homophobia among Black nationalists,[111] the two movements found common ground not only in their shared goals for liberation, but also in their mutual resistance to police harassment. As Timothy Stewart-Winter notes, 'Joined by their shared concern with combating the overzealous activities of law enforcement, black and gay activists found common cause', and their alliances 'stretched from the late 1960s to the early 1980s, fuelled by a backlash against police surveillance and intimidation of black militants'.[112] Many gay activists viewed 'fighting racism as central to gay liberation', and the Gay Liberation Front, founded in 1969, denounced racism and supported the Black Panther Party.[113] Likewise, in 1970 Huey Newton, the co-founder of the Black Panther Party, 'reevaluated his interpretation of homosexuality, insisting that the black liberation struggle could be strengthened with an alliance with the Gay Liberation movement',[114] and writing that 'homosexuals are not given freedom and liberty by anyone in the society. They might be the most oppressed in the society'.[115] Meanwhile, members of both the gay and Black communities endured and resisted mistreatment by the police. Raids on queer establishments were commonplace.[116] Newspaper stories about 'litigation and protests over violent rampages by drunken policemen, brutal beatings of African Americans, and police killings' supported 'the claim of [Black] activists that police abuses were widespread, were institutionalized, and required institutional reforms'.[117] Relations between the Black community and the police were so poor that the Black Panthers included in their party platform a demand for 'an immediate end to *police brutality* and [the] *murder* of Black people'.[118] As 'black organizations became more activist and formed self-defense groups to reduce police harassment within their communities', gays and lesbians formed 'similar police advocacy groups to stop police harassment at bars and cruising areas. In some cases, Black and gay organizations worked together to forge alliances to challenge police harassment and abuse'.[119] The focus on policing, identity and empowerment that were crucial to both the Black Power and gay rights movements are very much at issue in *Blacula* and *Scream Blacula Scream*.

Blacula begins in 1780 in Transylvania, where Prince Mamuwalde (William Marshall), representing the fictitious African Eboni tribe, meets Count Dracula (Charles Macaulay) in his castle to discuss relations between their two nations. They argue over the slave trade before Mamuwalde is bitten by Dracula, who renames the now-undead prince 'Blacula', locks him in a coffin and entombs him with his still-living wife, Luva (Vonetta McGee). The action then advances to 1972, when the interracial couple Bobby McCoy (Ted Harris) and Billy Schaffer (Rick Metzler), two flamboyantly queer interior decorators, buy the objects in Castle Dracula, including Blacula's coffin, and bring them to Los Angeles. Bobby and Billy inadvertently free the famished vampire and become his first victims. Blacula then meets and seduces Tina Williams (Vonetta McGee), a reincarnation of Luva, while being investigated by the Abraham Van Helsing-like Dr Gordon Thomas (Thalmus Rasulala), a pathologist for the Los Angeles Police Department (LAPD) and the boyfriend of Tina's sister, Michelle (Denise Nicholas). Eventually, Thomas succeeds in convincing his white colleague, Lt Jack Peters (Gordon Pinsent), that vampires are real and prowling the city. The two lead a small raid on Blacula's coven, before at last confronting its leader with a much larger group of policemen. After Peters stakes the vampirised Tina, Blacula kills himself by walking into the sunlight.

While authenticating and buffering *Blacula*, its frame complicates both functions. Drawing a direct line of descent from the legendary vampire to his near namesake, the opening narrative adds cachet to the film by linking it with Stoker's novel and prior adaptations. The frame also eases viewers into this new kind of horror movie by initially invoking a familiar cast and setting (Dracula, the vampire women, and imperilled visitors to a forbidding castle) before rendering the experience unfamiliar by adding Mamuwalde, Luva and the topic of slavery. Credit for this ingenious strategy is due to the lead, William Marshall, who explains how he argued against the film's original title, *Count Brown's in Town*, and for the frame scene:

> Blacula's straight[-]life name was Andrew Brown in the original script, the same as Andy's name in the [blackface] white comedy team of Amos and Andy. I wanted the picture to have a new framing story. A frame that would remove it completely from the stereotype of ignorant, conniving stupidity that evolved in the United States to justify slavery . . . I suggested an African hero who had never been subjected to slavery, an African prince traveling in Europe with his beloved wife, to persuade his 'brother' European aristocrats to oppose the African slave trade . . . While on this moral mission, he succumbs to European vampirism, which he didn't even know existed.[120]

Marshall's frame not only associates *Blacula* with its canonical antecedents, but also adds a compelling ideological dimension to the film by introducing slavery and relating it to vampirism, and by giving the titular Black vampire a rank equal if not superior to Dracula's. This approach was well received by many African American viewers, who responded enthusiastically to Mamuwalde's gravitas. Marshall recalls that 'the audience laughed, talked, and were excited to see the "African prince"'.[121] The authentication and buffering functions of *Blacula*'s frame are made more involved, in characteristically Gothic fashion, when Bobby and Billy challenge its verisimilitude. The estate agent (Eric Brotherson) for Castle Dracula who sells them the vampire's belongings insists, 'Count Dracula was no legend. He was terribly real'. 'Oh, I know', Billy responds, 'I've seen all of his movies'. The dramatic irony of his joke is not lost on viewers, who recognise that Billy is himself in a vampire movie and likely to be among Blacula's first victims. Thus, the usual dynamics of the Gothic frame are reversed. Even as the frame works to authenticate and buffer the framed narrative, the latter casts doubt on the former, highlights the tension between the two, and fosters an alienation effect.

The relationship between the frame and the framed narrative is further complicated, and queered, by camp. 'You are obviously not attuned to the antique market', Bobby tells the earnest estate agent. 'You see, where we come from, honey, the legend of Dracula, that's the absolute crème de la crème of camp! We're gonna get a fortune for these things.' He and Billy haggle with the agent over Blacula's coffin, commodifying it as a camp object while remaining heedless of its true significance as an artefact of suffering and a harbinger of death. The scene in which they unlock the coffin, inadvertently releasing Blacula, illustrates associations among camp, the Gothic and queerness that date from the eighteenth century. Defining camp as a 'mode of aestheticism' and a 'triumph of the epicene' that emphasises style over substance, Susan Sontag traces its origins to cultural expressions that include the original Gothic novels.[122] Robert Miles also discerns in these novels 'a recurrent interest in theatricality' as manifested in '"camp," pastiche, role-playing, excess and androgyny'.[123] Likewise, William Hughes and Andrew Smith contend that one key to 'the queer Gothic' is a 'camp quality'.[124]

The macabre campiness of the queer Gothic is amply demonstrated in the opening scene of the film's central story, which literalises the metaphors of flaming and screaming queens. Bobby, whom Billy calls a 'silly lamp queen', illuminates the warehouse that holds their purchases from Castle

Dracula with one of the oil lamps that Thomas will later throw at him, causing him to die by bursting into flames. Billy prances before Blacula's coffin and declares, 'I'm dying to open this!'. He then tells Bobby, 'I have a fantastic idea for this. You'll probably die if I tell you', and ominously elides sex and death by suggesting they replace the 'chintzy guest bed in the living room' with the coffin. Bobby breaks the heavy padlock on the coffin, moments before Billy cuts himself while opening a crate. In the foreground, Bobby wraps up Billy's cut. In the background, Blacula emerges from his coffin. As Bobby scolds him, Billy continues to complain: 'I'm gonna bleed to death! . . . Bobby, I'll die!'. At first merely hyperbolic, Billy's speech becomes almost hysterical before ultimately degenerating into screams. While the two men squabble, the vampire slowly and silently approaches them, mouth open and fangs bared. The scene is structured by juxtapositions: foreground/background and camp/non-camp. Billy's exaggerated desire to open the coffin, and his overreaction to a minor cut, contrasts with the real and fatal danger posed by Blacula, and with the relatively understated way in which the vampire stalks his prey. This contrast is a source of both humour and horror, though the latter predominates as the scene develops and its initial oppositions conflate. What starts as a campy performance of mortality and victimhood ends in brutal reality. Billy does indeed die – in fact, he bleeds to death – after the coffin is opened and Blacula attacks him.

This surprisingly explicit assault involves race and queerness in provocative ways. When Blacula approaches his two victims, ominous extradiegetic music builds as imposing low-angle shots of the vampire alternate with medium point-of-view shots from his perspective. When Billy and Bobby finally turn towards Blacula, close-ups of all three men show their respective terror and hunger. An extreme close-up of the vampire's mouth is followed immediately by a point-of-view shot of Billy's wounded arm. Snarling, the vampire sinks his fangs into Billy's body while the man screams (see Figure 1). A close-up moves along Billy's arm, from Blacula's lips to his own face, as his screams stop and eyes close. The camera then focuses on the vampire, his mouth and fangs bloody, as he stops drinking and looks upwards in ecstasy. When he resumes feeding on Billy, who is now prone and unresisting, Bobby ineffectually hits him with a wooden plank. Blacula strikes Bobby, knocking him backwards, then overpowers and bites him. His assault on Bobby, a Black man, is much less graphic and sexualised than his attack on Billy, a white man. This discrepancy might be explained by the fact that Billy is the ravenous vampire's very first victim, but his unique status in this respect likewise underscores his race.

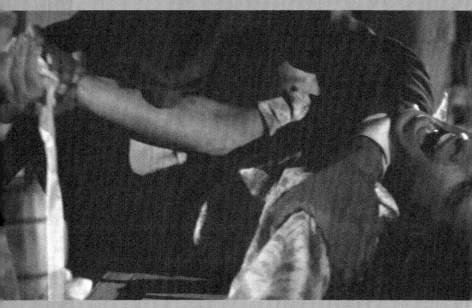

Figure 1. Blacula (William Marshall) attacks Billy Schaffer (Rick Metzler) in *Blacula* (1972). AIP/Photofest

Billy's whiteness holds both erotic and sociopolitical significance. It is essential to the fetishistic appeal a scene of interracial sadomasochism might have for viewers familiar with contemporary gay pornography, which was saturated by what Kevin J. Mumford terms 'black queerploitation' and defines as 'recurrent stereotypical depictions of hypersexual black men intended for gay readers'.[125] As he explains, 'like blaxploitation, black queerploitation played on themes of machismo and reversal of power relations in which subordinate black roles, such as a slave or prisoner, take sexual control of white men'.[126] Hence, the enslaved Blacula, who has in effect been bought by Billy, reverses their roles and takes possession of him. Billy's race is also noteworthy insofar as he is the only white person vampirised by Blacula. Furthermore, Billy is the only one of the vampire's victims who is buried, before being disinterred and staked by Thomas. Bobby's corpse, not Billy's, is prepared by the Black director of a funeral home, Swenson (Lance Taylor Sr), who explains to Thomas, '[Billy] was white. I don't get many whites in here'. Blacula goes to the mortuary to awaken Bobby, who later disappears from his coffin, but he leaves Billy in the ground. Vampirised, encoffined and abandoned to starve, Billy doubles Blacula, who tortures him as Dracula tortured Mamuwalde nearly two centuries earlier. As Blacula explains to Tina, when he visited Dracula 'on a mission to protest the slave trade', he was himself 'enslaved' and 'placed under the curse of the undead'. That the roles and races of the narrative frame are exchanged in the central story indicates an appropriate rebalancing and a condign retaliation, whereby the white enslaver becomes the enslaved. A similar dynamic is at work near the end of the film, when a group of white policemen hunt for Blacula in the chemical plant where he has hidden his coffin. 'This will be your inglorious tomb! Your tomb!', he warns them, as the Black man who was entombed by a white vampire becomes a Black vampire who entombs white men. That Thomas and Michelle are among this group complicates matters somewhat, though those whom Blacula actually kills in the chemical plant are all white policemen. His treating Bobby and Billy differently might well be a function of his racial animus, his quest for racial justice, or both.

That said, Billy's whiteness is arguably less important and certainly less emphasised than his queerness, which is underscored when the figuratively and literally screaming queen is penetrated, first by Blacula and then by Thomas. While being attacked by the vampire, Billy shrieks until he passes out from shock or loss of blood. Likewise, when Thomas disinters Billy and opens his coffin, Billy screams until his heart is pierced, during the most explicit and extended staking scene of the film. After knocking Billy back into his coffin and staking him with his bare hands, Thomas hammers the stake deep into the vampire's body by striking it three times with a shovel. The camerawork in these two scenes depicting a straight Black man penetrating and killing a queer white one complicates audience identification, particularly with respect to the male gaze. While the low-angle shots function as might be expected, the point-of-view shots are more problematic. The low-angle shots of Blacula as he approaches Bobby and Billy correspond with those of Thomas as he drives the stake into Billy's body. For a straight, Black male viewer, these shots might advance the empowerment via identification typically at work in Blaxploitation films. As Yvonne D. Sims notes, these films 'provided audiences who craved alternative heroes with an outlet in which they could, for the first time, identify with a protagonist who looked like them'.[127] Proving her point, William Marshall explained that young African American audience members were 'delighted' by seeing powerful Black characters onscreen in *Blacula*, and after watching it declared, 'There's our representation!'.[128] Blaxploitation films fostered identification between their protagonists and young Black men in particular. According to Amy Abugo Ongiri, these films 'focused intensely on an omnipotent, omnipresent African American masculinity, in effect catering to but also proscribing the group that could read and identify with these formulas as a spectatorial community', thereby promulgating 'a very specifically limited masculinist version of Black Power'.[129] Her observation is evidenced by the fact that while Thomas is in the grave staking Billy, Michelle is kneeling on the ground above it, echoing Billy's screams. In another instance of how *Blacula* aligns women and queer men, Michelle is the diegetic audience for this scene, as Bobby is for the scene in which Blacula attacks Billy. Their presence as spectators expands the film's opportunities for identification by providing characters with whom women and queer male viewers might identify. Michelle's spectatorship is conveyed by two shots in which, through her eyes, viewers watch Thomas dig up Billy's grave. After Billy and Thomas begin fighting, however, the camera no longer aligns with Michelle's point of view and again privileges the male gaze.

The shots of their struggle generate tensions between homoeroticism and homophobia that reproduce those in the scene of Blacula's initial attack, wherein Billy is both desired and destroyed. In the off-screen time between the two scenes, Billy has assumed some of Blacula's own phallic power and is a fanged aggressor rather than a prone and passive victim, the gash on whose arm signifies his castration. In the now-vampiric Billy's scene with Thomas, both the conflict and its representation are more balanced than in his earlier scene with Blacula, as objective shots of the action alternate with point-of-view shots from each man's perspective, encouraging viewers to share each subject position in turn. Those shots from Thomas's viewpoint show a monster that must be eradicated, while those from Billy's point of view depict not a vampire's prey, but a man determined to wipe out a monster. Although Billy is now a vampire who lunges at Thomas and attempts to bite him, he not only fails to penetrate his adversary but is himself penetrated by him, as he is by Blacula. Thomas punches him, hits him with a shovel and finally stakes him repeatedly. The homoerotic implications of this staking, which is represented in two explicit, objective medium shots, are vitiated by its brutality. Whereas Blacula's point-of-view shots focus on Billy's bloody arm, Thomas's concentrate on his mouth and fangs. Although both the wounded arm and the fanged mouth combine yonic and phallic characteristics, Billy's queer body has become repulsive and threatening rather than desirable.

Seeing through Billy's eyes, viewers experience themselves as battered and helpless, but Thomas's perspective empowers them. These alternating shots illustrate Harry M. Benshoff's insight that the 'processes of spectatorship are multiple and fluid, oscillating between masochistic and sadistic poles', and that (Blaxploitation) horror films may '[enable] socially oppressed people to contribute to their own oppression by consenting to the manufacture of their own identities as monstrous Others', or they may allow filmgoers to '[identify] with monsters out to topple dominant social institutions (that oppress both movie monsters and real-life minorities)'.[130] That both Billy and Thomas are members of minority groups complicates the scene of their struggle and its dynamics of identification, calling into question both the extent to which movements for queer and Black civil rights might co-operate, and the degree to which marginalised populations might empathise with each other.[131] In this instance, Billy's destruction suggests a zero-sum game and indicates a degree of homophobia. Michelle, horrified by what she has witnessed, keeps insisting that Billy was alive when Thomas staked him. 'He wasn't alive or dead', Thomas reassures her, underscoring the liminality of Billy's queerness-as-vampirism. After being unearthed and coming out of his coffin in a return of the repressed, his queerness amplified by his transformation into a vampire, Billy is finally put down for good. Yet his homophobic destruction by Thomas overwrites without effacing his homoerotic encounter with Blacula.

The scene between Billy and Thomas restages that in which Lucy is staked by Arthur, thereby indicating an alignment between transgressive women and queer men that is reinforced elsewhere in *Blacula*. For instance, when Peters speculates whether the Black Panthers might be involved in the murders of Billy, Bobby and Juanita Jones (Ketty Lester), Thomas disparages both his colleague's theory and Blacula's first victims by calling them 'two faggot interior decorators and a lady cabdriver'. Of the five people vampirised by Blacula, the first two are queer men. The next two, Juanita and Nancy (Emily Yancy), are women who contravene gender stereotypes. The last one is Tina, the reincarnation of Mamuwalde's beloved Luva. In an exception that proves the rule, Tina is transformed at her own request, after she has been shot by a policeman and is dying, so that she might join Blacula in a heteronormative (albeit vampiric) relationship that establishes him as a sympathetic character and the romantic lead. By contrast, Billy, Bobby, Juanita and Nancy are compelled to become vampires. The men are flamboyantly and stereotypically queer. Juanita is a cab driver whose sexual transgressiveness is underscored by Sam (Elisha Cook Jr), a morgue attendant who deals with her corpse. He tells Thomas, 'Fine job for a woman, runnin' a cab. You ask me, she's lookin' for something. You know what I mean, "lookin' for something"?'. Thomas ignores Sam's insinuation and dismisses him by asking for a cup of coffee. This request, together with the otherwise inexplicable fact that Sam's right hand has been replaced by a hook, indicates his symbolic castration and ineffectuality. While Sam implies that Juanita is driving a cab so that she can find sex partners, in fact she finds Blacula, whom she literally runs into while he is pursuing Tina on foot. After leaving her cab and discovering that he is miraculously uninjured, she lectures him: 'Chasin' tail could get you killed, you know'. Juanita's observation about Blacula echoes and reinforces Sam's about herself: she has, however inadvertently, chased the vampire and will now be killed for doing so. When she pointedly calls him 'boy', a derogatory term for an adult Black man,[132] he turns slowly towards her, his interest aroused by her audacity. Realising that she has gone too far, she tries to placate him while he approaches her with wide eyes, open mouth and protruding fangs. 'You take your hands off of me! I don't know you!', she cries, as he grabs her. For a moment, in a notable departure from his attacks on Billy and Bobby, it appears as though he is going to kiss her. He then moves his mouth away from hers and bites her throat, as she cries out and goes limp in his arms.

The sexual chemistry between Blacula and Juanita, unlike that between him and Billy, is largely the result of a contest between two strong figures. A woman cabbie and a military veteran wearing black leather trousers, a motorcycle jacket, and a United States Navy insignia pin on her Yellow Cab cap, Juanita is a Mina-like figure who blurs the conventional gender roles of her era. She is even more transgressive and formidable when she rises as a vampire and in effect takes her revenge on Sam for his disparaging remarks about her. Suspecting that Juanita is a vampire and seeking proof for his sceptical colleague Peters, Thomas calls Sam and asks him to remove her from the morgue's cold room, whose low temperature has kept her from resurrecting. Although Thomas emphasises that Sam is to lock the door of the room in which Juanita is thawing out, after removing her he forgets to do so. As she rises from a gurney, she casts a shadow that at once evokes *Nosferatu* and suggests the emergence of her shadow self. Like the vampirised Lucy, the reborn Juanita is now free from social constraints and able to realise her full potential as a gender outlaw. In a slow-motion sequence, Sam, his back to the room where Juanita has been lying, is talking on the phone in a medium shot before the scene cuts to a long shot of Juanita as she runs down a hall towards him and the camera, screaming, her hair loose, hands clawing, mouth open and fangs extended. As he turns towards her and himself begins to scream, close-ups of his face and hers alternate. At two points, her terrifying visage fills the screen in extreme close-up, point-of-view shots, forcing Sam and the viewer alike to confront her newly augmented energy and agency. In a vain attempt to ward her off, Sam raises his hook as she overpowers him. When Thomas and Peters arrive at the morgue, they destroy Juanita by exposing her to sunlight. Though Sam has presumably been vampirised, he never reappears.

While Blacula's fourth victim, Nancy, conforms more closely to gender norms than his previous three, her employment as a cocktail server and club photographer, her burlesque costume and her suggestive quips mark her as sexually transgressive. In a scene at the club where Nancy works, Mamuwalde, dressed in the evening clothes and cape he wears throughout most of the film, joins Tina's table at a party for Michelle's birthday. After his attack on Billy and Bobby, he removes this cape from his coffin and puts it on slowly and dramatically, spreading it out behind him as Dracula, in voiceover, intones, 'You shall be Blacula! A vampire like myself'. Mamuwalde thus assumes both the costume and the role that have been assigned to him. At the club, his standard-issue vampiric attire combines with the music played onstage to underscore the scene's theatricality. The real-life Hues Corporation performs songs that comment on the action and include lyrics such as 'Look the other way when he come by you' and 'I'm gonna get ya, babe', thereby functioning much as a soundtrack would do and blurring the line between the diegetic and extradiegetic.[133] Nancy serves Michelle and her friends champagne and takes their picture, upsetting Mamuwalde and causing him to leave. As he and Tina say goodbye, Nancy photographs them and, imitating Mae West, says archly, 'Oh, I think romance is in the air'. A young man who has joined the party, Skillet (Ji-Tu Cumbuka), observes of Mamuwalde's outfit, 'That's a bad cape. I'd like to beat him out of that cape'. His comment not only highlights how the cape serves as a metonym for the vampire, but also suggests that he and Mamuwalde might be interchangeable. Indeed, when Nancy leaves the club to develop her film, though Skillet asks if she would like his company, it is Blacula who follows her home. Again imitating West, Nancy tells Skillet, 'I know what would develop with you in a darkroom – and it wouldn't be my pictures', emphasising the punchline with a swing of her hips.

In the next scene, bathed in blood-red light that foreshadows Blacula's attack on her, Nancy develops the photographs in her kitchen, which is separated from the rest of her home by heavy drapes. Blacula enters her house, his shadow moving along a wall. After she discovers that the vampire is missing from the picture with Tina, she opens the darkroom drapes to reveal him standing in her living room. In a medium over-the-shoulder shot, with the camera positioned behind Nancy, Blacula glides towards her as if floating. A subsequent close-up shows his hand moving slowly down her torso as he bites her, before closing over the picture in her own hand and crushing it. The shot initially suggests the sensuality of their encounter, before shifting focus from her body to the true object of his desire, the photograph in which he does not appear. Nancy's costume, Blacula's costume, the drapes that open to showcase him as if he were appearing onstage, his unnatural movement, his shadow on the wall, the uncanny photograph – all highlight theatricality and (in)visibility. The staginess of the scene recalls the campiness of the one featuring Billy and Bobby, thereby reinforcing the alignment of queer men and transgressive women, while its emphasis on (mis)representation reveals why these people are targeted by Blacula.[134]

By vampirising members of marginalised groups, Blacula empowers them and renders them especially visible, albeit in paradoxical ways. His being released from imprisonment, though not enslavement, by a queer interracial couple indicates solidarity between the Black and gay communities. Indeed, in *Blacula* vampirism advances and aligns Black Power and gay rights, even as it represents empowered and visible African Americans and gays as monsters. Transformed into vampires and coming together as a community/coven, members of these two oppressed minority groups can cope with and even overcome the police. Significantly, given contemporary outrage about the number of Black people who were shot and killed by police, the vampires are immune to gunfire. Blacula alone easily and graphically kills several police officers. He never bites one, however, presumably because he is unwilling to augment their power, even though vampirising them would bind them to his will. Nancy does bite a policeman, Sgt Barnes (Logan Field), who joins Thomas, Peters and another officer, Johnson (uncredited), in a raid on a vampire coven. During this raid, Bobby is the first of the vampires to emerge from the shadows. He moves towards the officers while showing his fangs and licking his lips, acts that threaten the men by demonstrating his newfound phallic potency, and by conflating his vampiric and queer desires. Vampirism is also associated with queerness and camp by the fact that the vampires hide in the warehouse where Billy and Bobby's antiques are stored, and that, improbably, the men wear colourful hooded robes, while the women are clothed in sheer or satin dresses. Bobby is soon joined by several other vampires, all but perhaps one of them Black, who advance while the police retreat. As Johnson shoots a woman repeatedly, a close-up of his firing gun alternates with one of her face, which is hideous but calm. Completely unaffected by his bullets, she continues to approach him until he is jumped by another vampire. Encircled and overwhelmed, Johnson dies screaming. When Thomas begins incinerating members of the coven by throwing oil lamps at them, Barnes becomes a vampire and turns on Peters before being destroyed by Thomas. His transformation and betrayal not only represent the triumph of the Black and queer communities over the police, but also reverse the dynamic whereby the police infiltrated the Black Panthers in order to destroy the organisation from within.[135] Yet, thanks to Thomas, a Black man working with the otherwise white police force who is arguably an infiltrator of a different sort, the police ultimately prevail. Moreover, the queer and Black vampires merely transition from one form of oppression and bondage to another, since they are figuratively enslaved to vampirism and Blacula.

Their becoming visible as a result of their monstrous transformation is likewise progressive but problematic. Under orders from Peters, who now accepts the existence of vampires, the police surveil Bobby because of the interrelated threats that he poses – explicitly as a vampire and implicitly as a queer man. Watching and hoping to arrest him, the police demonstrate the long-term surveillance of gays and lesbians that finally came under challenge in the 1970s.[136] As might be expected, they go into action when Bobby meets another man. 'He's picked up a friend', Peters tells Thomas, as they move to intercept the pair. 'Let's go. That guy with him is in trouble.' Though the 'trouble' to which Peters refers is the threat that Bobby poses as a vampire, it also suggests legal trouble resulting from the man's accompanying Bobby to the warehouse, a rendezvous that calls to mind public gay sex of the sort long monitored and punished by the police.[137] That Bobby and the man he picks up draw the attention of the police but not those around them also indicates how for decades queer men and women were, paradoxically, at once visible to the police who surveilled them and invisible to the society in which they might pass as straight. With the acceleration of the gay rights movement in the 1970s, as Seth Dowland notes, 'their increasing visibility unsettled many Americans' who were 'accustomed to homosexuals' relative obscurity', to their 'remaining in the closet, concealed from public view'.[138] The contradictions of this newfound visibility and agency are illustrated in a conversation between the two officers in a patrol car who discover and track Bobby. One of them says, 'Hey, Danny, take a look at that fag. Isn't that the one? Sure looks like the one'.[139] His partner responds, 'How can you tell? They all look alike'. Bobby is both visible and invisible, as the officer refuses to see beyond a category and recognise an individual.

Similar dynamics involving prejudice, visibility, and tensions between surface and depth are at work with respect to the appearance of the vampires in both *Blacula* and *Scream Blacula Scream*, all of whom, regardless of race, have greenish-white skin. On the one hand, vampirism has erased a primary racial signifier and made everyone look the same, thus militating against racism. On the other hand, it has created a new category of difference and rendered those within it indistinguishable from one another. Further complicating matters is the fact that in these two films vampires can change their appearance. When aroused, Blacula and most of the other vampires become considerably more hirsute. The eyebrows of the men and women alike are bushier, and the men's sideburns and facial hair are fuller. Their hairiness signifies the emergence of their inner animality, which is linked with their monstrosity and thus with their racial and/or sexual nonconformity, which becomes truly monstrous only when it rises to the surface and is unmistakably visible. When it is submerged, the vampires can pass for human beings, as some members of racial or sexual minorities might pass for white or straight. Their performing an identity evokes the theatrical scene in Nancy's darkroom, together with the issues of mimesis and representation that it raises. Exercising their willing suspension of disbelief, viewers are expected to accept that though vampires are invisible to Nancy's camera, they appear on film in *Blacula*. Once again, the (in)visibility of African Americans and gays and lesbians is at issue, in both the diegetic and extradiegetic worlds. That they are showcased in *Blacula* and other Blaxploitation horror films is an unmistakable sign of progress, though their status as monsters remains contentious.

The representation of queer people and Black people as vampires reflects long-standing biases that gained salience in the 1970s, when *Blacula*, *Scream Blacula Scream* and *Ganja & Hess* were released. Of particular concern in the first two films is the speed and efficiency with which the vampires reproduce. A worried Thomas explains to Peters, 'Vampires multiply geometrically. First night there was one, second night two, third night four. It's a goddamn epidemic.' His metaphor of infection is apt, given that vampirism is in effect a blood-borne disease spread via parasites. The allegorical implications of the situation that Thomas describes become clear when we recognise how contagion, parasitism and reproduction informed contemporary thinking about gays and lesbians, and Black mothers on welfare. As Lee Edelman observes, in the West homosexuality has historically been 'conceived as a contagion, and the homosexual as a parasite waiting to feed upon the straight body'.[140] Daniel HoSang and Joseph E. Lowndes note that 'since the 1960s in particular', the notion of 'the parasite' has 'been constructed in highly racialized and gendered terms' and is exemplified by 'the [Black] mother on welfare'.[141] Observing how, according to 'heterofamilial logic', queerness 'not only refuses natural reproduction but also constitutes an unnatural form of reproduction', Valerie Rohy describes a 'fantasy of proliferation through seduction, influence, recruitment, pedagogy, predation, and contagion' that imagines queer men and women as 'capable of infinite growth, [and] naturally inclined to expand [their] unnatural ranks'.[142] This sort of thinking was expressed in 1977, when Anita Bryant's 'Save Our Children' campaign took out a full-page advertisement in the *Miami Herald* that read, 'Since homosexuals cannot reproduce, they *must* recruit'.[143]

From the late 1960s and through the 1970s, the reproductive capacities of Black women, like those of gays and lesbians, were viewed by many with alarm. As Jennifer Nelson explains, a number of advocates for population management 'championed birth control as a palliative against rebellions and riots among urban blacks as the civil rights movement shifted toward Black Power', and 'some white Americans' began to '[support] greater government funding for birth control in communities of color'.[144] Some physicians went even further, and 'the problem of sterilization abuse first came to popular public attention as members of Black Nationalist groups' showed that 'poor women of color were often sterilized without their knowledge'.[145] Opposing not only forced sterilisation but also birth control, these groups 'maintained that the path to a strong black nation lay in siring many children for the revolution'.[146]

Unchecked growth among marginalised populations is illustrated in *Blacula* during the raid at the warehouse, as monsters proliferate. Moments after Bobby appears, he is joined by two other vampires. A fourth vampire emerges, then a fifth, sixth, seventh, eighth and ninth. As members of the coven close in on the outnumbered police, the camera cuts quickly between the two groups. Medium shots alternate with close-ups from various angles, disorienting viewers and causing them to share the growing anxiety felt by the police. The confusing visuals of the scene are accompanied by distorted laughter whose source is uncertain. As the police begin fighting for their lives, even more vampires appear. Of the four who enter the warehouse, only two, Thomas and Peters, leave it – only to be confronted by yet another vampire, Blacula.

'The name is Blacula!': *Scream Blacula Scream*

In *Scream Blacula Scream*, the vampire is resurrected by Willis Daniels (Richard Lawson), who seeks to use him to displace Lisa Fortier (Pam Grier) as the leader of a group of voodoo practitioners. Blacula (William Marshall), however, vampirises and dominates Willis. The vampire meets Lisa and her boyfriend, Justin Carter (Don Mitchell), an affluent publisher and ex-police officer who owns a collection of African artefacts, including jewellery worn by Luva. After Blacula learns of Lisa's skill at voodoo, he persuades her to attempt to cure him of his vampirism. Meanwhile, Justin assists his former colleague, Lt Harley Dunlop (Michael Conrad) of the LAPD, who is white, in investigating murders committed by Blacula and those he has vampirised. The two men, together with a group of police officers, raid the house where the vampires live, and where Lisa is performing a ritual to cure Blacula that involves a doll made in his image. In the ensuing conflict, Willis is killed. Justin interrupts Lisa's ritual, which she refuses to resume after watching Blacula kill policemen in a fit of rage. When the vampire attacks Justin, she stabs the doll she has made of him. As Blacula screams, the film ends.

Scream Blacula Scream develops the relations among queerness, lineage and vampirism established in *Blacula*. Like its predecessor, it begins with a homoerotically charged vampiric attack. Shirtless and covered in a sheen of sweat, Willis has conducted a voodoo ritual to revive Blacula, which he believes has failed. As he sits at a table in the mansion where he is serving as caretaker, Blacula's shadow appears on the wall behind him. While the vampire advances, a point-of-view shot from his perspective shows the man's bare back. Rather than attack Willis from behind, Blacula grabs him by the neck and slowly turns his body towards himself, so that the men can look at each other. Close-ups alternate between the faces of the vampire and his victim, emphasising their proximity and intimacy. One extreme close-up lingers on Blacula's open mouth and protruding fangs, before a second shows his mouth on Willis's neck. The camera cuts to a window as Willis groans. This cut suggests that the assault will occur discreetly off-screen, but a moment later an extreme close-up shows Willis's hand clutching Blacula's cape, as the vampire's hand rests on the man's back. Thunder rumbles outside, underscoring the orgasmic quality of the moment. As Willis relaxes in Blacula's arms, his hand opens and moves down the vampire's torso. The next medium shot from behind Willis shows Blacula holding and biting the man, whose arms hang limply at his sides. The camera zooms in, as the vampire lifts his head and stares directly into it, his bloody lips and fangs glistening with the fluid from another man's body, breaking the fourth wall and confronting viewers with his homoerotic (blood)lust. The image freezes, and the extradiegetic music accompanying the opening credits begins. This extraordinarily queer sequence not only intensifies the eroticism of Blacula's attack on Billy, but also eliminates the complicating factors of interracial fetishisation and queer caricature informing that scene by depicting same-sex desire between two masculine Black men, thus offering queer African American viewers non-stereotypical though not necessarily sympathetic characters with whom they might identify. The scene does, however, replicate the tendency in gay pornography of the 1970s to depict Black men as either predators or victims (see Figure 2).[147]

It is followed by other queer scenes between Blacula and Willis that, while much less explicit, are perhaps even more remarkable. In one of the mansion's opulent, antique-filled rooms, Blacula drinks liquor from a brandy glass as Willis, dressed for a party, enters, singing. 'Hey, blood', he says to the vampire, emphasising both their racial and vampiric bonds. No mention is made of the previous attack, or of the man's subsequent transformation into a vampire. Standing in front of a cheval glass, Willis is upset to realise that he no longer casts a reflection. 'You got somethin' to do with this, man?', he asks Blacula, who replies, smiling slightly, 'I'm afraid that's one of the misfortunes of the cursed'. Growing increasingly distraught, Willis tells him, 'I don't mind bein' a vampire and all that shit, but this really ain't hip! I mean, a man has got to see his face!'. He then stands in front of Blacula and asks, 'How do I look, man?'. After they discuss the party that Willis plans to attend, which is hosted by Justin to show off his collection of Africana, Willis again asks, 'How do I look?'. Blacula ignores the question, and Willis wishes him goodnight. 'You go nowhere!', the vampire booms, then rises from the couch where he is sitting. During the rest of the scene, a low-angle shot renders Blacula more imposing and contrasts with a medium shot of the abashed Willis. 'You are never to leave this house without my permission. Your only justification for crawling on this earth is to serve me. If you ever dare to disobey, I will slice into your chest and pull your worthless life out', Blacula declares. Meekly, Willis responds, 'Right', and the scene ends. Newly queered, Willis has discovered and is troubled by his invisibility as a member of a marginalised population, one of the 'cursed'. Absent context, his bond with Blacula would appear to be a relationship of dominance and submission between a wealthy, older man and a kept younger one who has literally and figuratively lost sight of himself and now depends on the perspective of his superior. Moreover, it calls to mind the homoerotic, sadomasochistic connection between Dracula and Renfield.

Like Renfield, Willis both emulates his master and tries but fails to assert himself. When his friends Elaine (Barbara Rhoades) and Louis (Arnold Williams) arrive at the mansion to accompany him to the party, Blacula vampirises the latter in a scene similar to the one in which he bites Willis. After he pins Louis down on a staircase, a medium shot shows him sink his fangs into the man's neck. As the camera pans down Louis's body and he screams, his legs twitch orgasmically. Willis and Blacula then pursue Elaine through the house before the three of them, captured in a full shot, form a visual triangle that represents the triangular nature of the desire connecting them, which is strongest between the two men. Elaine faints, and Willis looks eagerly at Blacula, who silently assents to his unspoken request. Willis kneels down to bite Elaine, but before doing so

Figure 2. Blacula (William Marshall) attacks Willis Daniels (Richard Lawson) in *Scream Blacula Scream* (1973). AIP/Photofest

he again looks at Blacula for permission. A worm's-eye view from Willis's perspective underscores his abasement and his master's ascendancy.

The inequality and queerness of their relationship are likewise emphasised in a second scene that arranges them in a triangle with a woman. Shortly after Willis's girlfriend Denny (Lynne Moody) comes to the mansion, he attempts to vampirise her. When she sees his extended fangs, she laughs and says, 'Where did you get them teeth? Take that crap out yo' mouth!'. He responds to her verbally emasculating him by biting her, albeit with some difficulty, and when he finally penetrates her, she gasps in surprise and pleasure at his newfound potency. Later, though Blacula has forbidden the vampires to harm Lisa, Willis brags to Denny that he will find a way to punish her. Medium shots of one of the mansion's rooms cut between Willis standing in front of Denny and her sitting on a couch. The two are not in the frame together. As Blacula enters the room and says, 'You would dare?', a medium shot shows Willis in the foreground and Blacula in the background. When the vampire reveals himself, Willis turns towards him and a shot shows Blacula dominating the foreground to the left, his back to the camera, while Willis occupies the middle of the frame and Denny is to the right, barely visible. The framing underscores the imbalance in this triangular relationship, which is made even clearer when Willis, frightened and deflated, responds meekly to Blacula while Denny speaks out. 'Well, you just gonna let him bully you around?', she demands of her boyfriend. As Willis tries to placate Blacula, the master vampire hypnotises Denny into silence, showing how he can dominate a woman in a way that his minion cannot.

The outfit that Willis wears during this scene, including sunglasses, a fedora and a cape, speaks volumes about how he would fashion his masculinity. By vampirising Denny, he seeks to demonstrate to her, and to himself, that he is not simply playing a role, and that his phallic power, though drawn from another man, is real. Willis takes his performance of heteronormative masculinity further by assuming the distinctive hat and sunglasses of the pimp, a popular and virile character of Blaxploitation films,[148] together with a cape similar to Blacula's that is meant to signify how his machismo is enhanced by his vampirism. Yet Willis's costume indicates not his heterosexual prowess but his alterity, since the figure of the pimp is queered in a previous scene. Walking down a street in downtown Los Angeles, Blacula passes a prostitute before encountering two unnamed pimps, credited as Pimp #1 (Bob Minor), who wears sunglasses, and Pimp #2 (Al Jones), who wears a fedora. 'What's the matter, man', the second pimp asks him, 'don't you dig girls, or is that the reason for the cape?'. When the vampire ignores him, he shouts, 'Hey, faggot!', and demands money. 'Either you give it up, or we're gonna take it out on your black ass!', he threatens. What might be a scene of gay bashing turns into something very different, as Blacula angrily responds, 'You've made a slave of your sister, and you're still slaves, imitating your slave masters!'. He then knocks the first pimp through a plate-glass window and bites the second one. The scene aligns vampirism, pimping and prostitution as forms of slavery; thus, by vampirising at least one of the pimps, Blacula himself functions as a slave master. Though as an African prince he is ideally suited to represent Black pride and power, as an enslaved and enslaving vampire he is a deeply problematic figure.

This tension between Mamuwalde and Blacula is resolved at the end of the film, together with associated conflicts between science and the supernatural, and the present and the past. Science figures prominently in *Blacula* and *Scream Blacula Scream*, which, like *Blackenstein* and *Dr. Black, Mr. Hyde*, feature skilled Black women scientists. Michelle conducts research in a forensics lab, and Lisa, as Blacula observes, has 'exceptional powers in the exceedingly complex science of voodoo'. In fighting vampires, Michelle and Lisa join Thomas and Justin, who investigate vampirism and demonstrate its reality to their sceptical colleagues in the LAPD. Like Van Helsing, these men view science and the occult as complementary. Similarly, following Stoker's *Dracula* in drawing the past into the present, *Blacula* and *Scream Blacula Scream* seek to reconcile modern and long-established African (American) attitudes and practices. Though wholly contemporary characters, Justin and Lisa remain linked with their African heritage. They wear Afros[149] and are experts in Africana and voodoo. More broadly, the salience of lineage in *Scream Blacula Scream* is underscored by the fact that its plot turns on questions of inheritance. Willis brings the past, embodied by Blacula, back to life as part of his scheme against Lisa, who has been chosen as the successor to his mother, the recently deceased voodoo queen Mama Loa (uncredited). Lisa's being selected over Willis, the heir apparent, indicates that ability is more important than ancestry, and that on occasion the ways of the past must be set aside for the sake of the present and future. Looking beyond his own inheritance as a vampire and towards his lineage as a prince of the Eboni, Blacula hopes that Lisa can transform him back into Mamuwalde, and that he can return home to his tribe in Africa. As her voodoo starts to work on him, it seems that he might again fully inhabit his persona as Mamuwalde, the figure of living

African history who lectures Justin and his friend Walston, a professor of African Studies, on the artefacts of the Eboni Dynasty. But by beating and killing policemen in front of Lisa while she begs him to stop, he surrenders to his vampirism and reveals himself as the monster enslaved by Dracula centuries ago. Ultimately, he acknowledges as much. When Justin calls him 'Mamuwalde', he responds with fury, 'The name is Blacula!'.

Blood and the Cross: *Ganja & Hess*

In *Blacula*, religion plays a surprisingly minor role, appearing only when Thomas uses a large cross against Juanita and gives it to Tina for protection against Blacula. The cross and Christianity figure much more prominently in *Ganja & Hess*. The film centres on Dr Hess Green (Duane Jones), a wealthy anthropologist who researches the Myrthians, a fictional tribe of African blood drinkers from the ancient, pre-Christian past. His new assistant, George Meda (Bill Gunn), stabs Green with a Myrthian dagger before shooting himself. Vampirised by the knife, Green drinks the dead man's blood. He survives as a vampire by stealing blood bags from a hospital, and by drinking from a pimp he kills in self-defence. After Meda's wife Ganja (Marlene Clark) comes to Green's mansion in search of her husband, she and her host become romantically involved. She discovers Meda's death and marries Green, who vampirises her. He brings home a man (Richard Harrow) whom Ganja drains, and the two dispose of the body. Dissatisfied with his existence, Green attends a service at the church run by his chauffeur and stableman, Rev. Luther Williams (Sam L. Waymon). He then comes home and commits suicide by standing in front of a cross and allowing its shadow to fall on his heart. As the film ends, Ganja is looking out a window, watching the man she vampirised return from the dead.

The alignment of queerness, lineage and vampirism that informs previous iterations of *Dracula* is continued in *Ganja & Hess*, which complicates this nexus by involving Christianity.[150] In fact, the film is framed as a Christian allegory. As it begins, text appears onscreen describing how Green, 'while studying the ancient Black civilization of Myrthia, was stabbed . . . with a dagger, diseased from that ancient culture, whereupon he became addicted and could not die'. Medium shots and close-ups of western religious sculptures appear as a man sings a spiritual extradiegetically: 'I know it was the blood for me. / Tell you that one day when I was lost, / You know that He died upon the cross'. The scene moves to the interior of a church, where Williams is preaching onstage under a large cross. The diegetic sound fades and he begins speaking in voiceover, explaining that his employer Green is 'addicted to blood'. As shots show Williams driving Green to meet Meda at a museum, the minister's voiceover continues: 'And Jesus said unto them, "Who so eateth my flesh and drinketh my blood, hath eternal life"'. As might be expected from an opening frame provided by a minister, this one not only serves the Gothic functions of authentication and buffering, but also works in much the same fashion as scripture, transcending time by means of typology. In an authoritative voice that eases viewers into the occasionally disjointed narrative that follows his frame, Williams speaks first in the past tense and then in the present tense about future events, as if prophesying. He also construes Christ and Green as type and antitype, for the former's self-sacrifice via the cross prefigures the latter's. More problematically, though Williams contrasts African paganism with western Christianity, he also implicitly associates the two by accentuating the vampirism of the Eucharist. In an example of Gothic concentric narrative structure, embedded within his frame are two others. As Manthia Diawara and Phyllis R. Klotman observe, the film is told from the divergent perspectives of its three successive narrators: Williams, Meda and Ganja.[151] Christ is 'the hero of the minister's narrative, and the Africans – and Green, when he [follows] their example – [are] the villains'.[152] Meda and Ganja present very different viewpoints from that of Williams. Diawara and Klotman note that Meda is played by the film's director, Bill Gunn, whose 'metafilmic' narrative posits that 'blacks are damaged by both the minister's teleological conception of history and the white man's philosophy' of individualism and material success, which Green shares. As the film ends, Ganja, 'tired of being subservient to the church and to black men', is glad to be rid of her husbands, 'the self-destructive artist and the bourgeois patriarch',[153] and free to control her own life. Unsurprisingly, as the innermost narrative, hers is also the most transgressive.

The concentric narrative frames of *Ganja & Hess* engage contemporary debates about the strained relationship between Christianity and Black Power. In the late 1960s and early 1970s, as Albert J. Raboteau explains, 'Some activists accused [Christian] religious institutions of being otherworldly, conservative, and an obstacle to black liberation'.[154] Elijah Muhammad, the leader of the Black nationalist political-religious group the Nation of Islam, went so far as to claim that Christianity was the white man's religion. According to Mark L. Chapman, many 'began to view the black church as an "Uncle Tom" institution that was irrelevant to the concerns of youth during a new age of Black Power and black pride'.[155] In response to growing criticism, a new Black theology emerged, articulated by figures including the theologian James Cone and the clergyman Albert Cleage. Cone declared, 'Christianity is not alien to Black Power; it is Black Power', and he contended that 'Black rebellion is a manifestation of God himself actively involved in the present-day affairs of men for the purpose of liberating a people'.[156] He viewed this liberation in racial rather than individual terms, writing that 'freedom is *not doing what I will but becoming what I should*'.[157] Similarly, arguing that 'white society [was] corrupt because it [pursued] an individualistic concept of power', Cleage was 'concerned about the individualism that pervaded the theology of the black church', which he considered a 'slave theology' that emphasised 'individualistic otherworldly salvation' and formed 'one of the biggest stumbling blocks to black liberation'.[158] Central to his revisionist view of a community-focused Black Christianity was lineage, for he 'rejected the doctrine of the incarnation', argued that 'Jesus was a Black Messiah born to a black woman', and 'traced the genealogy of Jesus to prove his claim that Jesus was of African ancestry'.[159] 'We are not talking about God the Father', he declared. 'We are concerned here with the actual bloodline'.[160]

The outermost frame of *Ganja & Hess* rejects the Black theology of Cone and Cleage and depicts events in the film from a conventional Christian worldview, which prioritises individual salvation through Christ's sacrifice. In Green's case, such salvation means emancipation from his enslavement to vampirism – a release achieved, paradoxically, through the Eucharist. This process begins when Meda is stabbed with a Myrthian dagger that he has acquired and keeps on his nightstand. The text that begins the film claims that Meda stabs Green three times: 'one for God the Father, one for the Son and one for the Holy Ghost.' Since this text is extradiegetic, its source might be Williams, Gunn or a higher power. While Green is indeed stabbed three times, it seems odd to attribute a religious motive to Meda, who grabs the ancient dagger only because it is near at hand and he has failed to kill his employer with an axe. That said, the indeterminacy of the text's source encourages viewers to wonder not only who is speaking, but also why the events described occur. If the text functions as the voice of God, it indicates that an overarching theological and teleological narrative frame may be at work, and that Meda's stabbing Green could be part of a divine plan to bring him to Christ through the circuitous route of Myrthian vampirism. What appears to be a curse is thus revealed as a blessing.

The frame that Williams and perhaps the film itself attempt to impose on Green's life is challenged by Meda's experience of events. His perspective overlaps with that of Black theology, insofar as it stresses the welfare of the community, not the individual, and highlights African ancestry. Before shooting himself, Meda considers suicide by hanging. In a full shot, the camera pans down the tree in which he sits, his face obscured by leaves and darkness. Dominating the frame is a noose. Green finds Meda and attempts to dissuade him from self-harm by citing his own interest: 'It is my tree and my rope. You see, that would give the authorities the right to invade my privacy.' Unlike Meda, Green is fully visible in the foreground, his face illuminated by moonlight. The *mise en scène* and lighting undercut Green's selfishness by concealing Meda the individual and stressing his position as part of an entire race traumatised by lynching. The same wide focus on a people instead of a person is evident when Meda types up a suicide note 'to the black male children' that he reads aloud. 'Philosophy is a prison', it cautions. 'The result of individual thought is applicable only to itself.' In much the same way that he represents and addresses many African Americans, Meda exemplifies and embodies Black theology by functioning, together with Green, as a Black Christ figure. Before committing suicide, he takes a bath as though baptising himself. When he emerges from the bath, he is reflected in a mirror. As Meda points a gun at his heart, a wooden cross is positioned behind him. The scene cuts to Green, who has risen from the dead, as he approaches his bedroom mirror with a hand over his own heart, surprised to discover that his wounds have disappeared. The camera then returns to Meda, who shoots himself in the heart. When Green enters the bathroom where Meda is lying in a pool of blood, he appears first in a mirror. A subsequent shot shows him and Meda both in the foreground and in mirrors, highlighting their status as doppelgängers for each other and for Christ, an image of whom appears momentarily between two close-up shots of Meda's bloody body. Meda's sacrifice enables Green, who drinks his blood, to have eternal life, which he chooses to end by means of the cross. As he collapses in front of it, the camera cuts to Meda's own collapse after shooting himself, thereby underscoring the similarities between the men and their sacrifices.

The relationship between these two Black Christ figures calls attention to the queer potential of a man who gives his body to other men. In keeping with the pattern established by its precursors, the film introduces the homoerotic together with the vampiric. When Meda attacks Green, in a point-of-view shot from Meda's perspective Green is shown lying asleep in bed. Meda approaches the bed, over which hangs a painting of the risen Christ alongside a rack of antlers that connect with a small oval painting of Actaeon on a wardrobe. The antlers also evoke the Myrthian dagger, which is made of bone. The *mise en scène* indicates that the roles of hunter and hunted are reversible, and that Green, who will soon be penetrated by Meda and the dagger, will rise again to penetrate others, including the pimp whose throat he cuts before drinking from it. Moreover, this arrangement of objects at once juxtaposes and links western and African cultures, as do the opening shots of the film, suggesting that the tensions between traditions expressed within the narrative frames might be resolved. Meda swings at his victim with an axe but misses. The two shirtless men then grapple with each other in and around the bed, ending up on the floor. Finally, Meda grabs the dagger from Green's nightstand. The phallic qualities of this bone are established in an earlier scene that shows Green toying with it while lying in bed. In a medium shot, Meda stabs Green three times. The camera discreetly cuts to a record jacket on the nightstand before returning to Meda, who removes the dagger, tosses it onto the bed, and then climbs into bed himself. During the next and final time that the men appear together, Meda is lying naked in a pool of blood on the bathroom floor and Green is kneeling close to his body, lapping up his blood.

The image of a Black Christ recurs once more at the end of the film in Ganja's narrative. She looks out a window at a large swimming pool, behind which are a Greco-Roman pavilion and a fountain featuring a statue. In slow motion, the man Ganja has vampirised rises, nude, from the pool. The extradiegetic music and clapping, which increase in volume as he runs towards her, evoke that playing when Green dreams of a Myrthian woman who offers him her hand, and when he succumbs to his compulsion to drink blood. The camera cuts between the running man and Ganja, and when it returns to him, he freezes while jumping over the bloodied body of Green's servant Archie (Leonard Jackson), who has apparently been drained by Ganja in an act that emphasises her position above him. The music and clapping stop and the camera cuts to and zooms in on Ganja, who is watching coolly in a low-angle shot that reinforces her elevated status. It then cuts to a close-up in shallow focus from eye level and a different angle. Ganja's gaze shifts from the ground to the camera. Another cut shows her straight on, still looking directly into the camera. Her expression softens, and she smiles.

This remarkable sequence rejects both the conventional Christianity of Williams's frame and the Black theology of Meda's, favouring instead an

African-Christian synthesis informed by feminism. It begins with a third Black Christ figure, a man who seems to have risen from the dead and emerges from a pool of water as if reborn. The pool replicates both the pool of blood in which Meda dies and Green is born again as a vampire, and the bath in which Meda bathes before killing himself. Against the background of a classical pavilion and statue, this man recalls not only Christ but also the classical statues with which the film begins; thus, he seems to represent western religion and culture. Yet his vampirism is associated explicitly with Myrthians and implicitly with Christians, and the extradiegetic sound underscores his connection to the former. Whereas Ganja's deceased husband destroys himself because he cannot reconcile the conflict between western and African traditions, her resurrected lover unites them. Moreover, in running to join her, he varies the triangulation and substitution of previous vampiric narratives. Just as Ganja takes her husband's place at Green's side, so too does this man take Green's at her own – though Ganja and not Green now occupies the primary position of wealth and power. She thereby substitutes not only for Green but also for the Myrthian woman of his dreams, the tribal matriarch, becoming both a reincarnation of this ancient queen and the founding mother of a new vampiric bloodline.

Ganja & Hess follows its literary and cinematic antecedents by drawing together vampirism, queerness and lineage, and by employing this nexus to address issues of vital importance to contemporary readers and viewers. It radically departs from its predecessors, however, by empowering and elevating a female protagonist who survives and thrives. If Lucy and Mina in *Dracula* had been allowed to realise their potential as vampires instead of being staked or limited to traditional feminine roles, they might have evolved into characters as formidable as Ganja. Like Ellen in *Nosferatu* and Luva in *Blacula*, Ganja becomes involved with an aristocratic male vampire who destroys himself. Unlike these doomed women, she not only outlives but also displaces her demon lover, improbably coming to occupy the dominant and stable vertex of the triangular relationship that typically structures fictions and films about vampires. As a result, vampiric matriarchy of the sort extirpated in *Carmilla* is reinstated in *Ganja & Hess*. Ganja's smiling at viewers in her final close-up may well signify her satisfaction at how far the stories of vampires have come.

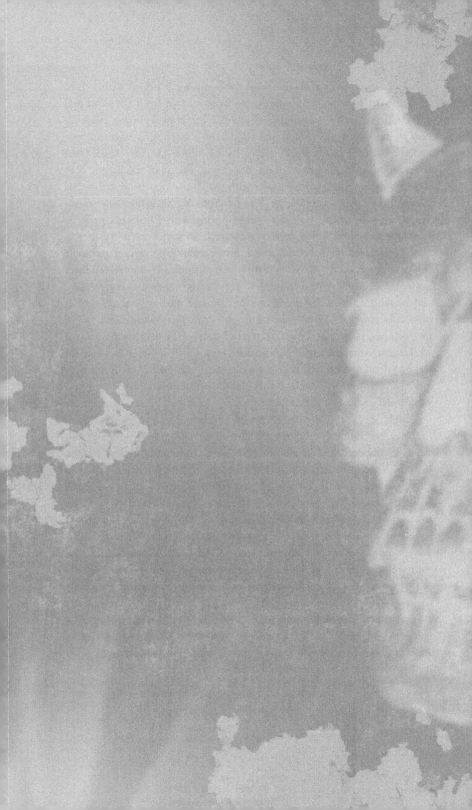

2
Making Monsters
Frankenstein's Creature

MARY SHELLEY'S *Frankenstein; or, The Modern Prometheus* (1818) is set in the eighteenth century and comprises concentric first-person narratives told by Robert Walton, who captains a ship heading towards the North Pole; Victor Frankenstein, who fashions a being and imbues him with life; and the unnamed Creature, who takes revenge on his creator. Embedded in Walton's letters to his sister Margaret are the stories of Frankenstein and his creation. Walton sees the Creature driving a sled and followed at a distance by Frankenstein, whom he brings aboard his ship. Frankenstein describes to Walton his childhood in Geneva among a prominent family consisting of his parents, Alphonse and Caroline; his brothers, Ernest and William; and Elizabeth, an orphan whom the family adopts. They also take in Justine, who cares for William. From childhood, Frankenstein is fascinated by the secrets of nature. His mother dies shortly before he begins studying at the University of Ingolstadt, which he leaves to pursue his own outré work. Ultimately, Frankenstein puts together a man from the pieces of human beings and animals. The Creature is a composite being whose parts Frankenstein finds not only in 'charnel houses' and 'the dissecting room', but also in 'the slaughter-house'.[1] Because 'the minuteness of the parts [forms] a great hindrance to [his] speed', he opts 'to make the being of a gigantic stature' and begins collecting what he euphemistically terms his 'materials'.[2]

After bringing his hideous creation to life, Frankenstein immediately abandons him and suffers a physical and mental breakdown. He is then reunited with a childhood friend, Henry Clerval, who nurses him back to health. On recovering, Frankenstein learns that William has been murdered by the Creature. Justine is executed for this crime after a miniature that Elizabeth gives William is found in her pocket, where it has been placed by the Creature. Frankenstein retreats to the Alps, where his creation confronts him and tells him of living in the woods and secretly aiding the De Lacey family, who reject him. Convinced that he will never be accepted by human beings, that he is 'a monster . . . from which all men [flee], and whom all men [disown]',[3] the Creature demands that Frankenstein make him a female companion to share his life apart from society. Frankenstein initially agrees, but in time he thinks better of his promise and destroys the body before it is complete. In retribution, the Creature kills Clerval, for whose murder Frankenstein is arrested. After a second breakdown, Frankenstein is released from prison and marries Elizabeth. On their wedding night, the Creature kills her. Alphonse dies shortly thereafter. Frankenstein pursues the Creature until the two reach the Arctic and Walton's ship. Not long after concluding his life story, Frankenstein dies. The Creature boards the ship, mourns Frankenstein, and vows to kill himself. He then drifts away on a raft of ice.

Creation, Collage and Justice: *Frankenstein*

Like the stitched-together being it portrays, *Frankenstein* is a collage whose monstrosity is closely bound up with its form. Although the theory and practice of collage are typically associated with the visual arts and modernist literature,[4] they unquestionably shape Shelley's novel. As Dennis R. Perry notes, Shelley is 'an adapter sewing together parts from older texts like the Prometheus myth, *Paradise Lost*, *The Rime of the Ancient Mariner*, *Faust*, and *Caleb Williams* to a create a monster that made conservative reviewers indignant enough to call the novel "a tissue of horrible and disgusting absurdity"'.[5] The narrative threads connecting the pieces of Frankenstein are not always taut, and sometimes the seams of the novel show, as when Walton describes to his sister a childhood they shared, Elizabeth tells Victor the life story of Justine, with whom they both grew up, or the Creature discovers *Paradise Lost*, *Plutarch's Lives* and *The Sorrows of Young Werther* in the middle of a forest. The thinness and scarring of the novel's textual membrane make it an even closer analogue to the Creature, whose 'skin scarcely [covers] the work of muscles and arteries beneath'.[6]

Likewise visible under the narrative surface of *Frankenstein* are the workings and connective tissue of collage, which manifest not only in the novel's patchwork of literary allusions, but also in its collocation of three different stories and storytellers. Scarlett Higgins contends that 'the juxtapositional force of collage' is 'disruptive of not just one given narrative but rather the larger formal and generic claims of narrative as a whole'.[7] Her insight indicates how the concentric structure of *Frankenstein* draws on both the classical Gothic frame and collage to challenge the conventions of linear, mimetic narrative, and to enrich the novel's Gothicism by emphasising the fragmentary, provisional nature of subjective experience and storytelling. Yet collage involves not only juxtaposition but also collation, for it both contrasts and aligns the accounts of Walton, Frankenstein and the Creature, whose similarities to one another become evident as their tales unfold. All three are autodidacts and travellers who are alone and seek companionship, and all three are to varying extents at odds with nature. They are in fact so similar as to function at times as doppelgängers for one another.[8] Doubling and collage are also central to the numerous cinematic duplicates of Shelley's novel, which '[create] "new" films out of the parts of previous ones'.[9] An amalgamation on which adaptations are continually being grafted, *Frankenstein* causes its readers and viewers to consider how the parts relate to the whole, and whether seamless integration is possible. Because the Creature is not well put together, he is deemed monstrous and cannot fit into society; thus, monstrosity is a function of both corporeal and social disintegration.

In proving this point, *Frankenstein* illustrates how monsters are made, not born. If the Creature were better assembled, he might not have become monstrous; but ultimately his mistreatment, not his construction, makes him 'the miserable monster whom [Frankenstein] [has] created'.[10] His descent into monstrosity begins when his own creator spurns him because of his ugliness, which is described as a disjunction between the parts and the whole – that is, a consequence of unsuccessful collage. As Frankenstein recalls, 'his hair was of a lustrous black, and flowing; his teeth of a pearly whiteness; but these luxuriances only formed a more horrid contrast with his watery eyes, that seemed almost of the same colour as the dun white sockets in which they were set, his shrivelled complexion, and straight black lips'.[11] This horrific incongruity leads the Creature to ask, 'Why did you form a monster so hideous that even you turned from me in disgust?', and to observe that '[his] form is a filthy type of [Frankenstein's], more horrid from its very resemblance'.[12] What the Creature cannot realise is that his external hideousness reflects and embodies his creator's internal monstrousness. Frankenstein admits as much, viewing the Creature 'nearly in the light of [his] own vampire, [his] own spirit let loose from the grave, and forced to destroy all that was dear to [him]'.[13] By killing Frankenstein's family members and closest friend, and by driving himself and his creator into the barren Arctic, the Creature completes a process begun by Frankenstein when he separates himself from (human) nature in the pursuit of his ambition to reproduce unnaturally, to become the 'creator and source' of 'a new species'.[14] As Frankenstein acknowledges, his 'eyes were insensible to the charms of nature. And the same feelings which made [him] neglect the scenes around [him] caused [him] also to forget those friends who were so many miles absent, and whom [he] had not seen for so long a time'.[15]

Frankenstein's alienation from his family and the natural world are at once the cause and the effect of his making monsters of himself and his creation. The latter, 'united by no link to any other being in existence', explains, 'If I have no ties and no affections, hatred and vice must be my portion', and asks to be 'linked to the chain of existence and events, from which [he] [is] now excluded'.[16] Ironically, Frankenstein seeks to rectify the damage caused by ruptures in the tissues of family and ecology by ripping apart his monstrous collage. 'You, my creator, would tear me to pieces', the Creature declares, and indeed Frankenstein does '[tear] to pieces' his second, female creation.[17] The Creature points out the moral inconsistency and unfairness of this behaviour, telling his maker, 'You accuse me of murder; and yet you would, with a satisfied conscience, destroy your own creature. Oh, praise the eternal justice of man!'.[18] His concern with (in)justice, together with the monstrous actions of himself and his creator, pose the problems related to crime, punishment and responsibility that inform *Frankenstein*.

Judgement figures prominently in the novel, as readers judge the relative culpability of creator and creation, the eponymous father (mis)judges his misbegotten son, and Walton judges whether Frankenstein is telling him the truth. Again, collage is essential. For instance, when William is murdered and Frankenstein spots the Creature in the mountains outside Geneva, he judges him a killer simply by virtue of his disorganised appearance. 'Nothing in human shape could have destroyed that fair child', he concludes. '*He* was the murderer!'.[19] Readers will eventually come to understand from the Creature's account that William's death might well have been an accident, but at this point the parts of the narrative have not yet combined into a whole to enable informed judgement. In keeping with the novel's structure and function as a collage, responsibility for William's murder is simultaneously individual and collective. Characters are charged with or take responsibility for a crime that they have not committed directly, and guilt is thereby distributed among them. The Creature kills William, yet Justine is arrested for and confesses to his murder, thus becoming, like the actual murderer, a 'monster'[20] rejected by a horrified society. Elizabeth, who gives William the locket that she believes causes his death, likewise confesses, 'O God! I have murdered my darling infant!'.[21] Frankenstein too declares himself 'the true murderer'[22] of William. After Justine is executed and Clerval is killed by the Creature, Frankenstein likewise indicts himself as 'the murderer of William, of Justine, and of Clerval'.[23] Even before his friend is murdered, he '[feels] as if [he] [has] committed some great crime', though he is 'guiltless'.[24] As guilt, blame and punishment circulate among those who are innocent of actual crime, true judgement becomes impossible.

Although the justice system plays a much larger role in *Frankenstein* than in later Gothic novels such as *Strange Case of Dr Jekyll and Mr Hyde* and *Dracula*, it proves dysfunctional and incapable of coping with a criminal such as the Creature. As a result, what passes for justice is meted out by individuals on one another and themselves. Justine and Frankenstein are charged with murders of which they are innocent, and the former is executed. The injustice of Justine's arrest and trial, a 'wretched mockery of justice',[25] is compounded by that of her sentence. An anguished Elizabeth declares that 'when one creature is murdered, another is immediately deprived of life in a slow torturing manner' and 'they call this retribution'.[26] She describes not only Justine's impending fate but also the circuitous dynamics of crime and punishment in *Frankenstein*, whose plot is driven by the Creature's vengeance and Frankenstein's attempts to respond to it in kind. This cycle accelerates after Frankenstein, having been judged innocent of Clerval's murder, seeks the aid of a magistrate in bringing his creation to justice. 'If it is in my power to seize the monster, be assured that he shall suffer punishment proportionate to his crimes',[27] this official tells Frankenstein. 'But I fear, from what you have yourself described to be his properties, that this will prove impracticable.'[28] Enraged, Frankenstein himself seeks to punish the Creature, whose sense of injustice is as strong as his creator's. 'Am I to be thought the only criminal, when all human kind sinned against me?',[29] he asks Frankenstein, from whom he '[determines] to seek that justice which [he] vainly [attempts] to gain from any other being that [wears] the human form'.[30] The Creature succeeds, at least temporarily, in persuading Frankenstein that there is 'some justice in his argument' and in determining 'that the justice due both to [the Creature] and [Frankenstein's] fellow-creatures [demands] of [Frankenstein] that [he] should comply with his request'.[31] Ultimately, however, Frankenstein passes a death sentence on his creation, and before his own death asks Walton to execute it. The transfer of punishment among the three doubles is complete when the Creature resolves to take his own life, telling Walton, 'Neither your's nor any man's death is needed to consummate the series of my being, and accomplish that which must be done; but it requires my own'.[32] He thus becomes his own judge and executioner.

Bad Brains: Frankenstein and The Curse of Frankenstein

Film adaptations and appropriations of *Frankenstein* not only function as grafts on the novel and extensions of its monstrous collage, but also retain its thematic focus on creation, collage and justice. *Frankenstein* (James Whale, 1931) and *The Curse of Frankenstein* (Terence Fisher, 1957) explore whether monsters are born or made, and how this process involves collage and (in)justice. *The Thing with Two Heads* and *Blackenstein* consider these issues from the perspective of race, illustrating how the American justice system, together with the medical and military establishments, can make Black men into monsters. Fisher's film contravenes Shelley's novel by positing that the Creature's monstrosity results from nature, not nurture, since it is the consequence of a damaged brain. Whale's film also features an inferior brain but explores the nature/nurture opposition with more subtlety. The Blaxploitation films accord with Shelley's theme that injustice and mistreatment create monsters. All four films adopt and adapt the novel's concern with who administers justice, and how. In Whale's film, it is executed by a mob. In Fisher's, it is promised by individuals but ultimately delivered by the state. In Frost's and Levey's, it is within the purview of the prison system and the police.

Before the action of Whale's *Frankenstein* begins, the actor playing Dr Waldman, Edward Van Sloan, cautions the audience about its potentially disturbing aspects. The scene shifts to Germany, where in a watchtower-turned-laboratory Henry Frankenstein (Colin Clive) and his hunchbacked assistant Fritz (Dwight Frye) assemble a being from pieces of cadavers. Seeking the final part of the Creature, Fritz sneaks into the medical school where Waldman has been lecturing on the differences between a normal and a criminal brain. After Fritz drops the jar containing the former, he brings Frankenstein the latter. Elizabeth Lavenza (Mae Clarke), who is concerned about her fiancé Frankenstein's well-being, joins their friend Victor Moritz (John Boles) and Waldman in an unannounced visit to his laboratory. The three witness the Creature's vivification by electricity during a thunderstorm. Waldman remains with Frankenstein, warns him that the Creature possesses a criminal brain, and urges him to destroy his creation. At first the Creature seems harmless, but after Fritz goads him into fear and anger with a torch, he is chained in a dungeon and finally kills his unrelenting tormentor. Frankenstein returns home to prepare for his marriage and leaves the Creature with Waldman, who pledges to destroy him but is instead strangled by him. The Creature leaves the watchtower and encounters Maria (Marilyn Harris), a child he plays with and accidentally kills. Villagers form search parties for the murderer, who attacks Frankenstein and takes him into a windmill. After the Creature hurls his creator out of the structure, the villagers set it ablaze and take Frankenstein home, where he recovers and weds Elizabeth.

In *Frankenstein*, collage manifests itself both formally and thematically. Whale's film was put together not only from Shelley's novel, but also from John Balderston's adaptation of Peggy Webling's play, *Frankenstein: An Adventure in the Macabre* (1927).[33] The stitching between the genres of theatre and film is conspicuous in Van Sloan's opening monologue. Not in costume but in evening clothes, and in his own persona rather than in character, the actor steps from behind stage curtains to address the audience. He speaks for 'Mr Carl Laemmle', the co-founder, owner and head of Universal Pictures, who 'feels it would be a little unkind to present this picture without just a word of friendly warning'. He continues, 'We are about to unfold the story of Frankenstein, a man of science who sought to create a man after his own image, without reckoning upon God', and concludes that the film 'will thrill you. It may shock you. It might even horrify you'. Although Van Sloan appears to break the fourth wall, he never looks directly into the camera and acknowledges that he is onstage in a film, not a play. Instead, his eyes move beyond and around viewers, across the space an audience would occupy in a theatre. The actor ostensibly addresses those watching Whale's 'picture', yet these viewers are excluded from his own gaze. As a result, he seems to be speaking from within a filmed play instead of a movie, and the suture between theatre and film is emphasised rather than elided.

The stitching among these two genres and a third, fiction, is evident in how Van Sloan's prologue reproduces the outermost, intertextual frame of Shelley's novel, together with its Gothic strategies of authentication and buffering. His citing Laemmle, Universal's patriarch, recalls her quoting from Milton, the father figure of the Romantics, on the title page of *Frankenstein*.[34] Both men lend paternal gravitas to the bizarre narratives that follow their invocation, ease viewers and readers from the familiar into the outré, and provide authoritative interpretive constructs whose themes seem clear: man should not challenge or emulate God, and sons ought not to oppose their fathers. In typically Gothic fashion, these fictional and cinematic frames cannot fully contain the transgressive stories they introduce; thus, the ligatures between them and these embedded narratives are strained. In Shelley's quotation from *Paradise Lost* (1667), the fallen Adam asks, 'Did I request thee, Maker, from my clay / To mould me man?'.[35] Representing the son's perspective rather than the father's, this provocative epigraph calls into question the justice of Adam's banishment and ultimate death sentence by suggesting that creators are responsible for their creations, and that they share culpability for the misdeeds of their progeny. It not only foreshadows the powerful and dynamic tensions between father and son that energise *Frankenstein*, but also indicates how these two seemingly opposed figures can be aligned, confused and conflated. Opposition and conflation are likewise balanced in the opening address of Whale's film, which is delivered by the actor playing the mentor and father figure against whom Frankenstein rebels in order to create a monster, in much the same way that Carl Laemmle Jr rebelled against his own father by producing monster movies.[36] Speaking through his patriarchal double, the senior Laemmle warns the audience against his son's illicit and dangerous creation, which he seeks to confine within a conventional ideological framework. Yet his ventriloquised address is designed to stimulate in the audience a Frankenstein-like curiosity about making a monster, while veiling this questionable intent with a theologically innocuous moral. Offering more enticement than admonition, Van Sloan functions less as a remonitory than as a carnival barker. His prologue involves Laemmle Sr in his son's monstrous film rather than distancing him from it, thereby problematising the opposition between father and son.

A closely related bifurcation, and one equally important to all iterations of *Frankenstein*, is that between man and monster. Whale's film illustrates how individuals within these categories may be transposed and blended, without offering a definitive answer to the question of whether monsters are born or made. The official theatrical poster by Karoly Grosz, Universal's art director, calls Frankenstein 'the man who made a monster', but Fritz is the one who turns a man into a monster by terrifying and tormenting Frankenstein's creation. That Fritz himself is a monster is made abundantly clear by his sadism, and his monstrosity may well be traced to the abuse that he has suffered as a hunchback, which he in turn inflicts on the only being more grotesque and abject than himself. Whether his deformity is the cause or consequence of his monstrosity is impossible to decide; it is probably both. Like Shakespeare's hunchbacked Richard III, Fritz may be 'determinèd to prove a villain'[37] because his handicap leaves him no other option, even as his twisted body serves as a metaphor for his warped psyche. The nature/nurture opposition collapses in his case, and perhaps in that of the Creature, whose monstrosity may result from his mistreatment, his abnormal brain, or both. Waldman believes the Creature is 'a fiend' because he possesses 'a criminal brain', but the doctor's lecture on the normal and criminal brains does nothing to establish causality. He describes 'the scarcity of convolutions on the frontal lobe' of the latter as compared with the former, and he points out 'the distinct degeneration of the middle frontal lobe' in the criminal brain before concluding, 'All of these degenerate characteristics check amazingly with the history of the dead man before us, whose life was one of brutality, of violence and murder'. But Waldman fails to clarify whether the man's life of crime was caused by or contributed to the degeneration of his brain. Though the Creature has an abnormal brain, might it have evolved if he had been treated with more kindness and compassion? By leaving open the question of causality, *Frankenstein* holds the categories of man and monster in unresolved tension, linked in an ontological collage.

The film likewise stitches together horror and humour, in a fashion that recalls the comic relief provided by frightened servants in classical Gothic novels.[36] The skeleton hanging in Waldman's lecture hall bounces after being touched by one of two doctors who have wheeled a cadaver into the room, causing the medical students to laugh for a few moments before turning their attention to cerebral anatomy. The skeleton jumps again when Fritz bumps into it, alarming him. That someone who traffics in corpses and body parts would be so nervous around them is a source of both irony and amusement for viewers. After being startled once more, this time by the sound of his own cane as it strikes a metal table, Fritz drops and shatters the jar containing the normal brain and picks up the jar holding its opposite. His comical anxiety and clumsiness yield deadly serious consequences when he is hanged by the Creature whose criminal brain he procures. When he steals this brain, his demise is literally foreshadowed. His own shadow and the one cast by the skeleton flank a large illustration of a skull on the classroom wall, prefiguring the shadow cast on the dungeon wall by Fritz's corpse as it hangs in the Creature's cell. Both this hanging corpse and the hanging skeleton also hark back to the hanged criminal whom Fritz reluctantly cuts down from a gibbet near the beginning of the film, in a scene with both comedic and horrific elements.

This correlation is problematic, for even viewers sympathetic to the Creature's torment might question whether he serves justice in executing Fritz, whose cruelty is monstrous but whose theft and graverobbing are hardly capital crimes. In contrast, the man whom Fritz releases from the gibbet is a killer hanging there in accordance with the Murder Act of 1752. Designed 'for better preventing the horrid Crime of Murder', the Act stipulated that 'some Terror and peculiar mark of Infamy be added to the Punishment of Death' for this crime.[39] Thus, the bodies of executed murderers were either 'sent to an appointed surgeon or anatomist for dissection, or turned over to the sheriff to be hung in chains'.[40] Both outcomes are depicted in *Frankenstein*, since Waldman identifies the body on display in his classroom as that of a murderer. In much the same way as the gibbeted man doubles Fritz, this cadaver mirrors the Creature, whom Waldman, with Frankenstein's consent, intends to execute and dissect as if meting out condign punishment for Fritz's murder. By killing one of the father figures who would kill him, the Creature at once temporarily eludes the consequences of his crime, destroys the outmoded patriarch whose upbraiding Frankenstein resents, and ultimately enables himself to throw his own negligent creator from a windmill.

The climactic scene in which he does so illustrates how in Whale's film, as in Shelley's novel and Milton's epic poem, the workings of crime and punishment are inextricable from the vengeance of fathers and sons. Moved by the wrath of the murdered Maria's father, a crowd of men is exhorted by the Burgomaster, who serves as a paternal surrogate for the village, to 'get [the Creature] alive if [they] can, but get him!'. When creator and creation appear together atop the windmill, the Burgomaster cries, 'There he is! The murderer!'. He seems to refer to the Creature, but since Frankenstein confesses that the death of Fritz is 'all [his] fault' and conspires with Waldman to commit a second murder, the appellation could apply to either of them. Their interchangeability and mutual culpability are illustrated when they circle each other around the wheel driving the windmill, staring through its spokes in alternating close-ups. In the end, both father and son appear condemned to death for their crimes. As the seemingly lifeless body of Frankenstein is taken home, the members of the mob abandon all restraint and cry 'Kill it!' while preparing to burn the Creature alive. In Shelley's novel, Frankenstein perishes whereas the Creature's demise is promised but unrealised. In the original cut of Whale's film, both father and son seem to die; but, in a scene that was added after test screenings revealed that viewers were dissatisfied with this outcome, Frankenstein is shown in a long shot recovering in bed while his father drinks 'to a son of the house of Frankenstein'.[41] His toast wishing for a grandson, and for the continuation of the Frankenstein patriarchy, ignores the problematic fact that the family already has a new son, the Creature, who will continue the cycle of paternal and filial transgression and retribution, of crime and punishment, in *The Bride of Frankenstein* (James Whale, 1935).

Like *Frankenstein*, *The Curse of Frankenstein* is a collage that explores the relationship between creation and justice. The film begins with a frame story set in 1860[42] wherein Victor Frankenstein (Peter Cushing), who is imprisoned and soon to be executed for the murder of his servant Justine (Valerie Gaunt), tells his life story to a priest (Alex Gallier) who visits him in his cell. At fifteen, Frankenstein is orphaned, gains control of his family's estate, and hires Paul Krempe (Robert Urquhart) to tutor him in science. After the two progress to the point where they can resurrect a puppy, they begin work on assembling a man and bringing him to life. Krempe, who is ambivalent about the experiment from its inception, withdraws from it soon after Elizabeth (Hazel Court), Frankenstein's cousin and fiancée, moves into the family home. Frankenstein scavenges or purchases most of the body parts for his creation, but to secure its principal component he kills a distinguished professor and removes his brain. This organ is damaged when Krempe confronts Frankenstein with his crime and grapples with him. Undeterred, Frankenstein vivifies the Creature (Christopher Lee), whose defective brain renders him violent and incapable of speech. After he escapes from his creator's laboratory and murders an old man whom he encounters in the woods, Frankenstein and Krempe track him down and the latter shoots him in the eye, killing him. They bury him, but Frankenstein later disinters and resurrects him. The Creature claims a second victim when Frankenstein arranges for him to murder Justine, who has been romantically involved with her employer, claims that she is pregnant with his child, and threatens to reveal his illicit experiments to the authorities if he refuses to marry her. Krempe, who has tried in vain to persuade Elizabeth to leave Frankenstein's house, returns to it at her invitation on the night before her wedding. The Creature menaces Elizabeth, before Frankenstein causes him to fall into a vat of acid. When the scientist concludes his narrative, the priest expresses disbelief. Krempe arrives in the cell, and though Frankenstein implores him to testify that the Creature killed Justine, he refuses to do so. He and Elizabeth leave the prison as Frankenstein is taken to the guillotine.

The significance of collage is apparent even before the diegetic action of *The Curse of Frankenstein* begins, and the mode becomes increasingly salient as the film progresses. An opening intertitle reads, 'More than a hundred years ago, in a mountain village in Switzerland, lived a man whose strange experiments with the dead have since become legend. The legend is still told with horror the world over . . . It is the legend of . . . The Curse of Frankenstein'. Like Shelley's epigraph from *Paradise Lost* and Van Sloan's monologue, this intertitle establishes both a formal and a thematic frame for the narrative that follows, thereby functioning as a crucial element of the cinematic collage. It stitches together not only past and present, but also fact and fiction. Frankenstein, viewers are to understand, did live and work in the mid-nineteenth century. In the years between his activities and the appearance of *The Curse of Frankenstein*, his experiments and reputation have gained global notoriety, passing from reality into myth and perhaps leaving in doubt the verisimilitude of the film recounting his biography. The concerns of the intertitle extend to the film's second concentric frame, which connects them with crime and punishment. To save himself from execution, Frankenstein must persuade his sceptical auditor that his extraordinary tale is true, and that Justine was murdered not by himself but by his creation. His attempt is futile, not only because there is no evidence to support his story and Krempe declines to corroborate it, but also because he lures Justine into an encounter with the Creature, thus murdering her by proxy.

Much of the film concentrates on why and how Frankenstein assembles the pieces of this homicidal being, and on the (meta)physical implications of his exceptional but damaged brain. Unlike Shelley's Frankenstein, who '[finds] it impossible' to 'renew life where death [has] apparently devoted the body to corruption',[43] Fisher's scientist is capable of resurrection but rejects it in favour of integration. 'It's no longer sufficient to bring the dead back to life', he declares to the dubious Krempe. 'Forget the whole. Now we must take the parts – limbs, organs – and then we must build . . . the most complex thing known to man, man himself.' Frankenstein becomes obsessed with collecting and bringing together the choicest components for what he hopes will be a superman 'with [the] perfect physique, with the hands of an artist and with the matured brain of a genius'. Bit by bit, he adds to his anatomical collage. He begins with a body cut down from a gibbet, grafts onto it the hands of the world's greatest sculptor, and adds eyes procured from a charnel house. The most important organ belongs to Prof Bernstein (Paul Hardtmuth), 'the greatest brain in Europe'. According to Frankenstein, this remarkable brain will not only control but also transfigure the stitched-together body parts, for 'when that brain starts to function within the frame, then the face and features will assume wisdom and understanding'. Considering the hideousness of his creation, in particular 'the scars on the face' caused by sutures, he understates, 'I admit he isn't a particularly good-looking specimen', but claims, 'A benevolent mind and the face assumes the patterns of benevolence. An evil mind, then an evil face'.

A function of the disarrangement of his parts, the Creature's ugliness poses the same causal problem as the hunchbacked Fritz's deformity: are monsters made or born? Despite his status as the archetypal monster-maker, Frankenstein holds to the latter theory and fully embraces biological determinism. The highwayman's body is sound, yet he replaces its hands because they are 'great clodhopping things', observing, 'No wonder he was a robber. With hands like those, he couldn't have been anything else'. Frankenstein's conclusion reflects the 'anthropological' as opposed to the 'environmental' school of thought about the origins of criminality, which two approaches were at odds during the mid-eighteenth and early nineteenth centuries.[44] Pursuing his deterministic line of thinking, Frankenstein attributes his creation's killer instincts and behaviour solely to the brain damage caused by Krempe. When Krempe characterises the Creature as 'a criminal lunatic' and points out that his first act after coming to life was to attempt to murder his creator, Frankenstein responds, 'That's the brain. When you attacked me, it was damaged. That makes it your fault'. After bringing the Creature back to life, he again blames Krempe: 'I chose a good brain, a brilliant one. It was you who damaged it. You who put a bullet in the wretched thing. This is your fault.' Confident that repairing or replacing the Creature's brain will eradicate his propensity for violence, Frankenstein is so absorbed in the parts of his monstrous collage that he is unable and unwilling to see it as a whole, and to acknowledge the role played by nurture as well as nature. 'Don't you see you've created a monster?', Krempe demands of him, to which question he responds, 'That doesn't matter'.

Frankenstein likewise ignores his colleague's observation that '[he] can't see the horror of what [he's] doing'. His focus on the parts rather than the whole blinds him to the ethical and legal implications of his work, leading him from crime to crime and eventually to a fitting punishment. He first steals from a gibbet the body of a highwayman that he acknowledges has been left 'as a warning to others', thereby not only working against the intent of the justice system to deter illegal behaviour, but also committing an offence of his own. He then engages in 'a little bribery' to acquire the Creature's hands and eyes. Frankenstein's wrongdoing escalates dramatically when he murders Bernstein for his brain. After inviting the elderly intellectual to his home, he lures him to the top of a flight of stairs to view a painting. Frankenstein urges Bernstein to move backwards, the better to see the picture, before pushing him through the banister to his death. The canvas, Rembrandt's *The Anatomy Lesson of Dr Nicolaes Tulp* (1632), portrays one of the public dissections permitted each year by the Amsterdam Guild of Surgeons. Seventeenth-century restrictions on dissection stipulated that the cadaver had to be that of an executed criminal. In this instance, it belonged to a thief who was hanged for his crimes.[45] By depicting the state of affairs before the 1832 Anatomy Act, which greatly expanded the supply of cadavers to doctors by enabling them to dissect donated bodies, Rembrandt's work underscores the monstrousness of both Bernstein's murder and the illegal and immoral means by which Frankenstein pursues his project.[46] By 1860, when *The Curse of Frankenstein* takes place, doctors had no need to turn to graverobbing and murder to obtain corpses for study.[47] Frankenstein's stealing body parts and killing Bernstein are therefore especially reprehensible deeds. Although he blames Krempe and the Creature for the deaths of the professor and Justine, the punishment for his crimes eventually falls where it belongs, on himself.

Making Black Men into Monsters: *The Thing with Two Heads* and *Blackenstein*

In *The Thing with Two Heads*, Dr Maxwell Kirshner (Ray Milland), a dying surgeon who seeks to prolong his life and work, develops an operation whereby his own head is grafted onto another man's body. The two heads share the body, until the transplanted one can assume full control of it and the original head can be removed. Assisting Kirshner is Dr Phillip Desmond (Roger Perry), who is struggling to find a volunteer for Kirshner's operation when Jack Moss (Roosevelt 'Rosey' Grier), an African American convict on death row, offers himself without understanding the nature of the surgery. Moss, who has been convicted of killing a police officer but proclaims his innocence, agrees to the experiment in order to gain time to clear his name. Kirshner hires another associate, Dr Fred Williams (Don Marshall), but marginalises him after discovering that he is Black. An unapologetic racist, Kirshner is outraged to awaken from surgery to discover his head on Moss's body (see Figure 3). Moss is even more upset to find Kirshner's head on his own body. He escapes from Kirshner's home, compelling Williams to drive the getaway car. After an extended chase sequence involving first Desmond and then the LAPD, Moss reaches the home of his girlfriend, Lila (Chelsea Brown). Williams agrees to excise Kirshner's head, but the surgeon gains control of Moss's body and returns to his laboratory. There, Williams confronts him before calling Desmond, who arrives to find Kirshner's disembodied head attached to machines that can sustain it temporarily. Kirshner asks Desmond to bring him another body, while Williams, Moss and Lila drive away.

The Thing with Two Heads demonstrates how the American judicial system tries but ultimately fails to make Black men into monsters. In a reversal of earlier cinematic set pieces in which electricity gives the Creature life, Moss is led to an electric chair evocative of the one used to restrain the Creature in *The Bride of Frankenstein*. Moments before being electrocuted, he announces his decision to donate his body to science, thereby reversing another convention: that the convicted criminal body, bereft of rights, is perforce rendered an object for anatomical investigation. The fact that Moss is to be operated on at all, however, underscores his perceived and interrelated criminality and monstrosity. Worried that his surgery might, as in centuries past, be seen as an extension and exacerbation of his punishment, the prison warden (Albert Zugsmith) hopes to keep it secret. 'We can't let any of this leak to the press', he tells Desmond. 'We're already having enough trouble with these executions without adding fuel to the fire.' The trouble to which he refers is both diegetic and extradiegetic. The latter involves the movement to abolish capital punishment, which gained a major victory in June 1972, the month before *The Thing with Two Heads* was released, when the Supreme Court ruled in *Furman v. Georgia* that the death penalty violated the Eighth Amendment's ban on cruel and unusual punishment. Concurring with the arguments presented by the Legal Defense and Educational Fund, a civil rights organisation and law firm, Justice William O. Douglas contended that 'the Negro, and the

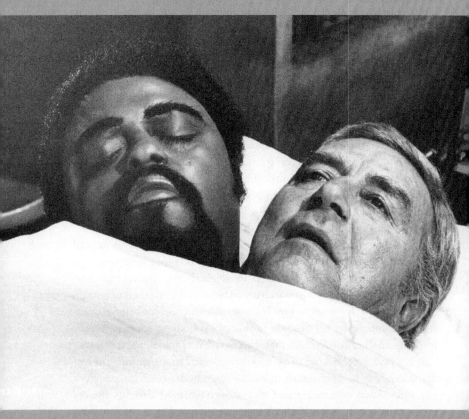

Figure 3. Jack Moss (Rosey Grier) is conjoined with Dr Maxwell Kirshner (Ray Milland) in *The Thing with Two Heads* (1972). AIP/Photofest

members of unpopular groups' such as the poor, were disproportionately condemned to death.[48] Undoubtedly, the death sentence had been meted out to many innocent Black men prior to *Furman v. Georgia*, under circumstances indicating that their race played a leading role in their punishment.[49] In one infamous and widely reported case, Wilbert Lee and Freddie Pitts were sentenced to death in 1963 for the murders of two white men, even though they proclaimed their innocence, another man confessed to committing the crimes, and an eyewitness recanted. In one of a series of trials conducted in 1972, three years before Lee and Pitts were ultimately pardoned, their attorney averred that the defendants, 'although totally innocent, were convicted because they were black'.[50]

The Thing with Two Heads engages the contemporary debate about race and capital punishment by putting Williams – and, by extension, viewers – in a position to judge and exonerate Moss. Kirshner serves as both prosecutor and would-be executioner, characterising Moss as a murderer yet himself premeditating homicide. 'You're the murderer, tryin' to cut off my head', Moss points out. 'That's different', Kirshner responds. He then tries to bribe Williams into turning Moss over to the police, offering him Desmond's place at his side, describing his plans to create a new medical facility and telling the doctor he has rejected out of bigotry, 'I need a man like you to head that department'. His expression suggests the creation of a second, more powerful and insidious two-headed monster, which Williams refuses to become. 'And in order to win all that acclaim and prestige, all I have to do is to help you cut off his head', he retorts, disgusted. Repelled by Kirshner's corruption, having learned the facts in Moss's case, and employing language that recalls the Murder Act, Williams tells his would-be colleague, 'I've heard enough to convince me that this man is innocent, and that you have no right to his body'. Kirshner replies, 'Williams, if you cut off my head that will be murder', not long before attempting to cut off Moss's own head. Williams intervenes, saying, 'You don't want to do that, doctor. You'd be killing an innocent man'. He then removes and preserves Kirshner's head, saving Moss's life and bodily autonomy while refuting Kirshner's accusation of murder. Williams leaves Kirshner even more monstrous but re-humanises Moss, not only by reversing the operation that has rendered his criminal monstrosity a grotesque spectacle, but also by enabling justice to be served – unless the officers of the LAPD, who function as an updated version of the bloodthirsty mob in Whale's *Frankenstein* and 'want Moss dead' because they believe he has killed one of them, catch up with him. Their doing so seems unlikely, given that their lengthy pursuit of Moss ends 'in the total demolition of fourteen police vehicles' and exposes the force's ineptitude. Yet the comedy of the film's chase scenes, in which Desmond pursues Moss and Williams before the police replace him, mitigates without eliminating the seriousness of how an alliance between the almost exclusively white medical and law-enforcement establishments forces a Black man to flee for his life.

The dangers posed to African American men by doctors and jailers, working independently and in combination, were all too clear by the early 1970s. *The Thing with Two Heads* mirrors both the Tuskegee Study of Untreated Syphilis in the Negro Male and medical experiments on Black prisoners.[51] The film appeared in theatres on 19 July 1972. Six days later, the Associated Press reporter Jean Heller broke news of the Tuskegee Study. For forty years, in a project sponsored by the United States Public Health Service and conducted in Alabama, medical personnel had withheld penicillin from 600 Black men infected with syphilis to examine how the disease progressed. These men believed that they were being treated for their disorder, when in fact they were being used as guinea pigs. This infamous study was finally stopped in 1973, and in 1974 the National Research Act led to the development of guidelines for research involving human subjects that emphasised informed consent, which had been absent from the Tuskegee Study.[52]

Also in 1974, the sometimes-shocking, decades-long experiments on prisoners at Philadelphia's Holmesburg Prison came to an end, after being exposed in the national press. The figure most closely associated with these experiments was the dermatologist Dr Albert Kligman, who on arriving at the prison in 1951 was thrilled by the boundless opportunities for research afforded by its inmates. 'All I saw before me were acres of skin', he recalled in 1966. 'It was like a farmer seeing a fertile field for the first time.'[53] Kligman and other researchers eagerly planted and harvested this field of flesh, offering prisoners $3 per procedure in return for their submission to a wide range of experiments. One inmate, Jesse Williams, described 'being burned by radiation and sulfuric acid', and 'immersing his arms in chemicals that had tanned his skin like leather'.[54] In a procedure that Frankenstein himself might have conducted, Williams had tissue from a cadaver implanted in his back 'to see if it would grow'; it did not.[55] Less gruesome but more alarming were tests involving dioxin, a carcinogenic element in Agent Orange, the defoliant used by the United States during the Vietnam War.[56] Also tested on inmates were psychotropic drugs that had serious and lasting effects.[57] Black prisoners were 'dramatically overrepresented' in these experiments, as they were in the prison population.[58] They volunteered for them not only for cash, but also because they felt they were being 'helpful' and 'contributing to research'.[59]

Moss too believes he is helping others. 'If you transplant somethin' from my body that makes a kid live, that's good', he tells Desmond. Like those who volunteered for the Tuskegee Study, who 'were incapable of understanding the facts of the experiment and forming their own conclusions',[60] and the inmates at Holmesburg Prison, who 'had about a third-grade level of reading comprehension [and] couldn't understand the consent forms',[61] Moss misunderstands the nature of the experiment to which he submits and therefore cannot properly consent to it. When he awakens from anaesthesia to find that he has been made into a 'two-headed monster', he exclaims, 'I didn't know you guys were gonna do this to me!'. That he commits crimes including kidnapping, theft and evading the police only after being operated on illustrates how injustice and exploitation, not biology, make him a monster.

His monstrous transformation ingeniously reworks the uncanny relationship in *Frankenstein* between creator and creation, combining these doppelgängers into one two-headed, bicoloured being while locating monstrosity only in the white head. As in Shelley's novel, the monster-maker is the true monster. Whereas Moss's monstrosity is temporary and circumstantial, Kirshner's is permanent and essential, a manifestation of his prejudice. Between their conjoined heads, the power struggle waged by Frankenstein and the Creature plays out as an embodied race war. In this closest of conflicts, Kirshner's racism is both monstrous and self-defeating, since it alienates him from Williams, whose profession makes him a potential ally. 'I don't understand you', Kirshner says after Williams rejects his bribe. 'The reason you don't understand, Doctor', Williams responds, 'is because you're a bigot. A bigot of the highest caliber. And because of that, you have underestimated me and my intelligence'. Kirshner's bigotry expresses itself both obviously, in his repeatedly calling Moss a 'black bastard', and subtly, in his desire to control Moss's body and extinguish his mind even before decapitating him. 'How am I ever going to control him?', he wonders, frustrated by the fact that his 'head won't begin to take control of [Moss's] body until ten to fourteen days' pass. Awakening attached to this body, the doctor remarks, 'It feels so strong. So magnificently, fantastically, beautifully strong'. To Kirshner, the Black man's body is a powerful tool to be used; his mind, a threat to be eliminated. When Moss is conscious, he dominates the body shared with Kirshner and makes decisions for them both. Kirshner demands that Moss 'give himself up and stop this insanity before we're all killed', but Moss retorts, 'What's this "we" stuff? They're not after you, they're after me. So I'll do the thinkin''. To stop Moss from thinking, Kirshner uses Moss's hand against his head by punching him unconscious, so that he can exercise complete control.

The contest between the two men allegorises race relations and the state of the civil rights movement in the late 1960s and early 1970s. As its title announces, *The Thing with Two Heads* depicts how misguided interracial integration dehumanises and renders monstrous the individuals it brings together, especially the minority partner.[62] The film debunks the notion that two heads are better than one, demonstrating how a struggle over leadership between the Black and white races is resolved only by separation. It thereby illustrates and advances the separatist rhetoric and ideology of Black nationalists such as Stokely Carmichael, who in 1966 contended that 'integration' was 'an insidious subterfuge for the maintenance of white supremacy', a dubious boon granted by white Americans to a minority of African Americans, and a manifestation of 'individual power' exercised by a few rather than 'group power' wielded by the many.[63] 'It is clear that the question is not one of integration or segregation', he argued, but a matter of '[controlling] the basic institutions that perpetuate racism by destroying them and building new ones', so that 'black people' come to occupy 'positions of power, doing and articulating for themselves'.[64] Because such control comes only from self-determination, 'We cannot have white people working in the black community'.[65] Integration therefore occurs within rather than between the races, as African Americans draw together to realise their potential as a community. Intraracial integration of this sort is apparent in *The Thing with Two Heads*. Moss rids himself of Kirshner's head and attains his freedom by co-operating with Williams, whom he likewise empowers to cut ties with Kirshner. Their solidarity transcends and upends the class division between them. 'You soul brother, you got a car?', Moss asks Williams, who responds, 'Yeah. Why?'. 'You're now the chauffeur', Moss tells the physician. Their united front outrages Kirshner, who mutters, 'I should have known your kind stick together'. That the film's Black characters do stick together is apparent in its final scene, which shows Williams driving Moss and his girlfriend Lila away from Kirshner's house. The three sing along to 'Oh Happy Day', a gospel song that underscores their shared Christian faith.

Racial solidarity is much less apparent in *Blackenstein*, whose plot turns on the betrayal of one African American man by another. The film depicts the ill-fated efforts of Dr Winifred Walker (Ivory Stone) to restore the physical and mental health of her fiancé, Eddie Turner (Joe DeSue), who loses his arms and legs after stepping on a land mine in Vietnam. Eddie is persecuted by a white orderly (Johnny Dennis) in the veterans hospital where he is (mis)treated. Seeking a cure for him, Winifred returns to work with her mentor, Dr Stein (John Hart), who experiments on two patients residing at his mansion in Los Angeles. Stein's DNA injections have enabled him to reverse the ageing process in Eleanor (Andrea King), an elderly woman who appears middle aged, and to graft legs onto the once-paraplegic Bruno (Nick Bolin). One of Bruno's legs is striped like a tiger's, as a result of the atavistic agency of the RNA formula with which Stein is supplementing his DNA injections. Stein and Winifred replace Eddie's arms and legs, and his recovery goes well until she rejects the advances of his assistant, Malcomb (Roosevelt Jackson), who seeks to eliminate his romantic rival by replacing Eddie's DNA solution with Bruno's RNA formula. Eddie degenerates into a being whose large forehead and protruding brow resemble those of the Creature in Whale's *Frankenstein* (see Figure 4). Each night, Eddie leaves his dungeon-like cell in Stein's basement to kill, dismember and sometimes devour people, beginning with the orderly who has abused him. One night Malcomb attempts to rape Winifred but is interrupted by Eddie, who strangles him before killing Eleanor, Bruno and Stein. He leaves Stein's house and terrorises one final victim before being brought down and torn to pieces by police dogs.

The forms and functions of collage are essential to *Blackenstein*, whose intertextuality involves both stitching characters together and pulling them apart. Its 'grafted title',[66] a portmanteau word that itself exemplifies the integration with which the film is so concerned, sutures creator and creation in a fashion that has become common since *Frankenstein: An Adventure in the Macabre* conflated the two by having Frankenstein give the Creature his own surname. Figuratively, both Winifred and Eddie are Black Frankensteins; moreover, she is a would-be bride of Frankenstein. Their association is counterbalanced by splitting Frankenstein into two creators, Winifred and Stein. Fritz is likewise divided into the orderly at the veterans hospital and Malcomb, both of whom follow their cinematic progenitor by ostensibly assisting doctors and scientists, while in fact subverting the plans of their superiors by indulging their own desires. To make the collage of *Blackenstein* even more involved, just as the grotesque Fritz doubles the Creature, so too the orderly and Malcomb double Eddie. The orderly is drafted to serve in Vietnam, as is Eddie, but is rejected because of an unspecified heart condition. Malcomb would replace Eddie as Winifred's love interest, and for a few moments does replace him in her bed. In yet another example of duplication, in *Blackenstein*, as in Whale's *Frankenstein*, the assistants emulate – and surpass – the scientists as monster-makers. The orderly taunts and torments Eddie, who later kills him as the Creature kills Fritz. Malcomb is likewise killed by Eddie, after turning him into a monster by means of a formula that renders him 'a throwback to the jungle' whose reversion is evidenced by his hairy hands and cannibalism, thereby underscoring the relationships among atavism, African Americans and the Creature that have been evident since the publication of Shelley's novel.[67]

In keeping with that text's emphasis on nurture rather than nature, Eddie becomes a primitive monster not because he has lost his arms and legs, but because he is brutalised after he returns home from Vietnam. Although Malcomb's tampering with Dr Stein's formula is as fictitious as the serum itself, Eddie's mistreatment in the veterans hospital reflects common real-world experiences. As Suzanne Gordon explains, 'following the war in Vietnam, the Department of Veterans Affairs (VA) healthcare system was viewed by many as a bleak backwater of inefficiency, indifference, and incompetence'.[68] Returning Vietnam veterans 'too often found themselves in hospital settings where VHA [Veterans Health Administration] underfunding and understaffing produced hospital conditions shockingly exposed in Ron Kovic's famous memoir, *Born on the Fourth of July*, and much protested by veterans' organizations'.[69] Kovic, a Vietnam veteran who was neglected and abused in VA hospitals, recalls an orderly who, when asked for assistance, responded, 'Vietnam don't mean nothing to me or any of these people. You can take your Vietnam and shove it up your ass'.[70] His comments echo those of the orderly in *Blackenstein*, who castigates rather than praises Eddie for his service to the nation. 'You didn't have to go', he tells Eddie, ridiculing him for falling for 'that old scam, patriotism' and telling him, 'Oh, blow it out your —'. As his monologue makes clear, the orderly is angry and bitter because he has been barred from fighting in Vietnam due to his bad heart, which functions as a metaphor for his cruelty. Like Fritz, he inflicts the degradation he has suffered due to his physical handicap on one even more disabled than himself. 'Why don't you take a look at yourself, eh?', he asks Eddie. 'You look like a creep, layin' there and lookin' up at me with those stupid eyes of yours!'. Together with his facial features, clothing and squared-off Afro, Eddie's expressive eyes link him to the Creature as played by Boris Karloff, whose forlorn gaze

Figure 4. Eddie Turner (Joe DeSue) degenerates into a monster in *Blackenstein* (1972). Exclusive International/Photofest

won over viewers otherwise horrified by his appearance. When *Frankenstein* began filming in 1931, Carl Laemmle Jr remarked that 'Karloff's eyes mirrored the suffering we needed'.[71]

Eddie's eyes not only generate sympathy from viewers, who share his disempowered perspective in low-angle shots of the orderly, but also call attention to the more subtly uncanny aspects of the scene, which extend beyond how the orderly and Eddie serve as doppelgängers.[72] Having lost all four limbs to a land mine, Eddie is symbolically and perhaps literally castrated; hence, he tells Winifred that they 'shouldn't see each other anymore'.[73] By linking vision with sexuality, his phrasing evokes Freud's discussion in 'The Uncanny' of 'the substitutive relation between the eye and the male organ which is seen to exist in dreams and myths and phantasies', and his observation that 'anxiety about one's eyes' is often 'a substitute for the dread of being castrated'.[74] Although Eddie is limbless, he retains his eyes, and his gaze is potent. Unnerved by it, the orderly brutally penetrates him with a phallic needle containing a sedative, growling, 'I'll close those eyes for you'. Like Stein, he repeatedly injects Eddie. Unlike the scientist, the orderly does so not to heal but to hurt. He attempts at once to emasculate and dehumanise Eddie, who reverses their positions after becoming Blackenstein. When Eddie attacks the orderly, an extradiegetic heartbeat reminds viewers that, despite his degeneration, he still has the good heart that his tormentor-turned-victim lacks. As the still-sympathetic audience sees through his eyes, Eddie tears off the orderly's right arm and leaves him lying helpless, thereby rendering the man a replica of his own former self. Like the orderly and Fritz, he hurts his victims in the same fashion that he has been hurt, by pulling them to pieces. Ironically, it is only after Eddie regains his arms and legs that he becomes truly monstrous; thus, his reintegration fosters disintegration.

By focusing on the promise of integration and the peril of disintegration, *Blackenstein* engages contemporary concerns about Black Vietnam veterans. 'The Vietnam War was the first American war fought in which integration was the official policy from the outbreak of hostilities', as Herman Graham explains.[75] During this conflict, there was 'a degree of integration among black and white Americans far exceeding that of any other war in our history as well as any other time or place in our domestic life', according to Whitney Young, the executive director of the National Urban League, an organisation that promoted civil rights.[76] Yet because many African Americans fighting in Vietnam felt 'like outsiders in the military', they 'began to segregate themselves from whites and developed their own black culture within the military'.⁷⁷ This tension between integration and separation became even more pronounced when Black veterans came home. After experiencing 'close interracial relationships in combat units in Vietnam, veterans reported racial polarization' in the United States.⁷⁸ They returned not 'as victorious units to the acclaim of their fellow citizens', but as 'individuals grateful to have survived', who were 'without recognition or social support'.⁷⁹ Their individualisation and isolation, combined with their shared experiences and concerns, led them to become 'an alienated solidary group'.⁸⁰ This oscillation between integration and disintegration led journalists, government officials and the general public to wonder which side Black veterans would take in the war at home over civil rights. Their role might 'range from full participation in society with a rejection of militancy, separatism and violence, to the use of guerrilla warfare skills in militant attempts at social change'.⁸¹

Like the veterans whose story it Gothicises, *Blackenstein* moves between these two poles before shifting abruptly from the political to the personal. Seeking to make Eddie 'completely whole again', Winifred works with Stein to reintegrate him: not only to put limbs back onto his body, but also to enable him to rejoin her and society. Their aims resemble those of the National Urban League's Veterans Affairs Project, which was formed 'to increase justice and opportunities for [Black] Servicemen and to assist them when they [became] veterans in obtaining employment, education, housing, and welfare benefits'.⁸² Winifred and Stein's project of reintegration goes awry when Malcomb interferes and sets Eddie on a radical path of multiple murder. Eddie's subsequent attack on the orderly indicates the film's initial and ephemeral alignment with the most combative form of Black Power. The orderly represents a bigoted white society that first sends Black men to Vietnam and then, projecting its own unfamiliar sense of failure and inferiority onto the Other, spurns and abuses them after they return home. That Eddie literally tears him apart signifies how Black militantism would dismember the white body politic.

The political import, if any, of Eddie's chewing on the arm that he has ripped off the orderly is much less clear and more problematic, since his cannibalism signifies his atavism and would wholly discredit him as a figure of Black Power by reinforcing a pernicious racial stereotype. Arguing along these lines and citing Eddie's gruesome assaults on women, Elizabeth Young contends that 'the self-consciously political development of the opening plot with the hospital orderly gives way to [the film's] manifestly apolitical – albeit misogynist – depiction of grotesque violence'.⁸³

Although Young overlooks Eddie's attacks on men, her point is well taken, for his subsequent victims hold personal rather than political significance. Eddie kills his fellow research subjects, Bruno and Eleanor, together with two of his three creators, Malcomb and Stein. He often targets couples: a middle-aged man and woman in bed; a pair of teenagers in a parked car; a man and woman behind a nightclub; and, finally, Winifred and Malcomb in her bedroom. Eddie's victims are both Black and white; thus, he is motivated not by race but by sex, and in particular by sexual assault. He intervenes when a woman resists a man's sexual advances, which in the final two scenes escalate into attempted rapes. During these assaults, Eddie appears to come to the woman's aid by dispatching her assailant, only to replace him by killing her, tearing away part of her body and consuming it.

Eddie's taste for human meat is puzzling, since it aligns with the anthropophagy of zombies rather than the vegetarianism of Shelley's Creature. His cannibalistic attacks are best understood as expressions of displaced and sublimated erotic desire. Angry at being denied Winifred and sexual satisfaction, he breaks apart couples and substitutes for the male partners, whose carnal appetites he replaces with his actual hunger for female flesh. His outré eating habits are never explained, though viewers can infer that they result from the regressive agency of the RNA formula, which is clumsily underscored when Malcomb switches Eddie's and Bruno's solutions and Stein is heard in voiceover repeating 'primeval theory', 'throwback', 'jungle' and 'prehistoric'. In keeping with the uncanny duplications and substitutions that characterise all iterations of *Frankenstein*, the swap between formulas parallels the exchanges among men. Eddie assumes the animalistic traits of both Bruno, another experimental subject, and Malcomb, at once his creator and a fellow monster. Malcomb's animalism, unlike Bruno's and Eddie's, results from inclination rather than experimentation, and it exemplifies the 'black-animal subtext' that underlies racist discourse and informs *Blackenstein*.[84] This association is most obvious when Eddie is attacked at the end of the film by police dogs that evoke the hounds pursuing the Creature in Whale's *Frankenstein*, but for their interchangeability with the monster they confront. Moments after Eddie tears at the throat of his final victim, he is ripped to pieces by two black Dobermanns. Both Eddie and the dogs growl as they fight, while close-ups of the combatants alternate with such rapidity that man and beasts conflate. During this dogfight, just as Eddie pulls off and carries away the orderly's right arm, so too one of the dogs pulls off and carries away his own right arm. If the dog intends to eat the appendage, as Eddie eats the orderly's arm, then its appetite for human flesh is yet another bond between man and animal in the dog-eat-dog world of the film.

Like *Night of the Living Dead* (George A. Romero, 1968), whose dénouement features German Shepherds evoking those that terrorised and attacked Black protestors during the 1963 demonstrations in Birmingham, Alabama, *Blackenstein* might have used dogs to illustrate how African Americans are rendered monstrous and victimised by the police. Instead, the film aligns man and beast in a fashion that reinscribes the earliest cinematic stereotypes and recalls the 'black brutes' of *The Birth of a Nation* (D. W. Griffith, 1915).[85] The resulting primitive, human-animal collage is a version of that originally created by Shelley's Frankenstein, though the malign, barbaric Eddie is a far cry from her interpretation of Jean-Jacques Rousseau's natural man. Furthermore, Eddie's deterioration from a sympathetic, speaking (if taciturn) subject into a murderous, growling monster reverses the trajectory of the Creature in Shelley's novel and Whale's *The Bride of Frankenstein*. Even the brain-damaged Creature in Fisher's *The Curse of Frankenstein* learns to follow simple commands. Though these versions of the Creature evolve rather than degenerate, all of them ultimately fall apart. Whale's is blown to bits, together with his bride and Frankenstein's laboratory, while Fisher's dissolves in a vat of acid. *The Thing with Two Heads* likewise depicts the Creature's fragmentation, though this result frees Moss from Kirshner. *Blackenstein* is far less optimistic. That Eddie loses his limbs in Vietnam, only to be put back together before being torn apart again in Los Angeles, ironically and gloomily signifies how Black servicemen were losing a two-front war abroad and at home. His story, like those of his precursors, depicts the ultimate failure of integration and collage, dwells on the inextricable link between creation and disintegration, and reveals how monsters are made – and unmade.

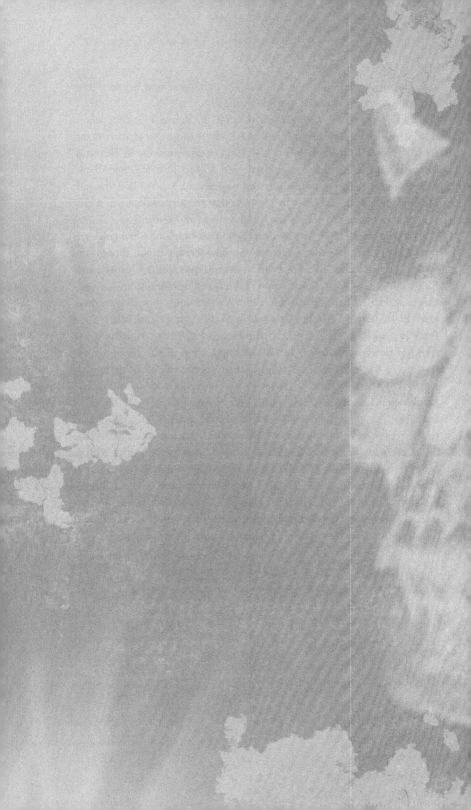

3

Beyond 'the animal within'
Jekyll/Hyde and the Werewolf

IN ROBERT LOUIS STEVENSON'S *Strange Case of Dr Jekyll and Mr Hyde*, Henry Jekyll, a distinguished scientist leading a double life, develops a chemical mixture that enables him to transform into the depraved Edward Hyde. Jekyll's friend and lawyer, Gabriel John Utterson, fears that Jekyll is being blackmailed by Hyde, whom Jekyll has made his sole beneficiary. After Hyde murders Sir Danvers Carew, a Member of Parliament and another of Utterson's clients, the lawyer assists the police in their search for the criminal, who disappears. When Jekyll first changes into Hyde without taking his potion, he asks for help from Dr Hastie Lanyon, a colleague from whom he has become estranged due to the unorthodox nature of his research. Having witnessed Jekyll transform into Hyde, Lanyon dies of shock. Before dying, he gives Utterson a letter detailing his encounter with Jekyll/Hyde, to be opened after Jekyll's own death or disappearance. Vainly attempting to create a new batch of the potion and thus maintain his original identity, Jekyll secludes himself for weeks. Poole, Jekyll's butler, comes to suspect that Hyde has murdered his master. He and Utterson break into Jekyll's laboratory, where they discover Hyde, dead from suicide. They also find a letter to Utterson in which Jekyll describes the causes and consequences of his fatal experiment. Through these letters, readers at last realise that Jekyll and Hyde are two aspects of the same man.

Jekyll at once acknowledges and rejects 'the thorough and primitive duality of man'.[1] Recognising that 'all human beings . . . are commingled out of good and evil', he nevertheless seeks to separate his composite self from his singular alter ego Hyde, 'who alone in the ranks of mankind [is] pure evil'.[2] Jekyll's focus on duality, together with the ways in which Stevenson's novella constructs, inverts and collapses not only its famous titular bifurcation but also multiple associated binary oppositions, naturally indicate a deconstructive approach to the text.[3] This method is also generically appropriate, given how closely deconstruction and the Gothic are interrelated. This connection is perhaps most obvious in Jacques Derrida's *Spectres of Marx* (1993), which relies on the figure of the ghost to develop the concept of 'hauntology'.[4] It also figures prominently in Derrida's foreword to Nicolas Abraham and Maria Torok's *The Wolf Man's Magic Word* (1986), which he begins by asking, 'What is a crypt?'.[5] Derrida and other practitioners of deconstruction routinely draw on Gothic tropes and conventions 'as an affective source for theory', invoking the (un)dead, the revenant and the crypt to instantiate their notions of linguistic instability.[6]

Although deconstruction is useful to understanding how *Jekyll and Hyde* relates to its cinematic adaptations, Jekyll's own idea of the self reveals that this theory is a place to begin, not to end. Jekyll and Hyde have come to emblematise and epitomise our bifurcation, yet Jekyll himself speculates that other researchers into the psyche 'will outstrip [him]' and that 'man will be ultimately known for a mere polity of multifarious, incongruous and independent denizens'.[7] Considering our duality is therefore just the first step towards appreciating our multiplicity. This concept, as developed by Gilles Deleuze, signifies not simply range or variety but 'a complex structure that does not reference a prior unity'.[8] A multiplicity in this sense is not a fragmented unity, for it has never been and never will be unified; it is an ever-changing patchwork. With respect to the psyche, multiplicity describes a subjectivity continually in flux. The influence of Jekyll's and Deleuze's insights into multiplicity is difficult to discern in canonical adaptations of Stevenson's novella, whose organising principle is duality as expressed in white/black, evolved/primitive, police/criminal and professional/unprofessional. *Dr. Black, Mr. Hyde* takes a very different and arguably more sophisticated approach to representing Jekyll/Hyde. It depicts how the divided self both reflects and reproduces the binary oppositions involved in professionalism, policing and family life. Yet it goes further than mainstream adaptations by building, in effect, on Jekyll's research into subjectivity, exploring not only division and opposition but also multiplicity and hybridity, particularly with respect to race.

Duality and Multiplicity in Stevenson's *Jekyll and Hyde*

Jekyll's transformation into Hyde signifies his degeneration into a being whose alterity has racial implications. Although the protean Hyde is not necessarily or only Black, both his colour and his character evoke the nineteenth-century association of Blackness with atavism. While Jekyll's hand is 'white and comely', Hyde's is 'of a dusky pallor and thickly shaded with a swart growth of hair', which characteristics underscore this 'apelike' throwback's proximity to the prehistoric forebears of humanity.[9] Hyde is 'the animal within' Jekyll, the beast 'caged in his flesh' who, in a primal return of the repressed, '[comes] out roaring'.[10] When cornered, this animal evinces a 'black sneering coolness' and 'so black a countenance' as to terrify those around him.[11] The exterior blackness of Hyde's complexion and expression is replicated by his interior 'black secrets', beside which 'Jekyll's worst would be like sunshine'.[12] This white/black bifurcation necessary to degeneration and racial difference is, however, prone to both collapse and transmutation into multiplicity. This tendency is particularly noteworthy with respect to how the novella's parallel white/black and exterior/interior oppositions function. These bifurcations manifest themselves most dramatically and violently when Hyde kills Sir Danvers Carew and causes the death of Dr Lanyon. Carew is an 'aged and beautiful gentleman with white hair', and as 'the moon [shines] on his face' his whitened visage seems to reveal a 'kindness of disposition'.[13] Likewise, the 'great' Lanyon's 'shock of hair prematurely white' indicates his compassion by suggesting that caring for 'his crowding patients' has taken its toll on his own health.[14] In portrayals of these men, exterior whiteness signifies interior benevolence and wisdom – attributes that the black Mr Hyde savagely attacks. These signifiers and roles are reversed when the doctor who confronts Hyde in the 'Story of the Door', who is initially 'of no particular . . . colour', becomes 'white with desire to kill him'.[15] In its devalued position, whiteness is associated not only with murderous rage but also with abject terror. On the night of Hyde's death, the terrified Poole's 'face [is] white', the footman Bradshaw is 'very white and nervous', and both Poole and Utterson are 'pale and fearful'.[16]

After the white/black binary opposition is inverted, it collapses when Jekyll and Hyde are revealed to be not two men but one. This conflation and revelation are prefigured long before Utterson discovers Jekyll's confession. As the usually 'pale' Hyde changes into Jekyll, his 'face [becomes] suddenly black' before the transformation is complete and he again turns 'pale' – now as his alter ego.[17] At the mention of Hyde, Jekyll '[grows] pale to the very lips, and there [comes] a blackness about his eyes'.[18] Likewise, Hyde's skin is neither black nor white but is of 'a dusky pallor'.[19] A variation of the white-black mixture characterising Jekyll and Hyde is also crucial to the formula that releases the latter. The 'salt of a white colour' that first activates and then inactivates Jekyll's concoction is useless without its 'unknown impurity which [lends] efficacy to the draught'.[20] While this initially undetected admixture must be either white or colourless, its presence emphasises the importance of what Jekyll judges to be 'impurity',[21] a quality that might instead be considered combination.

Indeed, as its ingredients are blended, Jekyll's potion transcends synthesis and evinces multiplicity. It contains materials of different colours and, as these combine, itself changes colour repeatedly. 'The mixture, which [is] at first of a reddish hue', begins 'to brighten in colour' before 'the compound [changes] to a dark purple' and ultimately to 'a watery green'.[22] That these shifting colours reflect those in Lanyon's face suggests a psychological multiplicity resulting from interpersonal rather than chemical catalysts. When Utterson mentions Jekyll's experiments, the 'red-faced' Lanyon '[flushes] suddenly purple'; and, after witnessing Hyde's transformation, 'the rosy man [grows] pale'.[23] As the changing colours of Lanyon's face subtly and ingeniously instantiate the notion of multiplicity, they also indicate the collapse of an exterior/interior opposition already complicated by Lanyon's being introduced as a man whose 'geniality' is 'somewhat theatrical to the eye' but '[reposes] on genuine feeling'.[24] His appearance seems to deceive, but in fact it reflects his true self. This involved bifurcation is elided entirely when Lanyon's visage becomes a readable signifier of his interior state and Utterson sees that he has 'his death-warrant written legibly upon his face'.[25] Lanyon's psychosomatic transformation is an example in miniature of Jekyll's discovery that the outer form is 'the mere aura and effulgence of certain of the powers that [make] up [the] spirit',[26] though, as Deleuze and Félix Guattari point out, the 'distinction to be made is not at all between exterior and interior, which are always relative, changing, and reversible, but between different types of multiplicities that co-exist, interpenetrate, and change places'.[27] Thus multiplicity may displace and erase binary oppositions of all sorts.

Jekyll and Hyde transcends dualism not only in how it conceives of and represents the psyche, but also in how it (de)constructs police/criminal and professional/unprofessional. The cane with which Hyde beats Carew to death is a gift from Utterson, and the provenance of this murder weapon illustrates how *Jekyll and Hyde* elides the division between the police and the criminal. Hyde's crime can be traced to Utterson, not only because it was committed with his cane, but also because the lawyer might have obviated Carew's murder had he involved the police in what he takes to be Hyde's crime of blackmailing Jekyll. Instead, Utterson substitutes for the police by surveilling Hyde. Likewise, rather than call the police to Jekyll's laboratory when he believes a murderer is lurking there, Utterson breaks down the door to Jekyll's cabinet himself. Only after Utterson is approached by the police does he cooperate with them, directing 'Inspector Newcomen of Scotland Yard',[28] a newcomer and latecomer to the strange case of Jekyll and Hyde, to the latter's hideout. Given Utterson's complicity in Carew's murder, small wonder that 'when he [glances] at the companion of his drive, he [is] conscious of some touch of that terror of the law and the law's officers'.[29] Enfield too has reason to fear the law, for while Utterson pursues extra-legal means of coping with Hyde's transgressions, Enfield employs illegal ones. Rather than calling for the police after witnessing Hyde trample a little girl, Enfield blackmails the criminal, thereby becoming a criminal himself. His term for Jekyll's home, 'Black Mail House',[30] is thus doubly appropriate and aligns the two blackmailers, Enfield and Hyde. Utterson is similarly though more subtly associated with Hyde's criminality when he begins his 'Search for Mr Hyde'.[31] In an uncanny reversal, the lawyer who has been 'haunted' by Hyde himself begins to 'haunt the door' to Jekyll's laboratory.[32]

Utterson and Enfield's illicit activities complicate both the police/criminal and the professional/unprofessional oppositions. That 'Utterson the lawyer',[33] as he is introduced, steps in for the police makes some sense, given his profession; but in doing so he violates the spirit if not the letter of the law. Moreover, by surveilling Hyde he casts off the repression that in *Jekyll and Hyde* is closely linked with professionalism. Jekyll describes 'the self-denying toils of [his] professional life',[34] and Utterson demonstrates professional restraint when tempted to unseal and read the mysterious enclosure with which Lanyon has entrusted him. 'A great curiosity [comes] on the trustee, to disregard [Lanyon's] prohibition' against opening the document before Jekyll's death or disappearance, but he observes 'professional honour' and leaves it 'in the inmost corner of his private safe'.[35]

Yet Utterson indulges rather than represses 'a singularly strong, almost an inordinate, curiosity to behold the features of the real Mr. Hyde'[36] by pursuing Jekyll's alter ego. Such curiosity is not only unprofessional but also dangerous, as Lanyon discovers when he dies soon after succumbing to 'the greed of curiosity'[37] and watching Hyde transform into Jekyll. Had Lanyon restrained himself, he might have reported to the police instead of confessing in a statement to Utterson his visit from a man 'hunted for in every corner of the land as the murderer of Carew'.[38] The consequences of his unprofessional curiosity are exacerbated rather than ameliorated by his belatedly observing professional decorum and remaining silent about what he sees 'under the seal of [his] profession',[39] for his excruciating reticence contributes to his premature death.

While Lanyon's and Utterson's interactions with Hyde draw them into unprofessional behaviour, Enfield, a 'well-known man about town',[40] has no professional obligations to uphold. Thus, though his blackmailing Hyde is arguably more serious than Lanyon's or Utterson's failing to report him to the police, it is also more understandable. Indeed, his doing so after 'coming home from some place at the end of the world'[41] links his being 'about town' with his crime, thereby strengthening his connection to his fellow blackmailer and man-about-town Hyde. The professional/unprofessional opposition is complicated, and related to that between police and criminal, when we recognise that not only the idle Enfield and Hyde but also the industrious lawyer Utterson and the Member of Parliament Carew are men about town on questionable and even unlawful business.

Duality in Adaptations of *Jekyll and Hyde*: the Animal Within as Racial Other

The multiplicity of Stevenson's novella is absent from *Dr. Jekyll and Mr. Hyde* as directed by John S. Robertson (1920), Rouben Mamoulian (1931) and Victor Fleming (1941). Robertson's silent film is arguably the most faithful to Stevenson's novella, though it departs from that text and establishes a tradition in adaptations of *Jekyll and Hyde* by adding not only a 'good' woman for Jekyll, as in Thomas Russell Sullivan's play, *Dr. Jekyll and Mr. Hyde* (1887), but also a 'bad' one for Hyde. All three films eliminate the narrative complexities of Stevenson's text, all change Carew into the father of Jekyll's fiancée, and all depict Jekyll not only as a research scientist but also as a practising physician who offers his services free of charge to the poor and unfortunate. More significantly, these canonical adaptations enact exterior/interior and white/Black dualities by depicting Hyde as 'the brute that [sleeps] within'[42] Jekyll, and by drawing on the racist conception of Jekyll's alter ego developed in Sullivan's play. As Daphne A. Brooks has shown, this theatrical adaptation, which debuted in Boston with Richard Mansfield in the lead before crossing the Atlantic, employs 'the theme of the "mongrel" other lurking literally within' to stage the expulsion of 'the (blackened) beast' from 'the play's Anglo hero'.[43] It thus functions to allegorise the segregationist objectives of an 'evolving Jim Crow culture' that sought to eradicate miscegenation and to protect whiteness 'from the threat of a "blackness" that was redefined as monstrous and deadly' when 'the end of slavery and Reconstruction threatened to obfuscate racial and class taxonomies',[44] thereby making multiplicity possible with respect to both race and class. Sullivan's allegory was energised by Mansfield's performance, which incorporated elements of minstrelsy and blackface. To embody Hyde, the actor emphasised his 'protruding lower lip' and crouched in an ape-like fashion while 'swaying and bounding'.[45]

In Robertson's and Mamoulian's films, John Barrymore's and Fredric March's performances of Hyde recall key aspects of Mansfield's stage characterisation. These include his 'stoop, his gait, his gruesomely "distorted fingers," and his rapid stage movements' – all of which in turn evoke the rapid movements and exaggerated positions of antebellum minstrel dancers.[46] The threateningly phallic quality of Barrymore's impossibly elongated prosthetic fingers resembles that of 'early minstrelsy', in which 'stiffness and extension of arms and legs announced themselves as unsuccessful sublimations of sexual desire'.[47] More obviously racist than Barrymore's fingers are March's bulging brow, sloping forehead, dark skin and broad nose, all of which features leave no doubt that Hyde is a degenerate racial Other.[48] This depiction is reinforced by the *mise en scène* in Mamoulian's adaptation. When Jekyll first transforms into Hyde, a point-of-view shot pans the laboratory before coming to rest on a black statue positioned near the mirror. This figure, which appears to be of Asiatic origin, has a long tail and seems to be an anthropomorphic primate similar to the statue of the monkey-god Hanuman, the desecration of whose temple leads to lycanthropy in Rudyard Kipling's 'The Mark of the Beast' (1890). As if ready to strike, it holds aloft a sceptre that doubles Hyde's deadly black cane. This phallic rod's bulbous end is tipped with two demonic-looking horns. When Hyde stares into the mirror to behold himself for the first time, this statue, a version of Stevenson's 'ugly idol in the glass',[49] is positioned alongside him within it as a dangerous Black doppelgänger. The first transformation scene in Fleming's adaptation is less blatantly racist, but Hyde (Spencer Tracy) still has darker skin and hair than Jekyll, together with bushy eyebrows and bulging eyes. His evil is more interior than that depicted in the other two films, though Fleming uses mostly objective shots to represent it.

Both Mamoulian and Fleming sharpen the police/criminal distinction that Stevenson blurs, and they associate the devalued term with Blackness and miscegenation. In Robertson's film, the police are offscreen searching for Hyde in Soho when he returns to Jekyll's home and attacks Millicent (Martha Mansfield), his alter ego's fiancée. By contrast, in the other two adaptations they are led by Lanyon into Jekyll's laboratory, where the doctor turns into Hyde and engages them in a fatal confrontation that results from and removes the latter's threat to white womanhood. In Mamoulian and Fleming's films, Carew's status as a pillar of the community is split from his transgressive behaviour,[50] and he is transformed from an apparently queer and cruising Member of Parliament who attempts to solicit Hyde[51] into the overprotective father of Jekyll's fiancée who stipulates a long engagement for the pair. Thus, Hyde results from Jekyll's sexual frustration by the patriarchy. Unable to wait for his wedding night, Jekyll changes into Hyde and pursues illicit erotic gratification with a working-class woman who remains unnoticed by the authorities until he murders her. His criminality is closely tied to his phallic black cane, which he deploys not only to poke women suggestively, but also to play 'apelike tricks'[52] on men and, ultimately, to bludgeon the frustrating patriarch to death. As Jekyll, he seeks reconciliation with his betrothed, before the stimulation of her proximity triggers his transformation into Hyde and the crucial scene in which he threatens her.

This scene's racial implications are stressed by both Mamoulian and Fleming. In Mamoulian's film, as Jekyll stands outside the home of his fiancée Muriel (Rose Hobart), watching her sob while he transforms into Hyde, his back to the camera, he is reduced to a faceless mass of black who recalls Utterson's dream of a Hyde with 'no face',[53] an apposite image of the amorphous racial and sexual dangers he poses. Fleming sets this scene outside the house but likewise shows from behind a looming black figure approaching Bea (Lana Turner), who is weeping on the ground and dressed entirely in white. The camera cuts from a shot of her embracing the legs of the man she believes to be Jekyll to a shallow-focus, close-up, low-angle shot of Hyde that draws attention to his hideousness and power, then moves to a high-angle shot of Bea to indicate her relative helplessness. Hyde lifts and grabs Bea while she screams for her father and faints. Mamoulian allows

Hyde to creep inside Muriel's home and embrace her from behind, kissing her shoulder, as she turns to confront him. In a close-up point-of-view shot that compels viewers to experience Muriel's peril and underscores Hyde's ugliness, he purses his thick, dark lips as if to kiss her. She screams to her father for help. Mamoulian and Fleming hark back to the postbellum America of Sullivan's theatrical adaptation, wherein 'asserting or restoring the *patriarchal powers* of the white-male-as protector was . . . central to rape panics' involving Black men and 'the white-woman-as victim'.[54] Mamoulian also engages 'the Scottsboro case, a sensational, racially charged rape trial widely reported in the media in 1931',[55] the year his adaptation was released. In both directors' films, after the father intervenes to stop Hyde from ravishing his daughter, the latter bludgeons him to death, thereby avenging not only his own grievance against the interfering patriarch but also Jekyll's. Hyde's breaking his cane while attacking Carew signifies the cost of assaulting the white patriarchy and the nullification of his own Black potency. In both films, the wronged woman calls for the police, who arrive immediately. In Fleming's film, a moment after Hyde's cane breaks, a police whistle sounds, tolling his death knell.

Having threatened white womanhood, clubbed down patriarchy and violated professional ethics, Jekyll/Hyde must be destroyed by the legal and medical establishments. Robertson's film, the only one to include Utterson (J. Malcolm Dunn), divides legal power between the lawyer and the police. When Hyde kills Sir George Carewe (Brandon Hurst), Poole (George Stevens) calls for the police and instructs a servant to find Utterson. In Mamoulian and Fleming's films, law and medicine are closely aligned when Lanyon directs the police to Hyde. In the latter they are conflated, for Lanyon actually shoots Hyde. This association and elision make sense, given that Jekyll has broken not only the laws of man but also those of nature. Mamoulian has Lanyon play judge and jury, while Fleming adds the role of executioner. Mamoulian's film includes a remarkable scene in which Lanyon (Holmes Herbert) sentences Jekyll to damnation. A two-shot shows Lanyon seated behind an enormous desk that evokes a judge's bench. Looming over Jekyll, he pronounces, 'You've committed the supreme blasphemy'. As Jekyll begs Lanyon for mercy, high-angle shots showing his abjection alternate with low-angle shots underscoring his judge's authority. Jekyll promises to give up both his drug and Muriel, but she proves to be the only catalyst necessary for him to transform into the bestial Hyde, who combats the legal and medical authorities in a manner that is unmistakably simian. He jumps around the room, swings from equipment, climbs up and hangs from bookshelves, and throws objects at the police before brandishing a knife and being shot down by an inspector. Spencer Tracy's Hyde is considerably less dextrous than Fredric March's, but he uses a club to attack the police before menacing Lanyon with a knife and being shot by him. Thus, law and medicine combine forces to put down the Black animal within and to restore the binary oppositions of the *status quo ante*.

Medical Ethics, Policing and the Single-Parent Family in *Dr. Black, Mr. Hyde*

Dr. Black, Mr. Hyde tells the story of Dr Henry Pride (Bernie Casey), a medical doctor and researcher living in Los Angeles around 1976. When he is a boy, his mother, a maid at a brothel, dies of alcoholism-related cirrhosis of the liver while the prostitutes she serves ignore her son's pleas for help. Seeking to atone for his inability to save his mother's life, the adult Pride works tirelessly to develop a formula to combat liver diseases through cellular regeneration. He is assisted by Dr Billie Worth (Rosalind Cash), his colleague and love interest, a 'good' woman who is balanced by a 'bad' woman, the prostitute Linda Monte (Marie O'Henry). Pride's formula transforms him into Hyde, an unnaturally strong albino who murders four prostitutes and a pimp, Silky. Lt Jackson (Ji-Tu Cumbuka), a Black detective, and Lt O'Connor (Milt Kogan), a white one, hunt for the killer. Hyde attempts to force Linda to take his experimental drug, but she escapes from him. Pursuing Linda and pursued by the police, Hyde climbs the Watts Towers, is shot by the police, and falls to the street. After transforming into Pride, he dies as Billie comforts him.

Dr. Black, Mr. Hyde addresses topics of deep and enduring concern to African American film audiences of the 1970s. Foremost among these are medical ethics and experimentation, the policing of Watts, a mostly Black neighbourhood in Los Angeles, and the perceived role of single-parent families in perpetuating a Black underclass. In speaking to these issues, the film engages with the exposure of the Tuskegee Study, the Watts riots (also known as the Watts Rebellion or Uprising) and the sociological reports on the Black family that followed the unrest.

The long-standing tension between Black Angelenos and the LAPD exploded in August 1965 during the Watts riots, when in response to police brutality, racism, and unequal living conditions, the residents of Watts and

Figure 5. Dr Henry Pride (Bernie Casey) transforms into his alter ego in *Dr. Black, Mr. Hyde* (1976). Dimension Pictures/Photofest

other areas destroyed property and battled the police and the National Guard.⁵⁶ The proximate cause of the event, a conflict between a Black motorist and the police, reflected years of mutual mistrust and animosity. Describing 'the complete deterioration' of the relationship between African Americans and the LAPD, Josh Sides notes, 'For black Los Angeles, the threat of police violence was a daily, and sometimes deadly, reality'.⁵⁷ Max Felker-Kantor explains that the 'unequal relation of power between the LAPD and the city's black and brown residents produced the conditions for the eruption of the largest urban uprising in American history'.⁵⁸ Two major reports were issued following this clash: *Violence in the City: an End or a Beginning?* (1965), by the California Governor's Commission on the Los Angeles Riots, and *The Negro Family: The Case for National Action* (1965), by the sociologist and Assistant Secretary of Labor Daniel Patrick Moynihan. The former traces the Watts riots to racial disparities in education, employment, health, and welfare, and emphasises closing 'a deep and longstanding schism between a substantial portion of the Negro community and the Police Department'.⁵⁹ The latter focuses not on the police but on the family – in particular, the Black family headed by a single mother, whose growth had steadily increased since the 1940s and accelerated after 1960.⁶⁰

Claiming that 'the Negro family in the urban ghettos is crumbling', *The Negro Family* considers the number of Black families headed by single mothers, notes that 'a fundamental fact of Negro American family life is the often reversed roles of husband and wife', and argues for 'the establishment of a stable Negro family structure'.⁶¹ A similar line of argument was pursued by the psychologist and first Black president of the American Psychological Association, Kenneth B. Clark. In *Dark Ghetto* (1965), Clark contends that an inverted 'sexual hierarchy has played a crucial role in the structure and pathology of the Negro family' by rendering the mother 'the dominant person' and the father almost irrelevant.⁶² The man's 'intolerable psychological position seems directly related to the continued high incidence of desertions and broken homes in Negro ghettos', Clark writes. 'The Negro woman has, in turn, been required to hold the family together', and 'her compensatory strength tended to perpetuate the weaker role of the Negro male'.⁶³ The 1967 report of the National Advisory Commission on Civil Disorders likewise points out that unemployed or underemployed Black men 'are often unable or unwilling to remain with their families. The handicap imposed on children growing up without fathers in an atmosphere of deprivation is increased as mothers are forced to work to provide support'.[64] The report also notes that 'the abrasive relationship between police and minority communities has been a major – and explosive – source of grievance, tension, and disorder'.[65] Having considered these and other issues, it concludes, 'Our Nation is moving toward two separate societies, one black, one white'.[66]

The white/Black opposition is crucial to *Dr. Black, Mr. Hyde*. It is interrelated not only with the film's focus on medical ethics, policing and the single-parent family, but also with the key divisions shared by Stevenson's novella and its canonical film adaptations: police/criminal and professional/unprofessional. Unlike the versions directed by Robertson, Mamoulian and Fleming, however, William Crain's film moves beyond duality towards multiplicity and hybridity. The most striking aspect of *Dr. Black, Mr. Hyde* is how, in appropriating earlier adaptations of *Jekyll and Hyde*, it offers more complex motives for Jekyll's research than sexual release and depicts Hyde not as an oversexed, dualistic animal within but as a multiplicitous embodiment of the tensions between Black pride and white privilege.

These tensions are apparent from the start of the film in a medical research centre at the University of California Los Angeles (UCLA), where Dr Pride's bona fides are established by visiting foreign scientists who note his having won a prestigious medical award. 'Dr. Pride tends to be very modest', explains Dr Worth, who is leading the group with Pride. This aspirational and progressive exposition depicts a Black man and woman as top-tier medical researchers at a time when less than two per cent of the physicians in the United States were African American[67] and fewer still were Black women, though in 1970 both African Americans and women began to enter the medical profession in greater numbers.[68] This scene also rationalises the extraordinary Dr Worth's surname while problematising the modest Dr Pride's. She proves her worth not only by conducting cutting-edge biochemical research alongside him, but also by volunteering at the Watts Towers Arts Center. The 1970s marked the rise of the Watts Towers as 'a pre-eminent site of black cultural activity', and the Arts Center 'played a crucial role' when the Black Arts Movement, the aesthetic expression of the Black Power movement, began to wane.[69] Worth's work, both at the Arts Center and at UCLA, demonstrates her commitment to the 'black pride and black self-determination'[70] that Jeffrey O. G. Ogbar identifies as central to Black Power. Moreover, the fact that both she and Pride style their hair in Afros signals their Black pride – as, of course, does his surname, though his pride is apparently mitigated by his humility. The extent to which Pride's name reflects his commitment to Black Power is an open question.

In the next scene, Pride steps into a silver Mercedes and drives from UCLA to Watts. As in Stevenson's novella, the neighbourhoods represent the two aspects of Jekyll/Hyde's psyche. Pride lives in an affluent area far from Watts, in a mansion that once served as the 'very high-class whorehouse' where his mother worked as a maid and died, and where he lived as a child. Unlike his fictional and filmic predecessors, Pride/Hyde has only one home for his two personas. Yet his home is *unheimlich*, at once very close to and very far from his experience as a poor boy raised by an alcoholic single mother in 'a room in the back' of the luxurious house. Pride/Hyde still enters and exits his house through the back, thereby revealing his inability to fully transcend his disadvantaged childhood. But the house that is now his home signifies not abasement but accomplishment, and his moving into it exemplifies the 'migration of middle-class African Americans out of Watts, South Central, Compton and West Adams into other, more affluent communities' that occurred in the 1960s and 1970s, a relocation that was viewed by some who remained in the impoverished neighbourhoods as 'a betrayal'[71] and that indicated an 'increasing differentiation and bifurcation' between rich and poor Black Angelenos.[72] This parallel is complicated by the fact that Pride is, in a sense, returning home; but where and how he lived from the date of his mother's death to the present, and how he gained wealth and status, are left unexplained. One thing is certain and significant: unlike Jekyll, who is born 'to a large fortune',[73] Pride has achieved success despite rather than because of his background.

Pride seeks to retain his connection to those less fortunate than himself by volunteering at a free clinic. The Watts Free Clinic in the film is based on the Watts Health Center, whose planning began where Pride conducts his research, at the UCLA School of Medicine.[74] This facility, which opened in 1967, was part of 'the Free Clinic Movement' whose clinics were designed to be not only free of charge but also 'free from judgment, moralizing, or bureaucratic red tape'.[75] Pride, however, does judge and moralise while seeing Linda, a prostitute whom he is treating for hepatitis. 'I don't want to sound like I'm preaching', he says while examining her, 'but obviously prostitution is not the healthiest job to have'. She responds with a judgement of her own, claiming that the well-educated, rich and accomplished Pride is a 'cop out' who 'dress[es] white' and 'think[s] white'. 'The only time you're ever around black people is when you're down here clearing your conscience', she declares. Pride believes he can retain his racial identity while working and living in the white world of UCLA and volunteering in the Black one of Watts, and that his two identities can coexist in harmony rather than in tension, but Linda emphasises their incompatibility. As the story develops, Pride/Hyde's interventions into her life and lifestyle become more insistent and dangerous. He first fails to persuade her to take his experimental drug and then, after she indicates her unwillingness to leave prostitution and threatens to inform the police about the murders he has committed as Hyde, he attempts to kill her.

Given the long-standing strain between the African American community in Watts and the LAPD, the police in *Dr. Black, Mr. Hyde* function differently from how they do in previous adaptations of *Jekyll and Hyde*. The disparity in policing and crime between Watts and the UCLA area is highlighted when Linda cries for help outside Pride's home and is assisted immediately by a private security guard, whereas after Hyde kills a prostitute in Watts the police are surprised not by the homicide but only by the fact that it 'isn't the usual type of ghetto murder'. As in Stevenson's text and Robertson's film, the police are marginalised; but in Crain's film they are kept on the periphery because of racial animus and anxiety. 'In the black community, Harry, nobody knows nothin', nobody sees nothin' and nobody hears nothin'', the Black Lt Jackson explains to his white colleague, Lt O'Connor. His point is illustrated when the bartender (Sam Laws) at the Moonlight Lounge in Watts refuses to answer their queries and tells them, 'We don't like questions around here'. Linda does, however, talk to the police. In this respect she differs from the Ivys of Mamoulian's and Fleming's films, who believe they are either beneath the notice or beyond the power of the authorities. Her trust is well placed, for Jackson and O'Connor, especially the former, are capable agents of the law. The open-minded Jackson is even willing to investigate Linda's improbable story of 'a black doctor who turns white'. Unlike Pride, Jackson is an educated, professional African American who exists comfortably in both the white and Black worlds. He code-switches easily, telling the reticent bartender, 'Brother man, this situation is rapidly becoming insalubrious. Meaning we about to stomp a mudhole in yo ass'. In this scene he plays good cop to O'Connor's bad cop, demonstrating the potential for interracial co-operation. Such co-operation is a force for both good and evil, as indicated by the fact that these two detectives are mirrored by their criminal counterparts, the Black pimp Silky (Stu Gilliam) and the white pimp and pusher Preston (Marc Alaimo). Racial integration is similarly evident in the precinct where Jackson and O'Connor work, which is full of Black and white cops, criminals, and law-abiding citizens alike.

Thus, the portrait of the LAPD painted by *Dr. Black, Mr. Hyde* is more positive than might be expected, although not without its flaws. Even in the climactic confrontation with Hyde at the Watts Towers that ends the film, the police mostly demonstrate good judgement and self-control. 'Surround him but don't shoot. I don't want any needless bloodshed', O'Connor instructs the uniformed officers. Jackson is more sensible still and acts to restrain his partner. When the latter wants to use a dog to bring down Hyde, the former objects, 'He'll kill a dog, Harry!'. When O'Connor does eventually release a dog, in a scene that rewrites the ending of *Blackenstein*, Hyde does indeed kill it. Jackson likewise warns, 'You can't fire on these towers, Harry. It would be like firing on the Lincoln Monument'. His simile logically aligns the Watts Towers, which 'transformed into an emblem of black cultural nationalism after the Watts uprising',[76] with a memorial linked to emancipation. Hyde's carrying Linda to these towers before dropping her and seeking sanctuary inside them at once echoes the scene in which Linda meets him there and asks him to surrender to the police, signifies his attempt to hide within and perhaps destroy a symbol of Black pride, much as he hides within and destroys Pride, and, as Cynthia Erb observes, renders him a variation on King Kong.[77] Pride/Hyde does find emancipation at the Towers, though only in death.

If Hyde is interpreted as an expression of the monstrous inner whiteness that hides within Pride, then his being drawn to Watts in general and to the Watts Towers in particular might be explained by his desire to destroy the neighbourhood and what it represents. In the end, when he refuses to climb down from the Towers, the police do fire repeatedly on both him and the structure, killing the former and damaging the latter. His hiding is also explicated by the film's title, *Dr. Black, Mr. Hyde*, which aligns Black with pride and Hyde, implicitly, with shame. Hyde is created not only by a serum, but also by Pride's shame at being unable to save his mother's life – and, unconsciously, by his shamefully trading Black pride for white privilege. While climbing the Towers, Hyde cries out repeatedly, thereby recalling his namesake in Stevenson's novella, who when surprised by Poole '[gives] a kind of cry' and '[cries] out like a rat'.[78] Apropos of King Kong and degeneration discourse, his cries are certainly bestial and atavistic, as is his protruding brow. They are also a pre-verbal *cri de coeur* that echoes his vain cries for help for his mother, expresses his childish anguish at losing both his mother and Linda, and underscores how Hyde represents the infantile, id-like aspects of Pride's psyche.

This primitive part of Pride's mind is ascendant when he tries to inject Linda with his serum to cure her hepatitis, in a scene that parallels the horrors of sexual and scientific mistreatment. When she balks at being injected, he probes, 'What if I insist?'. She appears unfazed by his implied threat of violation, but as he approaches her with needle in hand, she shrinks from him. 'What are you doing with that?', she asks, alarmed. She then agrees to take the drug if he does so first, but after witnessing his ghastly transformation, she flees. This scene at Pride's home echoes two earlier ones at the free clinic, where he treats Linda by giving her vitamin shots as the two of them exchange double entendres. In all three scenes, needle and penis are conflated. 'Your needle's the only needle stuck in my ass', a nude Linda tells Pride in an examination room moments before he stands behind her, his pelvis suggestively aligned with her backside, to deliver an injection. This penis-needle conflation not only associates Pride with pimps and johns, but also illustrates how the cause of and treatment for Linda's hepatitis are symbolically identical. These twin phallic symbols also underscore the patriarchal power over women held by pimps and physicians alike, which is abused when Pride unethically (mis)treats Linda's hepatitis with a cure that is actually a more virulent disease.

Pride's attempted experiment on her, and his failed experiment on an elderly Black woman at his hospital, conflate sickness and remedy while linking him to the Tuskegee Study and the Black physicians who were implicated in it. Many who commented on this research averred that 'American society was so racist that scientists could abuse blacks with impunity'.[79] Complicating this view of events was the fact that the Tuskegee Veteran's Affairs Hospital, the Andrew Hospital and the Tuskegee Institute, all of which were involved in the study for decades, 'were African-American institutions', and that 'many young African-American nurses and doctors participated in the project, apparently bolstering their professional resumes by doing so'.[80] Pride is aligned with these disgraced medical professionals, and led to a moral and professional fall, when, like the Jekyll of Fleming's film, he finds his experiments on animals to be inconclusive and requires a human subject. When an aged patient gravely ill with liver disease is admitted into his ward, he suggests to Billie, 'This could be a good chance to try out that serum'. Shocked, she responds, 'No, you can't try that serum on a human. That's not right'. 'What is right?', he asks her, 'To stand around and watch somebody die, not trying to save them? Is that right? That's how my mother died, remember that?'. Here Pride obliquely indicts the Tuskegee doctors who did nothing for their patients suffering from syphilis. That Linda's liver condition stems from hepatitis, a sexually transmitted disease, also evokes the Tuskegee study, as does Billie's remark that Pride is willing to treat the gravely ill patient 'as a guinea pig', and Linda's refusal to allow Pride/Hyde to 'use [her] for some type of human guinea pig'. In describing the Tuskegee Study, the *New York Times* ran a front-page story describing 'human beings with syphilis, who were induced to serve as guinea pigs'.[81] The same metaphor was employed by the *Los Angeles Times*, which described the hundreds of Black men persuaded to participate in the study as 'human guinea pigs', and by the *Washington Post*, which argued that experiments 'on human beings are ethically sound if the guinea pigs are fully informed of the facts and danger'.[82]

Pride emulates the Tuskegee researchers not by inaction, but by breaching medical ethics: he succumbs to temptation and injects the liver patient with his experimental formula. Unbeknown to Pride, she turns into an albino and attacks her nurse. After Pride is informed of her death, he tries the serum on himself and becomes Hyde. When Billie discovers missing doses of the experimental drug, she confronts her colleague with his dangerous unprofessionalism. 'If we get involved in anything illegal, it could ruin us', she tells him. He ignores her and removes another dose of the serum from the lab; thus, his fixation on his mother's illness and death at once drives and imperils his research.

Viewed through the lenses of the sociology and psychology of the 1960s and 1970s, Pride's obsession is an extreme magnification of the deleterious effects that being raised by a single mother might have on an African American child, especially a boy.[83] As *The Negro Family* explains, such effects are lifelong, for 'the child learns a way of looking at life in his early years through which all later experience is viewed and which profoundly shapes his adult conduct'.[84] Traumatised in childhood when his mother died from cirrhosis of the liver and he was helpless to save her, in adulthood Pride seeks a cure for liver disease as the next best thing to resurrecting her. He tries to inject Linda with his serum because she functions as his mother's doppelgänger, and her becoming Mrs Hyde would provide him with a symbolic mother, wife and mirror image. When Pride declines a dinner date with Billie, he jokes, 'I have this very heavy thing going with a guinea pig in the lab'. She replies, 'I knew there was another woman'. Their joking assumes Oedipal significance when Linda, 'some type of human guinea pig', accepts a dinner 'date' with Pride. Linda chooses prostitution in lieu of being 'a maid in some tacky hotel', varying the experience of Pride's mother – who lived, worked and died as a maid in the mansion that he has bought and (again) made his home. Pride's mother 'drank a lot', and her alcoholism-induced cirrhosis corresponds with Linda's sexually transmitted hepatitis. Linda also acts maternally by helping to support her friend Bernice's children. Explaining her assistance, she tells Pride, 'I guess that's the mother image in me'. Her expression is literalised, and her internal mother externalised, when she appears in a mirror with Bernice, who is clothed in a maternally dowdy robe and cap while Linda wears a form-fitting dress and puts on a wig. Dressed for work, Linda offers Bernice money for her son's birthday, thereby illustrating how, like Pride/Hyde, she is bifurcated: both a prostitute and a mother surrogate.

This bifurcation makes her a fitting counterpart for Pride, the man she concedes to '[thinking she] was in love with'. Indeed, when Bernice asks Linda, 'When you gonna get a man of your own, and settle down?', and she responds, 'I almost did, once', her cryptic reply might be construed as a reference to her earlier 'date' with Pride, which ends with Hyde's trying to transform her into a female version of himself. A Linda-Hyde pairing is certainly logical, not only as the converse of the Billie-Pride relationship, but also because Linda's maternal qualities are complemented by Pride's paternal ones. Her giving money to Bernice is duplicated by his offering a needy mother money for her son's vitamins and telling Linda, 'That is the father in me'. Linda stands no chance with Pride, but she might with Hyde.

Pride's seeking to cure Linda's liver disease and his own primal trauma by changing her into a double of both his mother and himself, in the (un)homely former brothel where she died while the prostitutes working there ignored his cries for help, is powerfully deconstructive and uncanny. Mother/son, male/female, self/other and familiar/unfamiliar – all these binary oppositions collapse. No longer a helpless boy, Pride can at once save (a double for) his diseased mother, join her in an Oedipal bond, and see his own monstrous albinism comfortably mirrored by his mother-mate. Pride's wish, however, is complicated by his hatred for prostitutes. As he confesses to Linda, 'I despise them all for letting my mother die! All of them!'. Her being among the despised renders him ambivalent towards her – as, arguably, he was towards his alcoholic mother, who left him alone 'while she would go out and clean up the filth . . . and look after those ladies of the evening'. Repelled by prostitutes but attracted to Linda as a mother figure, Hyde copes with her rejection of him and his serum by '[cleaning] up the filth' – or, as O'Connor puts it, '[cleaning] up the community' – and murdering his first streetwalker. He thereby emulates the mother whose life and death helped create him, while also expressing Pride's unconscious aggression against and desire for his mother (surrogate). Regarding such aggression, Russell Campbell explains that 'male feelings of hostility toward women that find expression in the perpetration of violence against a prostitute may have their roots in resentment against the mother', and 'a number of films make such a link explicit' by either making mothers prostitutes or, as in *Dr. Black, Mr. Hyde*, associating the killer's mother with prostitution.[85]

Pride/Hyde's unique pathology distinguishes him from other film versions of Jekyll/Hyde who are motivated by sexual repression/expression. Unlike them, he is not separated by a powerful patriarch from his love interest, sexually frustrated and sublimating his libido into his research. In fact, until Pride begins using the serum on himself, he and Billie seem to have a healthy and stable relationship. Hyde is born not from Pride's sexual desire, but from his unconscious wish to resurrect his mother. While this wish certainly has Oedipal aspects, it is very different from conventional lust. Likewise, though Pride's injecting Linda with vitamin shots and Hyde's attempting to do so with the experimental serum are symbolically sexual, both men seek to cure her, not to ravish her. Linda repeatedly makes suggestive comments to Pride, and he consistently deflects them. When he asks her to dinner in order to persuade her to take his experimental drug, she asks, 'Am I for dessert?', and he responds, 'It's not like that at all'. He wants to offer her 'fatherly advice' and emphasises that 'there will be no hanky panky'. When dinner concludes and he invites her to his home for 'a surprise', she says, 'You get the check and I pay the bill'. He replies, 'It's not like that'. Although Linda wants Pride, as the Ivys of Mamoulian's and Fleming's films want Jekyll, her desire, unlike theirs, is unrequited. Pride longs not for Linda but for his mother, and as Hyde he attempts to transform the former into the latter.

Pride's own transformation into Hyde discloses a final unconscious motivation: his wish to be white. His desire, at once political and personal, is a mechanism for both coping and survival. Kelly Miller, a colleague of W. E. B. Du Bois and a fellow prominent member of the NAACP, claimed that to live in the United States 'the Negro must get along, get white, or get out'.[86] Pride, who seems to accommodate himself to white hegemony before turning into Hyde and eventually being killed, pursues each of these options in turn but focuses on the second. His yearning for whiteness is analysed by Kenneth B. Clark, whose studies in the 1940s of how and why Black children rejected Black dolls and embraced white ones became well known. In *Dark Ghetto*, Clark describes how white racism shapes the dynamics of 'the Negro's complex and debilitating prejudice against himself'.[87] To protect themselves from such racism, he writes, 'Many Negroes live sporadically in a world of fantasy, and fantasy takes different forms at different ages. In childhood the delusion is a simple one – the child may pretend that he is really white'.[88] Pride has the means to turn this fantasy into reality. 'Look at my hands', he tells Linda after changing into Hyde. 'Look at my face'. In a medium close-up that provides the viewer with some distance from Hyde's ghastly features, the camera cuts between his face, which she calls 'horrible', and her own horrified countenance. 'In a moment, you'll look like me', Hyde says to Linda, evoking her telling Pride, 'If I was white, I just might have a chance [with you]'. Hyde's parallel attempts to win Linda's maternal approval and change her into a mirror image of himself fail, for they prove her right about his racial insecurity. Repelled by his horrific whiteness and refusing to become like him, she cries, 'I won't!', and flees. Her embracing Blackness and his desiring whiteness permeate *Dr. Black, Mr. Hyde*.

Horror in Black and White: Multiplicity and Hybridity in *Dr. Black, Mr. Hyde*

This white/Black opposition is ubiquitous in the film's *mise en scène*. Pride first appears in a white lab coat, in a white hospital building, in bright white light. Tellingly, he wears white not only at work but also at home, where he dresses in white pyjamas and a white robe. Billie likewise wears a white lab coat, which covers a black blouse. Her outfit is reversed by the black suit and white shirt that Pride wears to the hospital, before removing his black suit jacket and putting on a white lab coat. These scenes illustrate how often 'white is the positive term, holding priority and privilege over black'.[89] The film associates whiteness with scientific objectivity, expertise and purity. Whiteness is also linked with wealth, for both the well-funded hospital and Pride's mansion are white. More complexly, dressing in white suggests alignment with, if not assimilation into, white hegemony. Billie's wearing black underneath white indicates that though she is 'essentially' Black, her professional role requires her to assume whiteness. Conversely, Pride's wearing a white shirt under a black suit jacket signifies his acceptance of white values and ideology, thereby reinforcing Linda's critique. His trading a black suit jacket for a white lab coat, while retaining his black trousers, bifurcates both his outfit and his symbolic significance: white above the waist and black below it, his clothing replicates the white/Black opposition, reinforces the conventional hierarchy of its constituents, and hints at the potent sexuality stereotypically associated with Blackness. This association, and that between Blackness and villainy, is strengthened and illustrated by the black hat worn by Silky, an abusive, knife-wielding, African American criminal.

While white/Black often functions conventionally in *Dr. Black, Mr. Hyde*, the film follows Stevenson's *Jekyll and Hyde* and departs from canonical film adaptations by occasionally reversing and conflating the elements of this opposition. In a significant scene, Preston, a white pimp, supplies the drug-addled Silky, a Black pimp, with cocaine on the condition that he convince Linda to return to work for him. That Silky wears a black hat, and Preston a black suit, signifies their relative degrees of turpitude and underscores the latter's dominance over the former. Yet, both figuratively and literally, white is more significant than Black in this scene. Preston's influence, though not solely a function of his whiteness, is closely connected with it. He is a white man who employs a white drug to control a Black man – and, through him, a Black woman. Preston's power play is enacted in his 'office', a restroom whose fixtures are white, a venue that – together with Silky's calling the cocaine 'shit' – emphasises the execrable nature of Preston's business. The white pimp's malignity, however, pales beside that of the murderous albino Hyde, who kills Silky by crushing him against a wall with Pride's Rolls-Royce. In Pride/Hyde, described by Lt O'Connor as a 'black doctor that turns white at night', the associated binary oppositions white/Black and good/evil appear to be reversed. Making this point and citing the film's original title,[90] Cynthia Erb claims,

> *Dr. Black and Mr. White* inverts the traditional dichotomy, so that black is the norm and white has extremely destructive connotations. When Pride changes, he goes from being a handsome black man to a grotesque white monster. Emphasis is put on the lavish white car he drives, its headlights cutting through the darkness.[91]

The film's initial title makes explicit what its subsequent title, *Dr. Black, Mr. Hyde*, leaves implicit: that the devalued term, *Hyde*, is bound up with the typically privileged term, *white*. By substituting *Black* for Jekyll but not *White* for Hyde, the title sacrifices symmetry for suggestiveness, enabling a degree of slippage between the latter two terms. This indeterminacy is appropriate, given that, contrary to Erb and O'Connor, Pride's killer car is not white but silver and grey, and Hyde is not white but albino. Both car and driver thus function not to invert but to collapse the white/Black binary opposition.

A blend of the colours black and white, grey appears not only on Dr Pride's Rolls-Royce Silver Dawn, but also on Silky's grey cape. Silver, a metallic form of grey, accompanies grey in Dr Pride's two-tone Rolls-Royce, his silver Mercedes with grey interior, Silky's silver Cadillac, and the silver-headed cane that Silky sports while wearing a grey cape and evoking the classic Victorian gentleman's evening costume of both Jekyll and Hyde. Black and white are also combined with silver and grey to underscore the latter's liminality: both Pride's Rolls-Royce and Silky's Cadillac have white-wall tyres; Silky wears a black hat with his cape and cane; and, when Silky is pinned by Pride's car, shots of him in a white suit are cut with those of the car's spinning whitewall tyres. The status symbols owned by Pride and Silky are literal grey areas, and figurative indications of the moral compromises that these Black men have made while succeeding in a white world. More positively, the silver car driven by Jackson and O'Connor, an interracial pair of detectives, signifies a productive combination of Black and white.

Hyde's colour is an overdetermined signifier that may be considered from multiple perspectives. From one perspective, it functions as whiteface, a form of reverse minstrelsy. Whiteface, a theatrical practice that dates from the 1890s, must be distinguished from 'passing', an attempt by 'black citizens who visually appear white' to 'assimilate into the majority-white culture', for 'unlike racial passers . . . whiteface minstrels' assume whiteness to 'reveal its loopholes, its constructed nature, and even its terror'.[92] The terror of whiteness is on full display as Hyde rampages through Watts, killing people and destroying property. That he is terrifying rather than terrorised illustrates how whiteface enables *Dr. Black, Mr. Hyde* to overturn the stereotype of the Black coward described by William L. Van Deburg, who observes, 'Cowardly black literary and theatrical characters were terrified of graveyards, haunted houses, [and] funeral parlors', and 'some temporarily turned chalky white with fear'.[93] Hyde's version of whiteness inspires fear in others rather than exaggerating and rendering comical his own fear. It thus reproduces a tactic first deployed in the antebellum period, when 'in the works of African American writers . . . slaves use ghost stories to undermine white authority'.[94] These stories inverted those of the slave masters, who used tales of spectres to 'limit slave movements and discourage runaways' by '[endowing] places along possible escape routes with violent ghosts'.[95] In rewritings of these stories, slaves turn superstition against their masters. In one, 'John tries to fetch water for his master, but a bullfrog frightens him. He tells the story of a hopping haint [ghost] to his master, who must accept the explanation to encourage further superstition in his slave. By embracing superstition, John forces his master to get his own water'.[96] Locating Hyde's terrifying whiteface in this subversive African American storytelling tradition enables us to appreciate how it appropriates the Jekyll/Hyde figure and inverts canonical, white adaptations of *Jekyll and Hyde*, not only by reversing the white/Black binary opposition, but also by questioning the meaning and stability of whiteness. The obvious artificiality of Hyde's white makeup highlights the fact that whiteness is not essential but constructed, not deep but superficial, not permanent but transitory.

Shifting focus, we see that the ghostly white Hyde is also uncanny, as Jackson recognises by calling him a 'haint'. A word used in the South for a haunt or ghost, *haint* refers not only to Hyde's pale complexion but also, and more profoundly, to his being racially and ontologically (un)familiar. As Freud explains, the uncanny often manifests in the form of 'spirits and ghosts', operating as a kind of psychic haunting whereby 'something familiar which has been repressed' re-emerges into consciousness.[97] Hyde is thus doubly uncanny, at once a doppelgänger and a ghost that signifies both the return of Pride's repressed Blackness and the worst of his assumed whiteness. His uncanniness is enhanced by the fact that he is not simply white. In Watts, he is told by a man on the street that he is 'on the wrong side of town', a comment indicating that he is perceived as white. Likewise, after resuming his identity as Pride, Hyde is overlooked by Silky and others hunting for him. Yet, as Pride notes when recording the results of his experiments, his formula results not in whiteness but in albinism, a 'total reduction in pigmentation'. Thus, Hyde is not only or even principally a Black man who turns white, one whose inner whiteness is figured as monstrousness in an inversion of the stereotypical white/Black opposition, but a Black man who loses his colour. His status and significance are elucidated by the narrator of *Moby-Dick* (1851), who considers what 'in the Albino man so peculiarly repels and often shocks the eye' and concludes that his 'whiteness is not so much a color as the visible absence of color', a 'blankness, full of meaning'.[98] Not whiteness but a lack of Blackness, Hyde's albinism is the result of Pride's misguided attempt to incorporate himself into the white power structure. He renders himself neither Black nor white, becoming a third, colourless kind of being who, like his unique precursor in Stevenson's novella, is 'the first creature of that sort' to exist.[99] Pride/Hyde's uncanny hybridity is emphasised and augmented by Jackson's description of Hyde as 'a cross between the Abominable Snowman and Willie the Werewolf'. Each creature is itself a human-animal hybrid that doubles Hyde's animality within Pride's humanity. Pride/Hyde is therefore a hybrid of two hybrids, each of whom is a racial signifier for horror in Black or white.

Hybrids are often perceived as monsters,[100] since both groups consist of 'the in between, the mixed, the ambivalent as implied in the ancient Greek root of the word "monsters": *teras*, which means both horrible and wonderful'.[101] Pride/Hyde's augmented hybridity is monstrous in the original sense of the word, both horrible and wonderful. It not only illustrates the horror of losing one's racial identity, but also offers prospects for multiplicity that move beyond binary thinking about race, looking backward to the utopian America envisioned by Charles Waddell Chesnutt and forward to current ideas of hybridity. In 'What Is a White Man?' (1889), Chesnutt notes that 'where the intermingling of the races has made such progress as it has in this country, the line which separates the races must in many instances have been practically obliterated'.[102] In 'The Future American' (1900), he imagines the 'amalgamation' or fusion of racial and ethnic groups and the collapse of associated binary oppositions. Chesnutt contends that 'the future American ethnic type' will result from 'a mingling . . . of the various racial varieties which make up the present population of the United States'.[103] Once Americans became 'a composite and homogeneous people', the 'elements of racial discord' would disappear, since 'there would be no inferior race to domineer over; there would be no superior race to oppress'.[104]

While the Los Angeles of *Dr. Black, Mr. Hyde* is very far indeed from Chesnutt's ideal, the ways in which the film collapses the white/Black binary opposition and imagines a third, hybrid category that transcends race align with our current appreciation for how hybridity might deconstruct artificial racial distinctions and yield intercultural understanding. As Nikos Papastergiadis explains, when identity depends on 'an exclusive boundary between "us" and "them", the hybrid, born out of the transgression of this boundary, figures as a form of danger, loss and degeneration. If, however, the boundary is marked positively – to solicit exchange and inclusion – then the hybrid may yield strength and vitality'.[105] Pride/Hyde is a liminal figure not only insofar as he is capable of transforming from one state into another, but also by virtue of his being able to navigate both the 'Black' and 'white' worlds constructed in the film. Although *Dr. Black, Mr. Hyde* focuses on the horrors and perils of liminality, hybridity and multiplicity, it nonetheless recognises their immense potential.

The Hunter and the Hunted: *The Beast Must Die*

Hybridity is also central to films about Jekyll/Hyde's bifurcated and shape-shifting close relation, the werewolf.[106] As Howard L. Malchow observes, 'The resonance of the racial half-breed with this form of gothic monstrosity is inescapable'.[107] The 'black', bestial half of this hybrid creature is often linked with Black men, who historically have been depicted in films as animalistic 'sexual monsters'.[108] It makes symbolic sense, then, that in *Dr. Black, Mr. Hyde* the werewolf-like Hyde chases prostitutes and goes berserk at the Moonlight Lounge. As the hunter becomes the prey in the film's climactic scene, an inarticulate Hyde cries like a beast and fights to the death another animal sent to bring him down. This stereotypical association of Black masculine identity with animalism in general and the werewolf in particular is exploded in *The Beast Must Die*, which inverts both binary oppositions and audience expectations as it moves beyond duality towards multiplicity.

The Beast Must Die is drawn from a work of fiction: 'There Shall Be No Darkness' (1950), a story by James Blish that depicts how guests at a country manor cope with a werewolf in their midst. The adaptation departs from its source by casting Black actors as the wealthy Tom and Caroline Newcliffe (Calvin Lockhart and Marlene Clark). In another important change, whereas Blish's story reveals the identity of the werewolf in the exposition, Paul Annett's film makes a point of obscuring it. The movie begins with an onscreen announcement and voiceover: 'This film is a detective story – in which you are the detective'. Viewers are encouraged to identify the werewolf during 'the werewolf break', which occurs fifteen minutes before the film concludes and provides thirty seconds for answers. In *The Beast Must Die*, Newcliffe, a successful businessman and hunter, invites to his estate in the English countryside a group of five people, one of whom he suspects of being a werewolf. He and his wife host Arthur Bennington (Charles Gray), a diplomat linked with the mysterious disappearance of two colleagues; Jan and Davina Gilmore (Michael Gambon and Ciaran Madden), a noted pianist and his wife shadowed by grisly murders; Paul Foote (Tom Chadbon), an artist imprisoned for cannibalism; and Dr Christopher Lundgren (Peter Cushing), an archaeologist whose speciality is lycanthropy. The house and grounds are equipped with cameras, microphones and motion sensors monitored by Pavel (Anton Diffring), an expert in security. Newcliffe subjects his guests to various tests for lycanthropy, none of which are successful until wolfsbane pollen is spread within the group. A werewolf appears, killing Pavel, a helicopter pilot, Bennington, and finally Caroline's dog, whose wounds she attempts to treat. Newcliffe then asks his remaining guests to put a silver bullet in their mouths. When Caroline does so, she transforms into a werewolf and attacks her husband, who shoots her with a silver bullet. Lundgren reasons that Caroline was infected with lycanthropy by her dog's wounds. After the werewolf kills Foote, Newcliffe's top suspect, the hunter confronts the beast in the woods and shoots it with a silver bullet. The werewolf is revealed to be the pianist Gilmore, who has bitten and infected Newcliffe during their struggle. The film ends after the hunter returns to his mansion and shoots himself to avoid becoming the beast he has hunted.

The Beast Must Die uses the hunter/hunted binary opposition not only to reverse the white/Black bifurcation, but also to challenge the assumptions of its audience with respect to race relations. The film begins with a nine-minute chase sequence. Aerial shots alternate with those closer to the ground as a white helicopter pilot watches a Black man clad entirely in black running through the woods, while a truck full of white men wearing uniforms and armed with rifles follows him. Cameras in the trees surveil the man, whose locations are conveyed to his pursuers by a white man with a European accent who is wearing a jacket and tie and sitting in a control room. As this man directs the chase and watches it on a television screen, close-ups emphasise his piercing blue eyes. Camera angles encourage the audience to identify with the pursuers rather than the pursued. Aerial point-of-view shots from the perspective of the helicopter pilot not only underscore the disparity in power between the hunters and the hunted, but also parallel shots of the television screen seen through the blue eyes of the man in the control room. The alignment between this man and viewers is especially strong, given that both he and they see events not directly but through the mediation of a camera and screen. In contrast with the aerial shots, the two point-of-view shots from the perspective of the man being chased are low-angle shots of the canopy of trees and a surveillance camera, both of which images disempower him by reinforcing his being trapped and watched. Viewers who have been prepared to serve as werewolf hunters might logically conclude from the action, camera shots and *mise en scène* that the Black man running through the woods is a werewolf, though not the werewolf whose identity they are invited to ascertain. Whereas white viewers might find identifying with the white hunters natural, Black viewers might resign themselves to empathising with the Black underdog. This man is targeted and released by three successive hunters. As the audience begins to conclude that these men are playing some sort of game rather than hunting in earnest, they are directed to 'intercept and kill' their prey. Exhausted and dirty, he emerges onto an expanse of lawn in front of a mansion where a group of well-dressed people are having lunch. As they look quizzically at him, the hunters confront him and open fire. He collapses to the ground and a woman screams. The members of the party on the lawn rush towards him. The sequence ends with his rising and laughing.

The next scene shrewdly subverts viewers' expectations about race, wealth and power. The man in black is now not on the ground but in the control room, standing in front of a bank of television screens and watching with wry amusement a recording of the scene that viewers have just witnessed. After he and the blue-eyed European discuss cameras, microphones and sensors, he concludes, 'You've earned your money, Pavel'. The audience now realises that this Black man is not an intruder on the white man's estate, but the owner of the estate and the white man's employer; not one who is hunted like an animal, but a world-class hunter who is preparing for the most challenging hunt of his life by testing the surveillance system that he has bought with 'a great deal of money'. He is Tom Newcliffe, a self-made millionaire businessman, 'a big man' and 'a born hunter' who tells Pavel, 'In this world, you're either the hunter or the hunted'. The revelation that a Black man holds such wealth and power renders this scene far more surprising and significant than the one in which the identity of the werewolf is revealed. Newcliffe has invited a group of the white elite to his estate, so that he can hunt and kill one of them. These remarkable and progressive inversions of the white/Black and hunter/hunted binary oppositions are underscored near the climax of the film, when Newcliffe ascends in his helicopter to shoot at a white man turned werewolf (see Figure 6).

The film inverts yet another key bifurcation by tracing lycanthropic infection not to an exotic Other but to a white, western man. In so doing, it departs significantly from its cinematic precursors. Although these films theorise that anybody could become a werewolf, in practice transforming into such an outré creature serves as a condign punishment for men who

Figure 6 Tom Newcliffe (Calvin Lockhart) targets the werewolf in *The Beast Must Die* (1974). Cinerama Releasing Corporation/Photofest

journey into foreign territory. In *Werewolf of London* (Stuart Walker, 1935), the werewolf Yogami (Warner Oland) infects Wilfred Glendon (Henry Hull) when the English botanist strays too far afield into Tibet. In *The Wolf Man* (George Waggner, 1941), Bela (Bela Lugosi) infects Larry Talbot (Lon Chaney Jr) after the Welshman ventures into the gypsy's camp. *The Curse of the Werewolf* (Terence Fisher, 1961) stems from a beggar (Richard Wordsworth) who unwisely enters a strange castle in a strange land. These lycanthropic trajectories are reversed and otherwise complicated in *The Beast Must Die*. Remarkably, infection spreads from a white man to a Black woman and a Black man. No exotic locales, figures or even forces are involved, for lycanthropy is presented as a non-geographically specific disease whose physiology Lundgren explains in excruciating scientific detail. Anyone from anywhere – man or woman, Black or white, foreign or domestic – could be the werewolf, as the 'werewolf break' emphasises by showing each of the suspects in turn and asking viewers to choose one. This interval illustrates how the film avoids the typical binary oppositions associated with lycanthropy in favour of multiplicity.

While complicating white/Black and hunter/hunted, *The Beast Must Die* subtly references the Black Panther Party, a Black Power movement that began in 1966 and continued until 1982. Central to the Black Panthers was 'the practice of armed self-defense against the police',[109] and their 'most publicized characteristic . . . was an emphasis on the gun'.[110] Using both 'loaded guns and cameras',[111] the Black Panthers were known for policing the police by following and surveilling law-enforcement officers with 'cameras [and] tape recorders'.[112] Newcliffe, who refuses to involve the police in the killings at his estate, likewise deploys guns, cameras and recording equipment. He also dresses very much like one of the Black Panthers, who were famous for their 'trademark leather jackets, black pants, and black boots', so much so that their 'leather jackets came to symbolize Black Power and armed self-defense'.[113] When Newcliffe prepares for his first night of hunting the werewolf, he is already wearing black trousers and boots. He then completes the distinctive outfit of the Black Panthers, but for their berets.[114] Standing in the control room with his back to a gun cabinet filled with rifles, he strips to the waist and dons a leather jacket without first putting on a shirt. Newcliffe then turns towards the cabinet, selects and inspects a rifle, and picks up a gun belt. In the foreground of the shot is a section of the control panel for his cameras and microphones. This image brings together the Black Panthers' guns, surveillance equipment and clothing, though this last is more symbolic than practical.

Unlike Newcliffe's rifle, his glossy black leather jacket serves little purpose in hunting the werewolf and contrasts with the neutral, camouflage-coloured outfits worn by the white hunters at the start of the film. The jacket's function is primarily representational, as the framing of the scene indicates. In a medium long shot, the leather of a club chair in the foreground parallels and contrasts with the leather of the jacket. The former signifies wealth and refinement, while the latter, an animal hide that covers the hunter's own bare skin, draws a metonymical link between him and the creature that he pursues, another man who wears the skin of a beast. This association, reinforced by the fact that both the jacket and the werewolf (as a wolf) are black, is even more conspicuous later in the film, when Newcliffe wears a form-fitting black leather jumpsuit that renders him a man-as-panther stalking a man-as-wolf. His form, if not his function, aligns with the symbol of the Black Panther Party as described by one of its founders, Stokely Carmichael. 'We chose for the emblem a black panther', Carmichael explains, because the animal represents 'the strength and dignity of black people' and 'never strikes back until he's back so far into the wall, he's got nothing to do but spring out'.[115] Unlike his animal double, Newcliffe strikes first, instigating a confrontation in which the roles of hunter and prey are continually in flux.

The reversible nature of surveillance and hunting in *The Beast Must Die* evokes how the Black Panthers not only surveilled and followed the authorities, but also were surveilled and followed by them. The FBI's secret and illegal Counterintelligence Program (COINTELPRO) was established in 1956 to combat communism and operated until 1971, when several of its dossiers were stolen and leaked to the media. In the 1960s, the Black Panthers became one of its key targets. Its 'massive program of surveillance' deployed both electronic devices and agents, not to gather intelligence but to induce paranoia among those surveilled.[116] COINTELPRO also fomented suspicion within the Black Panthers by using 'informers and agents provocateurs' who, after being invited into the organisation, worked to disrupt its internal functions.[117] In *The Beast Must Die*, the increasingly agitated Newcliffe is viewed as paranoid by nearly everyone except for the werewolf himself, who functions in much the same strategic fashion as a COINTELPRO infiltrator. His first target is not Newcliffe but his surveillance system, which the werewolf disables by killing Pavel and wrecking the control room, the better to conduct his own surveillance of the man tracking him. In employing human reasoning, the creature demonstrates an intelligence at once human, animal and hybrid, a multiplicitous consciousness unusual for a werewolf.[118]

His complex and developing subject position is shared by the audience, as the dynamics of surveillance and hunting continually shift. Throughout the film, Newcliffe is both the hunter and the hunted. After guns, cameras and sensors are aimed at him, he turns them on the werewolf. As he stalks this beast, the beast, in both wolf and human forms, stalks him. He is menaced by an unseen antagonist with an axe, a pitchfork and an arrow. The arrow is revealed to have been shot by Foote, who tells him, 'Been tracking you. Hunting the hunter'. In retrospect, viewers come to understand that not Foote but the werewolf, Gilmore, must have been responsible for the first two attacks. Point-of-view shots in each scene compel the audience to align with the unknown assailant, again becoming hunters even while continuing to serve as detectives attempting to determine whose eyes they are looking through. The result is a commingled subjectivity that serves as another instance of multiplicity in the film.

In exploring and depicting multiplicity, especially in relation to subjectivity and race, *The Beast Must Die* follows *Dr. Black, Mr. Hyde* and diverges from other iterations of the Jekyll/Hyde figure not only by drawing on the binary oppositions structuring Stevenson's *Jekyll and Hyde*, but also by manifesting its proto-deconstructive insight that such bifurcations are inherently unstable and subject to transposition and elision. Furthermore, both *The Beast Must Die* and *Dr. Black, Mr. Hyde* engage the pressing social and political concerns of Black viewers in the 1970s. These progressive films are by no means unproblematic, however, as their endings demonstrate. In *The Beast Must Die*, the roles of hunter and hunted stop reversing and finally combine when Newcliffe, infected by Gilmore's lycanthropy, shoots himself. Like Caroline and Gilmore, he has become a beast; or, more accurately, he is revealed as the beast he already has become. Caroline indicates that her husband's metamorphosis precedes and foreshadows his infection, telling him, 'You've let your passion for hunting turn into a blood lust.' Hence his changes, from man into symbolic panther into actual werewolf, are less a matter of kind than of degree. According to the film's extradiegetic title and its protagonist's diegetic decree to his guests, 'the beast must die' and so he does, after killing Caroline and Gilmore and arguably being responsible for the deaths of three more people. Newcliffe's death sentence replicates those of Pride/Hyde and Jekyll/Hyde, both of whom seem to die as punishment for having killed. Yet their true crimes may be not capital but Promethean. The implications of this interpretation are much more troubling in *The Beast Must Die* and *Dr. Black, Mr. Hyde* than in *Jekyll and Hyde*, given the significance of race relations in the films. Billie asks Pride, 'Are you trying to work yourself to death?'. Likewise, Caroline tells Newcliffe, 'You have to win all the time'. These women recognise what their achievement-obsessed partners cannot: that a Black man determined to succeed at all costs in a white world can become a monster who destroys others and, ultimately, himself.

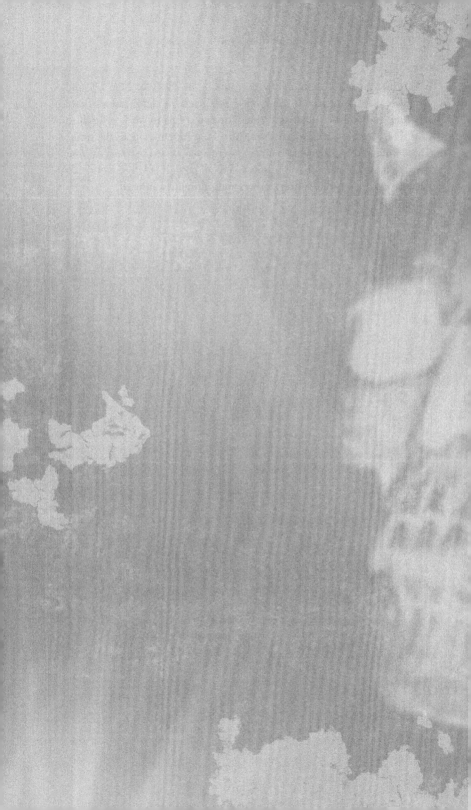

4

Body and Soul

The Zombie and the Evil Spirit

WHILE THE WORKS of Bram Stoker, Mary Shelley and Robert Louis Stevenson have canonised the vampire, Frankenstein's Creature and Jekyll/Hyde, literary representations of two other important and interrelated Gothic figures, the zombie and the evil spirit, are diffuse though hardly uncommon. The first popular book in English to depict the zombie is ostensibly non-fiction, though unquestionably in the Gothic mode. In *The Magic Island* (1929), a highly unconventional Haitian travelogue, the American journalist, adventurer and occultist William Seabrook recounts tales of 'the *zombie*', a 'dead body which is made to walk and act and move as if it were alive' by the bokor, a sorcerer who makes of it 'a servant or slave'.[1] After *The Magic Island* popularised the term *zombie*, the authors of pulp fiction followed Seabrook's lead and published lurid stories of the creature in American magazines such as *Weird Tales*, *Thrilling Mystery* and *Argosy* during the late 1920s and early 1930s.[2] Long before the zombie first appeared in print, tales of evil spirits had proven popular. Ann B. Tracy finds either demons or Satan himself in twenty-two Gothic novels published between 1790 and 1830.[3] Major texts featuring the diabolical include William Beckford's *Vathek* (1786), Matthew Lewis's *The Monk* (1796), Charlotte Dacre's *Zofloya* (1806) and James Hogg's *The Private Memoirs and Confessions of a Justified Sinner* (1824). In the twentieth century, Ira Levin's *Rosemary's Baby* (1967), the story of a woman impregnated by the Devil, and William Peter Blatty's *The Exorcist* (1971), which depicts the ordeal of a girl possessed by a demon, were bestsellers.

Zombies and evil spirits also became popular and enduring figures in a wide variety of films. Not long after *The Magic Island* was published, zombies first appeared on-screen in Victor Halperin's *White Zombie* (1932), a film inspired by Seabrook's text, and they returned in the director's *Revolt of the Zombies* (1936). *I Walked with a Zombie* (Jacques Tourneur, 1943) is among the better traditional films in its expansive category, which extends to comedies such as *The Ghost Breakers* (George Marshall, 1940), *King of the Zombies* (Jean Yarbrough, 1941) and *Zombies on Broadway* (Gordon Douglas, 1945). *Night of the Living Dead* marked a turning point in the genre, not only by depicting zombies as cannibals, but also by casting an African American actor, Duane Jones, in the lead role. As Romero was completing his film, he learned that Martin Luther King Jr had been assassinated. 'From that moment on', he recalls, 'it became impossible to view *Night of the Living Dead* as anything but a racial "statement"'.[4] Racial issues, always central to zombie films, are especially prominent in *Ouanga* (George Terwilliger, 1936), which propagates racist stereotypes and exploits anxieties about miscegenation. The film was remade with an all-Black cast and without zombies as *The Devil's Daughter* (Arthur H. Leonard, 1939).

Movies portraying evil spirits are as varied in tone and tenor as those portraying zombies. Mephistopheles made his cinematic debut in *Le Manoir du Diable* (Georges Méliès, 1896). From the 1900s through to the 1970s, Satan and his demons were portrayed in works ranging from horror movies to musicals and comedies, including *The Devil* and *The Sorrows of Satan* (D. W. Griffith, 1908, 1926), *Satanas* and *Faust* (F. W. Murnau, 1920, 1926), *Leaves from Satan's Book* (Carl Theodor Dreyer, 1920), *Damn Yankees* (George Abbott and Stanley Donen, 1958), *Bedazzled* (Stanley Donen, 1967), and *The Devil Rides Out* (Terence Fisher, 1968). *Rosemary's Baby* (Roman Polanski, 1968) and *The Exorcist* (William Friedkin, 1973) memorably adapted their fictional precursors. Shortly after these two landmark works were released, Blaxploitation films featuring zombies and evil spirits began to appear. *Sugar Hill* and *The House on Skull Mountain* involve zombies. *Abby*, *Lord Shango*, *J. D.'s Revenge* and *Petey Wheatstraw* portray women and men who are possessed.

Although zombies and evil spirits seem to be very different figures, they are in fact quite closely linked. Both zombiism and possession dissociate body and soul. Moreover, both zombies and the possessed are alienated from their own identities and made to serve the will of another, whether a bokor or a spirit, in a condition that amounts to slavery. Paul Christopher Johnson points out that 'the zombie is precisely a reprise of the slave, a body owned and occupied yet simultaneously empty and agentless, movement minus will'.[5] Likewise, 'spirit possession [indexes] the absence of control, the body without will, and, by extension, the figure of the slave'.[6] The figure of the zombie-as-slave holds historical as well as imaginary resonance, given that it emerges from the Vodou[7] religion as practised in Haiti by enslaved Africans who rebelled against their masters.[8] Its historicity renders it paradoxical, since, as Sarah J. Lauro observes, the Haitian zombie is a creature that 'incorporates a people's history of both enslavement and political resistance'.[9] Psychological and spiritual rather than historical tension is evident in how self and other at once conflict and conflate in relations between the zombie and the bokor, and between the possessed individual and the possessing spirit. These contradictory relationships illustrate what Freud terms the 'doubling, dividing and interchanging of the self' that characterises the uncanny.[10] Indeed, zombies and those possessed by evil spirits are profoundly uncanny. As Freud notes, 'apparent death and the re-animation of the dead' are 'most uncanny themes', as are 'spirits and ghosts'.[11] Moreover, both zombies and the possessed generate 'uncertainty' as to whether they are 'human [beings]' or '[automata]' acting without volition.[12]

Uncanny doubling and the loss of agency are essential to narratives of zombies and the possessed, as are the (dis)empowerment of women and conflicts between and about religions. First explored in pulp fiction and Gothic novels, these topics are revisited in mainstream cinematic representations of zombies and evil spirits. They are viewed from a fresh perspective in Blaxploitation films, which use them to join contemporary discussions of autonomy, the role of women and the status of religion in the African American community. As adaptations and appropriations, these films might well be compared with zombies and the possessed, insofar as they are reanimated or inhabited by what Jean-François Lyotard calls 'master-narratives'.[13] While lines of influence may be traced among these three categories of texts, their thematic and adaptive trajectories are far less direct than those of the works already considered, given the lack of central, original fictions from which to plot such courses. This chapter will therefore focus on how Blaxploitation films depict and deploy zombies and evil spirits, drawing connections to fictional and cinematic antecedents as appropriate.

Voodoo Woman: *Sugar Hill*

In *Sugar Hill*, Diana 'Sugar' Hill (Marki Bey) is a fashion photographer in New Orleans whose boyfriend Langston (Larry Don Johnson), the owner of Club Haiti, refuses to sell his business to the white mob boss Morgan (Robert Quarry), who has him killed. Sugar inherits the nightclub and is in turn pressured by Morgan to sell it. She plays for time with the gangster while methodically plotting against him and his minions. To empower herself and enable her revenge, Sugar seeks help from an elderly voodoo queen, Mama Maitresse (Zara Cully), who summons Baron Samedi (Don Pedro Colley), the loa (god) of the dead. He not only provides Sugar with the zombies of enslaved men and women to help kill those who killed Langston, but also participates in and relishes their murders. These strange homicides are investigated by Valentine (Richard Lawson), Sugar's ex-boyfriend and a police lieutenant, who suspects but cannot prove her involvement in them. Ultimately, the detective is injured via voodoo and sidelined, Morgan is killed, and the mobster's girlfriend, Celeste (Betty Anne Rees), is taken by Baron Samedi into the underworld as payment for his supernatural services.

From its noteworthy first scene, *Sugar Hill* links the uncanny and the empowerment of women. The film starts with what seems to be a genuine Vodou ceremony, which involves a man vigorously beating on drums, snake-wielding dancers, and a chicken whose throat is cut and whose blood is offered to a loa. In an indication that all might not be as it appears, the action is accompanied not by diegetic drumming, but by an extradiegetic soul song, 'Supernatural Voodoo Woman', whose lyrics foreshadow Sugar's plot for revenge and warn, 'Do her wrong and you won't see the light'. As the dancing ends, together with the song and the film's opening credits, applause begins and the camera cuts to a medium shot of a sign that reads 'Club Haiti'. Viewers realise that the song was diegetic after all, and that they have been watching not an actual Vodou ritual but a performance of voodoo, a simulacrum that uncannily doubles the zombie film in which it takes place.

This initial duplication is followed by another, as Sugar returns to her decaying family home in search of her own doppelgänger, Mama Maitresse, the elderly voodoo priestess who represents the 'Supernatural Voodoo Woman' that Sugar will become by the conclusion of the film. Why this elderly woman is living alone in Hill Mansion is never made clear, nor are her history and relationship with Sugar. But her function as a surrogate mother is apparent from the moment Sugar steps through the cobweb-shrouded front door and calls, 'Mama? Mama Maitresse?'. Her alliterative name signifies the combined origins of her power: she is at once a source of life and a mistress of death. 'Why have you come back here?', Mama Maitresse demands of Sugar, pointing out that she has 'always been a disbeliever' and asking, 'Why do you now believe?'. 'Because I want [my enemies] dead!', Sugar responds. Thus, the sepulchral house to which she returns, in which she seeks death and is reborn as the acolyte of a religion she once rejected, functions as a classically Gothic womb/tomb, and as an uncanny site for the return of the repressed. It is an *unheimlich* home where, in the terms established by the film, 'real' voodoo is practised, one that contrasts with Club Haiti, where voodoo is a commodity and a spectacle. The efficacy of the faith as practised by Mama Maitresse is quite dramatically demonstrated. After the voodoo queen conducts a ritual at her home altar, she and Sugar venture into the woods beyond the house and, at a second altar in a graveyard for slaves, she invokes Baron Samedi.

In *Sugar Hill*, voodoo is privileged and Christianity devalued. The film reverses the traditional syncretic but unequal relationship between these two faiths, in which the latter is 'visible and official', while the former is 'unofficial and, until recently, largely secretive'.[14] The only character explicitly associated with Christianity, Preacher ('Big Walter' Price), is a minor one whose status as a legitimate member of the clergy is questionable. Though he wears a clerical collar, he is shown not ministering to a congregation but rather playing a piano and singing in a bar. Moreover, Preacher is implicated in criminal activity when King (Raymond E. Simpson), a member of Morgan's gang, assumes that he knows who killed his fellow mobsters and interrogates him. Christianity and crime are likewise associated when Morgan and his henchmen meet their ends. King cries out, 'Dear God!', before Sugar uses a voodoo doll to dispatch him. O'Brien (Ed Geldart), another member of Morgan's gang shouts, 'Oh my God!' before he is killed. Morgan himself yells, 'Jesus, God, no!' and 'For God's sake, help me!' as he dies. In marked contrast with Christianity, voodoo is construed as a force for justice that substitutes for police power. In a conversation with Valentine about criminals, Sugar asks him, 'Do they ever pay?'. His response, 'They'll pay, in time', fails to satisfy her, and she savours the prospect of watching Langston's killers die. Voodoo empowers Sugar to realise her ambition, and to punish those guilty of murder expeditiously, appropriately and absolutely – or, in the words of Baron Samedi, 'nicely, neatly, superbly'. 'I'm passin' sentence, and the sentence is death',

Sugar tells Tank, the first of Morgan's men to be killed, before she has zombies decapitate him. When another gangster, George, calls 'crazy' a voodoo ritual designed to compel him to stab himself to death, she responds, 'No, it's justice'.

The connection that Sugar draws between justice and voodoo is also made by Valentine, who shares with her his growing suspicion that the men's deaths are a supernatural 'punishment' for their past crimes, and eventually consults Dr Parkhurst (J. Randall Bell), an expert in voodoo, for assistance with his strange case. Parkhurst, who oversees the Voodoo Museum and Research Library, provides Valentine with a desk where the detective conducts his own research and concludes, 'This voodoo is fascinating stuff'. Sitting on top of the desk is a wooden cross painted with an image of Christ. While this definitively Christian object seems out of place in a space devoted to voodoo, it indicates the syncretism of the two religions and the fact that 'the cross is extremely important in voodoo cosmology'.[15] By evoking the ultimate martyrdom, it also reminds viewers that Valentine, like his namesake St Valentine, will be martyred (albeit in a relatively inconsequential manner) when Sugar's voodoo spell causes him to break his leg and end his investigation. Moreover, it signifies that Valentine has reached a spiritual crossroads at which he has come to believe in zombies. As Jan Lundius and Mats Lundahl explain, in voodoo 'the crossroads and the cross' are closely linked with the spirits of the dead and their leader, Baron Samedi.[16] Joseph A. Brown likewise observes, 'In African and African American spirituality, no place is more sacred than the crossroads', where 'the ethical decisions are made' and 'the visitations of the spirits take place'.[17] It therefore makes perfect sense that Parkhurst stands close to the cross on Valentine's desk while telling the detective about his meeting Mama Maitresse at 'a road junction', and that locating this crossroads leads Valentine to Hill Mansion, Sugar, Mama Maitresse and Baron Samedi. After meeting them, his suspicions about the involvement of zombies in the murders are strengthened to the point where he must be stopped by Sugar's spell.

Sugar's close association with Baron Samedi and his zombies both advances and complicates her uncanny empowerment, while involving it with mastery and slavery. She kneels before the 'King of graveyards' and, apparently confusing him with his nearest Christian analogue, Satan, offers him her soul in return for 'the power to destroy [her] enemies'. But the being whom Madame Maitresse describes as 'a great lover', who is flanked by his zombie 'brides' in their diaphanous graveclothes, seeks an exchange of another sort. 'It ain't souls I'm interested in', he declares, laughing and leering at Sugar. Realising that he wants her body rather than her soul, she looks down for a moment, discomfited, but perseveres and raises her eyes to meet his gaze again. During their conversation, in shot-reverse shot the camera alternates between close-ups of the two. Baron Samedi is filmed glaring down at Sugar in a low-angle shot that underscores his regal status, while she looks up at him in a modified low-angle shot that indicates her own indomitability. 'You're not afraid of me', he remarks in surprise, before fulfilling his end of their bargain by calling up from their graves 'an army of the dead who await [her] orders'. These zombies are identified as slaves, first in life and then in death. As they claw their way out of the ground, their wrists are bound in shackles, though their chains have been broken. Somewhat cryptically, Baron Samedi declares, 'All here who are pledged to obey the will of Baron Samedi, slave and master, master and slave, awake!'. Since all those who rise from the dead are explicitly coded as slaves, it seems that in speaking of a 'master' he refers to himself and establishes a master/slave binary opposition. Yet his use of chiasmus suggests a potential inversion or even conflation of these terms.

In keeping with Baron Samedi's correlative language, the film demonstrates how the roles of master and slave are to some extent interchangeable. Morgan masters his henchmen and his girlfriend Celeste, before himself being mastered by his adversaries and hunted by zombie slaves through the woods, as if he were not the master of a criminal organisation but a runaway slave. Conversely, the zombies literally and figuratively arise, armed with machetes, to master their enemies in what under different circumstances would be a slave revolt. They then employ these blades, at once signifiers of oppression and weapons of liberation, to cut down the white men whose ancestors enslaved them. That the machetes were most likely used by living slaves to harvest sugar cane associates them with Sugar, whose name is not only a term of endearment given to her by Langston, but also a signifier of her value and potential commodification by either Morgan or Baron Samedi. Both seek to possess Sugar but instead settle for Celeste, who, like Mama Maitresse, functions as her doppelgänger.

While Morgan would master Sugar, Baron Samedi not only allows her to be her own master, but also enables her to continue to master others. Morgan appreciates Sugar, 'an honest working girl' who contrasts with Celeste, a kept woman. But Morgan also seeks to control Sugar, and when he cannot do so he comes to hate and fear her. Once Morgan realises that Sugar is manipulating him rather than the reverse, he repeatedly calls her a 'bitch'. When confronted with her ineffable supernatural powers, he no longer has any term to describe her and cries, 'What the hell are you?'. Morgan's fear of Sugar, an emerging voodoo queen, echoes the masculine dread of the feminine vividly described by William Seabrook in *The Magic Island*. During a Vodou ceremony, while listening to the 'howling choral of the women', the author experiences 'a terror of the dark, all-engulfing womb'.[18] His primal fear is realised in *Sugar Hill* when, in another iteration of the womb/tomb motif, Morgan is sucked down into quicksand and suffocates while Sugar watches impassively. Baron Samedi then complements her on how well she has dispatched Langston's killers, and enquires into her plans for Celeste, whom Morgan had hoped to exchange for Sugar. The two women are indeed swapped, though not by the mob boss. Sugar suggests that, as 'the price [he] asked for [their] bargain', Baron Samedi take Celeste instead of her to the underworld. 'I would prefer you', he tells Sugar. 'But she will have to do'.

Baron Samedi's preference for Sugar is significant, given the otherwise stereotypical dynamics of miscegenation at work in the scene, which evokes the one in which Ann Darrow is sacrificed to the eponymous gigantic ape in *King Kong* (Merian C. Cooper and Ernest B. Schoedsack, 1932). 'Won't you join me?', Baron Samedi asks the horrified white woman, while drums pound. Like Kong's, his eyes bulge as he leers at her, his mouth open wide as if to consume her. Struggling and screaming, Celeste is held between Baron Samedi's brides in a shot that evokes how Ann, likewise struggling and screaming, is tied between the pillars on Kong's sacrificial altar. The two scenes conclude in the same fashion, as the bride-to-be is carried away by her monstrous mate. Having calculated her way out of her double's awful fate, thereby demonstrating the superiority recognised by both Morgan and Baron Samedi, Sugar observes Celeste's downfall with wry amusement.

She now carries the cane that Baron Samedi has provided for her as a parting gift, which supplements her yonic capability with phallic potency. Though Baron Samedi's cane is 'often adorned with an erect phallus'[19] that duplicates the cigar the Baron smokes, in this instance its silver tip is in the shape of an African American man's head, which adornment suggests headship and power over others. Unsurprisingly, Sugar holds the cane between her legs. Sporting an Afro, the signifier of Black pride and power, and wearing a form-fitting white trouser suit that signifies both purity and puissance, she has become a fully empowered phallic woman, one of those whom Stephane Dunn characterises as the 'heroines of blaxploitation who [are] shown using traditional masculine tools and feminine sexual power to enter and survive in racist, patriarchal worlds'.[20] Whether Sugar, to paraphrase Audre Lorde, can use the master's tools to dismantle the master's house remains an open question.[21] There is no doubt, however, that she now possesses part of that figurative house, together with her family home and Club Haiti. She is also poised to take the place of Mama Maitresse, whom she tells, 'It's over, Mama. You can rest now'. Sugar's transfiguration into a voodoo queen is underscored in the film's final scene. As the camera pulls away from Sugar and Mama Maitresse and their image freezes, 'Supernatural Voodoo Woman' plays over the end credits.

A House Divided: *The House on Skull Mountain*

As *The House on Skull Mountain* begins, Pauline Christophe (Mary J. Todd McKenzie), an old woman and a practitioner of voodoo who lives and dies in her eponymous mansion outside Atlanta atop a skull-shaped mountain, is receiving last rites. She sends letters summoning four of her great-grandchildren, who arrive after her death. The first to come, Lorena Christophe (Janee Michelle) and Phillipe Wilette (Mike Evans), are followed by Harriet Johnson (Xernona Clayton) and finally by Dr Andrew Cunningham (Victor French), a professor of anthropology who was raised in an orphanage and is the only white member of the family. Seeking to exterminate Pauline's line and to advance his own family, her long-time butler, Thomas Pettitone (Jean Durand), surreptitiously uses voodoo against the Christophes, while his wife, Louette (Ella Woods), observes them and remains silent about his machinations until interrogated by Andrew. Thomas kills first Phillipe and then Harriet, before putting Lorena into a trance and compelling her to descend into a cavernous sub-basement of the house. There, Thomas presides over a voodoo ceremony involving drummers and several frenzied dancers. After killing Louette for betraying him to Andrew, Thomas draws Lorena, whom he intends to marry, into the dance. He is confronted by Andrew, and the two men duel to a draw with machetes. During the film's climax, Thomas raises Pauline from the dead as a zombie and orders her to destroy the professor. Andrew himself employs voodoo to redirect Pauline's wrath at Thomas, whom she kills. In the end, Andrew remains in the mansion to study his family's history and his own genealogy, while Lorena departs.

The main structure of the house on Skull Mountain expresses the uncanny doubling of western and African influences. The architecture of the house's ground and upper floors is wholly European. The mansion is in the style of an English country manor of the Tudor type, with a steep roof and lead-lined bay windows. Its imposing interior features wainscotting, coffered ceilings, a sweeping bifurcated staircase and large fireplaces with elaborate mantels. The décor, however, blends the European and African, combining traditional oil paintings and tapestries with tribal masks, drums, shields and spears, in addition to the skins of exotic animals. This hybridisation is evident from the first scene of the film, which highlights the syncretism of Catholicism and voodoo. Having administered the Sacrament of Last Rites to Pauline, a priest leaves his last rites box, containing a crucifix and candles, on her nightstand. A priestess in her own right, the old woman then opens a similar box containing voodoo dolls immediately before she dies, as if performing an uncanny version of the Catholic sacrament. In another instance of religious and cultural combination, a bead necklace associated with the loa Damballa, the creator-god, sits in a bell jar near both carved African figurines and European-style china plates. As Thomas explains, this necklace is reminder of how Damballa possessed Henri Christophe, Pauline's great-great-grandfather, inspiring him to become a leading Haitian revolutionary, the nation's first president, and ultimately Henry I of Haiti. A formal oil portrait of Henri in western military dress hangs on the wall opposite the necklace. In other bell jars throughout the house, wangas (charms) are placed alongside decorative dried plants. The aesthetic and cultural conglomeration of the house's main floors reflects the converging and diverging nature and history of both Haiti and the Christophe family. The latter originates in Africa and flourishes in Haiti, itself a hybrid of the African and European, then migrates throughout the United States and divides along both generational and geographic lines, before coming together again near Atlanta at the behest of its matriarch.

In contrast with the blended main and upper floors of the Christophe mansion, the sub-basement is largely homogenous, though it still signifies the religious syncretism of the rest of the house. Connected to the basement of the dwelling via a lift shaft, this area appears to be a natural cavern without distinguishing features. Here, European influence is almost entirely absent but for the contemporary clothing of some of those participating in the ecstatic dancing of the voodoo ceremonies. That these rituals take place beneath the house indicates how voodoo has served as a foundation for the Christophe family, whose wealth and power are based on Henri's possession by Damballa. Syncretism manifests itself more darkly in this subterranean region, which evokes death and sacrifice in voodoo and Christianity alike. In this sacred space, Louette is ritually stabbed to death by Thomas, her death a sacrifice both to an unspecified voodoo god or gods and to the man's ambition to elevate the Pettitone family and end the Christophe line. A much greater sacrifice is indicated by the fact that this place of death is part of Skull Mountain, which uncannily doubles Golgotha, the skull-shaped hill in Jerusalem where Christ was crucified. This allusion is strengthened by the fact that the Christophe family name contains the word *Christ*, that Pauline rises as a zombie on the third day after her death, and that her own name calls to mind the writings of the Apostle Paul, especially his account that Christ 'rose again the third day' (*KJV*, 1 Cor. 15: 4).

Another link between resurrection and the Christophe family is established in the coat of arms embedded in the window of 'Pauline's favourite room', a shrine of sorts where the portraits of Henri and other ancestors hang. The Christophe family crest, an angel, signifies life after death or life that transcends death. The family motto, '*Ad Mortem Fidelis*' ('Unto Death Faithful') is an oddly transposed and ambiguous variation of *Ad Fidelis Mortem* ('Faithful Unto Death'). This transposition not only privileges death but also calls attention to a subtle uncertainty. Given the dual meanings of *unto*, the motto indicates that the family is either faithful *until* death or faithful *to* death. The latter construction explains why the Christophe home was built on Skull Mountain, an enormous *memento mori*, and it might indicate a hope for transfiguration through death. The former interpretation aligns with the fact that, after death, the zombified Pauline turns against her own family. Of course, as a zombie, Pauline has little choice but to do the bidding of Thomas, a bokor, who declares, 'Pauline Christophe, I have summoned you to do my will!'.

Both Pauline's zombification by Thomas and her release by Andrew highlight the leading role of the family in *The House on Skull Mountain*. Once the possessor of the Christophe home, fortune and status, the zombified Pauline becomes, in an uncanny reversal, the possession of her own servant, protégé and surrogate son, whom she has empowered by instructing in voodoo for two decades, and who would take her possessions by taking possession of Lorena. Thomas boasts to Andrew, 'Lorena is mine! She obeys none but me!'. He then explains, 'Through Lorena, the powers of the priesthood will be mine'. Without a family of his own on which to draw, Thomas needs to access the potency of the Christophes by compelling Lorena to marry him. Andrew, who has begun a romantic relationship with Lorena, threatens his plans and must be killed. Accordingly, after summoning Pauline from the dead, Thomas commands her to 'touch [Andrew]' and 'feel his warm flesh'. The extreme diegetic and extradiegetic horror induced by the notion of Pauline's touching her great-grandson derives from the sense that 'zombies are untouchable',[22] combined with the incest taboo. To forestall this illicit and presumably fatal contact, Andrew makes use of the knowledge of voodoo he began to cultivate in college, when his bloodline led him to be 'fascinated by it' without knowing why.

He frees both Pauline and Lorena, and dispossesses Thomas, by calling on the family of loa, who both double and constitute part of his own extended family. He begins by invoking Granne (Grandma) Erzulie, 'mother of all', and asking her to 'restore [Pauline's] soul'. A member of the Erzulie, an all-female clan of spirits, Granne, who 'represents the wisdom gained by experience and maturity, and grandmotherly kindness and love',[23] is an uncanny double for Pauline. As Andrew himself points out, she is also a syncretic double for 'the Virgin Mary, [who] is just another aspect or manifestation of the goddess'. The professor then invokes Damballa, the 'father of all Christophes', who is their paterfamilias by virtue of his having possessed Henri. In response, Thomas calls on L'inglesou, 'a loa who lives in the wild areas of Haiti and kills anyone who offends him'.[24] His invocation of this solitary loa, for whom he functions as a *de facto* avatar, is unsuccessful. Pauline, freed from his control, points at Thomas and propels him through a window to his demise. As she does so, a skull is superimposed on her face, reminding viewers of the Christophe family's motto and close association with death and resurrection. Pauline has been reborn as a zombie and risen from her grave, a womb/tomb that doubles the yonic cavern under the house, where Louette is killed and from which Andrew and Lorena emerge with new understanding.

Whereas he embraces their insight into the occult, she rejects it. Andrew feels compelled to remain in the house on Skull Mountain and 'study it' to verify his status as a Christophe.[25] His intention to 'explore' both the house and his own identity underscore their close association, thereby indicating how the former might be read in Freudian terms. The upper floors align with the conscious mind; the subterranean area, with the unconscious. Whereas Andrew seeks to integrate these physical and psychological regions, Lorena '[wants] to forget there ever was a Skull Mountain', though Andrew reminds her, 'It's gonna be very hard for you to do, because half of this place is yours and always will be'. Days after first being brought together, the two relatives separate again, as splits develop between male and female, and between investigation and repression. In the Gothic tradition epitomised by the house of Usher, the house of Christophe represents both the combination and the division of the family and the psyche.

Possession and the Patriarchy: *Abby*

In *Abby*, also known as *Possess My Soul* and *The Blaxorcist*,[26] during an archaeological expedition to Nigeria, Bishop Garnet Williams (William Marshall) opens an ancient container that he finds in a cave and unleashes Eshu, a Yoruba trickster spirit of chaos, crossroads, duality and sexuality. Eshu travels to the home of the Bishop's son, the Reverend Emmett Williams (Terry Carter), and daughter-in-law, Abby Williams (Carol Speed), in Louisville. The spirit possesses Abby, who transforms from a pious Christian into a physically and sexually aggressive monster. She kills two members of her church before Bishop Williams exorcises Eshu from her body. *Abby* was withdrawn from theatrical release after Warner Brothers sued American International Pictures for copyright infringement of *The Exorcist*.[27]

Like *The Exorcist*, in which the twelve-year-old Regan MacNeil writhes on her bed while spouting obscenities at two Catholic priests, *Abby* illustrates the dangers posed by unbridled female sexuality to patriarchal religious authority. Christopher J. Olson and Carrie Lynn D. Reinhard contend that although *Abby* '[establishes] the Church's power', it 'depicts this institution as under threat from feminine sexuality and agency', and it construes 'assertive female sexuality as a transgressive and emasculating force'.[28] Boundary-breaking and uncanny, Abby/Eshu blurs the lines between self and other, Christianity and the Yoruba religion, and feminine and masculine. As Harry M. Benshoff notes, the possessed woman, who 'has facial hair and a deep voice', blends 'male and female'.[29] Her actions as well as her appearance are stereotypically masculine, particularly with respect to her preacher husband Emmett, whom she dominates and humiliates. In a role-reversing scene that inverts and perverts the Christian wedding rite, she throws him onto their bed, declaring, 'I'm gonna show you what a real marriage ceremony is like! You are gonna love and obey me!'. Climbing on top of Emmett, Abby/Eshu hits him repeatedly while he cries out in fear and confusion. In a point-of-view shot from his perspective, half of her face is in shadow, indicating her divided nature. Her wide-open mouth underscores her sexual voracity, while reverberating, distorted laughter whose source seems at once diegetic and extradiegetic indicates both the uncanny doubling of possession and the strange mirth of carnivalesque inversion and the grotesque. As Mikhail Bakhtin describes it, this sort of 'laughter [is] sent to earth by the devil' and, like Abby/Eshu, it '[looks] at man and at the world with the eyes of angry satire'.[30] Laughing and speaking through Abby's body, which he has made grotesque by entering and occupying it, Eshu mocks the conventions of piety and propriety alike.

Other bedroom scenes between Abby/Eshu and Emmett demonstrate not only how queer female sexuality and the Yoruba religion challenge conventional masculinity and Christianity, but also how Emmett's own gender fluidity renders him especially vulnerable to such a challenge. In the first scene of the couple in bed, Emmett is awakened by Eshu's entering their home and wakes Abby in turn, anxiously describing the odd phenomena that he has experienced. That he seeks comfort from her indicates an initial reversal of traditional gender roles, which recurs when she tells him, 'That's a pretty silly excuse just because you want to have some fun', thereby dismissing his genuine fear, misinterpreting it as an erotic ploy, and projecting her own desire onto him. After he accepts her sexual invitation, she assures him that he is 'the best lover a girl could have'. Once Eshu takes complete possession of her, she is far more aggressive and less complimentary. One night as she lies in bed watching television, he emerges from the bathroom wearing a towel as if it were a loincloth, imprudently attempting biblical roleplay to seduce her. 'I am black, *and* comely as the curtains of Solomon, O ye daughters of Jerusalem', he intones, assuming the persona of the female lover who speaks in the introduction to the Song of Solomon, and modifying the biblical language ('black, *but* comely') to affirm Black pride (*KJV*, S. of S. 1. 5; my emphasis). '*Make me* kiss thee with the kisses of my mouth', he continues, again changing the original: '*Let him* kiss me with the kisses of his mouth' (*KJV*, S. of S. 1: 2; my emphasis). Emmett's speaking in a woman's voice uncannily replicates Abby/Eshu's speaking in a man's voice. He likewise transposes gender roles by transferring erotic agency from the man to the woman, asking to be compelled to engage in sexual activity by his wife rather than assuming that she will demurely permit him to initiate such activity. Abby/Eshu responds to Emmett's ill-advised, gender-bending foreplay by characterising sex in what might be construed as a stereotypically manly fashion as 'just an animal lust' and bellowing, 'You ain't got enough to satisfy me!', before kicking him in the groin and laughing wildly. Her physical assault, at once masculine and emasculating, figures castration, fear of which Freud identifies as both the origin of the uncanny and crucial to resolving the Oedipus complex.

These uncanny and Oedipal dynamics shape Emmett's relationship with his father, Garnet. As two clerics, the men at once double and differ from one another. The son emulates his father by following a religious path, but he also criticises how he practises his vocation, implying during a family dinner that Garnet's working alone in Nigeria reveals his egotism. When Abby asks, 'Now what are you comin' down on your father like that for? He's doing God's will, just like you', her husband retorts, 'Sometimes I wonder whose will he's really doing'. After Abby's perceptive brother Cass (Austin Stoker) observes, 'It sounds like Emmett's a bit jealous', the pastor responds, 'I'm not jealous. He's got his work to do and I've got mine. Besides, I'm better off than he is. I've got someone to share the load'. Emmett's telling comparison, motivated by his unresolved Oedipal rivalry, highlights the unexplained absence of his father's wife and his own mother. Both vacancies could be filled by Abby, who, from a Freudian point of view, has already taken the place of Emmett's mother and might likewise take that of Garnet's wife. Seeking to realise these possibilities, Abby/Eshu exacerbates the Oedipal conflict between father and son by lusting after the former. Her desire is made explicit in both senses of the word. After Emmett contacts Garnet and asks him to return home from Nigeria, Abby/Eshu tells him, 'I want to thank you for callin' that motherfuckin' father of yours!'. Likewise, when Garnet arrives to conduct his exorcism, the spirit greets him with 'Hello, motherfucker!'. The obscenity functions not only as an insult, but also as a signifier of Garnet's past and possibly future sexual role vis-à-vis Emmett's mother and wife, and as an indication of the possessed Abby's own wish. Sitting with father and son, Abby/Eshu caresses the elder Williams lasciviously, calls him 'a very handsome man', and leers at his 'powerful arms' and 'strong muscles' while her husband watches in horror. Reaching for Garnet's crotch, she says, 'I bet your muscles are strong all over', before he pushes her away.

Abby/Eshu has already lured a few men into sex, and implies that Garnet too might yield to seduction, having led a double life. 'I know you, you old chameleon. You might have fooled your son, but I know your hypocrisy. Wanna hear your mother's opinion of your wonderful father, Emmett?'. Because this opinion is never shared by the spirit, and because Garnet's wife is entirely absent from the film, viewers are left to speculate as to how he transgressed during his marriage. That he did so, and that Eshu speaks the truth about marital duplicity, is indicated by Garnet's closing his eyes in anguish after the spirit's provocative remarks, and by a previous scene in which the possessed Abby exposes the church organist, Mrs Wiggins (Nancy Lee Owens). 'Wiggins isn't your name, you damn liar!', Abby/Eshu declares, 'Horace Wiggins never married you!'. Like the putative Mrs Wiggins, Garnet hides something related to his marriage, perhaps infidelity to his wife. The revelation that he harbours such a secret echoes the release of Eshu from the object containing him and signifies the return of the repressed. The unconscious wishes that Garnet represses stem from his Oedipal conflict with Emmett: to possess his daughter-in-law and to subjugate his son.

Both wishes are advanced, and the second is realised, by the Bishop's logically questionable but psychologically intelligible decision to open a container that he knows is associated with a force for destruction and chaos. A canister made of ebony and embossed with admonitory symbols of the spirit that it imprisons, including a cockscomb, a whirlwind and an erect penis, this overdetermined object is at once a phallic symbol for the priapic 'god of sexuality' and a yonic 'ceremonial vessel' that is 'more hollow than solid'. Accordingly, it is linked with both Garnet and Abby. He unlocks this phallus-shaped puzzle box by twisting the penis that adorns it, thereby demonstrating that the solution to the enigma of Abby's strange behaviour is the phallic power of the patriarch by whose agency she is first possessed and then exorcised. Moreover, both Abby's body and the Yoruba canister are vessels for Eshu, who returns to the former after being exorcised from the latter in a ceremony that demonstrates Garnet's authority over both the spirit and Emmett, who are associated as the insubordinate sons of commanding fathers. Their alignment is indicated by Eshu's declaring, 'You know what it's all about. Jealousy! They're all jealous of my magnificent powers!'. He denies his own jealousy of a greater spirit, Olorun, the Supreme Being of the Yoruba religion and father of the other orishas (deities), and projects it onto the men who would dispossess him of Abby.

In much the same fashion, Emmett denies his own jealousy of Garnet, whose releasing Eshu forces the son, who is unable to cope with his wife's increasingly violent and disturbing actions, to seek spiritual guidance from his father, to whom he submits entirely. That Emmett always calls Garnet 'Father', thereby conflating his paternal and pastoral titles, underscores both his filial and his clerical submission. As the film makes clear, both natural and supernatural sons must bow to their fathers. Garnet exorcises Abby by calling on the patriarchal power of Olorun, who easily takes her from his son Eshu. Olorun is 'acknowledged by all the divinities as the Head to whom all authority belongs and all allegiance is due',[31] for 'fathers demand service'.[32] In Abby, unlike in *The Exorcist*, fathers supersede their sons. Whereas the senior priest in Friedkin's film, Father Merrin (Max von Sydow), dies and is replaced by the junior one, Father Karras (Jason Miller), in Girdler's movie Emmett is reduced to helping his brother-in-law Cass hold down Abby while Garnet performs the exorcism. Moreover, while Karras takes the demon into his own body, Eshu's offer to transfer from Abby's body into Garnet's is rejected by the Bishop as unnecessary, given the spirit's inferiority to Olorun and imminent defeat by Him.

In depicting how both Emmett and Abby submit to Garnet, *Abby* indicates that younger men and all women in the Black church[33] must accept the authority of patriarchal pastors. 'Hold her, in the name of the Lord God Jehovah!', the Bishop orders Emmett and Cass. His command emphasises the ascendancy of the divine father, the need to restrain a woman who has become powerful and unruly, and the leading roles played in this restraint by her husband, brother and father-in-law, in relation to whom her subordinate status as wife, sister and daughter-in-law is determined. 'Now spread her arms in the form of the Holy Cross, symbol of balance', Garnet continues, 'and lay her on the floor'. His instructions reveal his intention to rebalance Abby's relationships with the church and the men who run it, and to ground her – that is, to render her prone and submissive. When she attempts to defy him by levitating, he commands 'Down!' and brings her back to earth, both literally and figuratively. In the final stage of the exorcism, Garnet joins hands with the two other men and is illuminated in 'the Christ's light', forming a tripartite variation on the Father, Son and Holy Spirit, and embodying the function of the cross to realign relations between the human and the divine through sacrifice. In this instance, the sacrifice is Abby's dominance over men, which she gains when Eshu amplifies and makes horrific her already considerable influence within the church. As Cass notes, Abby '[takes] on a seven-day schedule', working with the youth programme, singing in the choir and providing marriage counselling to members of the congregation. 'Wherever would I be without you?', her husband asks. 'Still tryin' to work your way through seminary', Abby answers. When Eshu further empowers her, Garnet asserts that the spirit in her body is not actually Eshu but a lesser being impersonating the orisha. His assertion conveniently avoids the fact that Eshu 'keeps balance and harmony as part of his vital role in the divine scheme of things',[34] and its implication that Abby's possession, not her exorcism, properly rebalances the status of men and women in the church.

Such an adjustment is in keeping with the Yoruba religion. As C. Eric Lincoln and Lawrence H. Mamiya explain, because 'traditional African religions have usually given women a greater role' than Christian denominations have done, their involvement in the latter has meant a considerable diminution of their authority, such that 'the offices of preacher and pastor' in 'black churches [have remained] a male preserve'.[35] This situation had begun to improve when *Abby* was released in 1974. According to Bettye Collier-Thomas, 'the 1970s represent a turning point in the struggle of black women for equality in the church and society', a moment when 'almost a century of protest had brought legislative changes that made it technically possible for women to occupy any position they desired', though they were still underrepresented in church leadership positions.[36] That Abby cannot recall her possession by Eshu after being exorcised indicates how thoroughly the film bearing her name seeks to repress her transitory empowerment, and how it aligns itself with conservative elements within the Black church.

Yet forces for change and conflicts within the church are also apparent in *Abby*. The tensions between Emmett and Garnet, which manifest along religious as well as familial lines, reproduce those within their denomination. Although this church is never named, since Emmett is a reverend who leads a Protestant congregation and Garnet is a bishop, both are almost certainly clergymen in the African Methodist Episcopal (AME) Church. As Dennis C. Dickerson explains, the AME Church is a 'freedom church' founded in the nineteenth century, which 'pursued liberationist activities on both sides of the Atlantic' in 'strong opposition to slavery, segregation, and colonialism' and in support of 'black self-determination'.[37] As the AME Church grew, its 'emancipationist ethos' came into 'dynamic tension with the necessities and requirements of institutionalization'.[38] Garnet, who teaches university courses in African religions and often works abroad, exemplifies the Church's commitment to foreign outreach and, in the contemporary world outside *Abby*, would be included among the 'intellectuals of AME background who envisaged themselves as pan-Africanists and their denomination, at least historically, as an institutional expression of black Atlantic identity'.[39] Conversely, the AME Church's focus on domestic development is represented by Emmett, who criticises his father for his solitary work abroad and implies that he would be better off tending to the church at home. The limits of Emmett's attitude are underscored by his inability to cope with Eshu, and by his turning to Garnet to exorcise a transnational entity that has journeyed from Nigeria to Louisville.

Eshu's status as the orisha of the crossroads indicates not only the ideological turn taken by Emmett, but also how in the late 1960s and early 1970s the Black church was at a crossroads with respect to its administration, theology and liturgy. Inspired by the Black Power movement's emphasis on self-determination, African Americans in largely white congregations sought a greater degree of ecclesial authority and autonomy. In the Catholic Church, this objective was a function of both Black Power and the Second Vatican Council, which ended in 1965 and focused on modernising the Church. As Matthew J. Cressler explains, 'In 1968 Black Catholic activists began to interpret Vatican II as an opportunity to incorporate Black Power in Catholic life', and to '[call] for control of Catholic institutions in Black communities'.[40] Meanwhile, intellectual leaders of the AME Church, together with Black scholars in the Catholic Church and other denominations, were developing the tenets of Black theology, which construed Christian theory and practice as means of liberating oppressed Black people worldwide.[41] In a perversion of this call for liberation, Eshu tells Emmett and Cass, 'Come to me. It is the only way to break your chains, the only way to know true freedom. Believe in me. I will free you'. Voiced by a woman whom Eshu has enslaved, this promise of freedom is paradoxical at best and disingenuous at worst. The spirit offers not the liberatory potential of Black theology, but the false freedom of egotism and hedonism, which amounts to spiritual enslavement. By instructing Emmett and Cass to ignore Eshu's deceitful pledge to liberate them, Garnet articulates one of the central themes of Black theology and echoes its creator James Cone, who argued for subordinating the individual's will to that of the race and averred that 'unrestricted freedom is a form of slavery'.[42]

Attempting to 'free Abby' from such slavery, Garnet combines the liturgies of the Christian and Yoruba faiths, calling on Jehovah, Olorun and Christ alike. Having begun the rite of exorcism by using a cross, the Bishop continues it by donning a kufi and layering a dashiki over his clerical collar, before finally drawing the cross from under his tribal clothing and deploying it once more (see Figure 7). His doing so complicates the film's initial opposition between Christianity and the Yoruba religion, figures a comprehensive approach to faith, and highlights 'the Yoruba genius for syncretism'.[43] It also exemplifies how the Black Power movement altered religious rituals. For instance, after Black priests had begun to 'incorporate African and African American cultural traditions into Catholic liturgy', an 'African Mass' was held in Chicago in 1968, complete with 'the beat of jungle music' and musicians wearing 'African robes'.[44] Judged alongside such real-world liturgical innovations, Garnet's exorcism is progressive insofar as it features the Yoruba religion. Yet his goal of disempowering *Abby* and repositioning her as a helpmate to Emmett is quite conservative. That Garnet's own wife is missing from *Abby* evinces Jacquelyn Grant's contention that Black theology rendered women 'invisible', thereby invalidating 'its liberation struggle'.[45] As the film ends, Abby is free from Eshu but possessed by her husband and father-in-law.

The Spirit and the Flesh: *Lord Shango*

Lord Shango takes place in a town in Tennessee, located near a Yoruba village of emigrants from Africa. Jenny (Marlene Clark) and her teen-aged daughter Billie (Avis McCarther) live with Memphis (Wally Taylor), Jenny's partner and Billie's surrogate father. The two women are baptised in a river by Reverend Slater (John R. Russell), a Baptist minister, while Jabo (Lawrence Cook), a once-successful drum player turned alcoholic, observes from a distance. After Billie's Yoruba boyfriend Femi (Bill Overton) wades into the river and angrily interrupts her baptism, Deacon Davis (B. A. Ward) and Deacon Tibbles (Stanley Greene), together with Memphis, submerge and accidentally drown him. Jenny and Billie attend his funeral in the Yoruba village. Seeing Femi in a vision, Billie mistakes Memphis for Femi and has sex with him. She then runs away, while Jenny throws Memphis out of the house and leaves the church. Months later, Jabo appears at the construction site where Memphis works, telling him that he has three chances to atone for killing Femi. As Jabo watches, Memphis accidentally slashes himself with a table saw in a scene crosscut with a Yoruba drumming ceremony. Jenny attends a Yoruba religious rite, where she sacrifices her baptism medallion to Shango, the god of thunder and lightning, in exchange for a child. This ceremony causes Davis to die of a heart attack. Billie comes home, pregnant. When Billie and Jenny return to the Yoruba village and sacrifice a dog, Billie has a second vision of Femi, who assures her that they will soon be reunited, as Tibbles is killed by

Figure 7   Bishop Garnet Williams (William Marshall) employs syncretic clothing and objects in *Abby* (1974). AIP/Photofest

another dog. Jenny demands that Memphis marry Billie. While driving to work, Memphis is nearly hit by a train, as Jabo watches and drums pound. Jenny takes Jabo home, where he explains that he paid Shango's price for becoming a great drummer with the lives of his wife and daughter. Jenny and Jabo then engage in a sexual encounter with ritualistic overtones. The next day, at her wedding, Billie is possessed by Femi and refuses to marry Memphis (see Figure 8). Jabo, possessed by Shango himself, coaxes Femi's spirit out of Billie's body. After marrying Memphis, Billie sees Femi in a third vision. He tells her not to worry about the baby and to join him in the afterlife. Imperilled at work for the third time, Memphis is rescued from a fall by Jabo/Shango. Both Memphis and Jabo come home to Jenny, who tells Memphis that Billie has left with Femi and herself leaves with Jabo, carrying her newborn grandchild.

Lord Shango is replete with doppelgängers. Associations among them include but transcend the uncanny bond between a possessing spirit and a possessed individual, demonstrating how this relationship structures the entire film. By having sex with and eventually marrying Billie, Memphis doubles Femi, who is likewise doubled by Jabo when he dances with Billie at the Hurricane Club, where Jenny works as a server. 'It was like being with Femi', Billie tells her mother afterward, indicating that Jabo was possessed by Femi. Jabo likewise doubles Femi by playing father to Billie's child at the end of the film. His paternal role also causes him to double Memphis, who appears to be the actual father of Billie's child, though she claims it belongs to Femi. This unborn child itself doubles both Femi and Billie. 'There's always a struggle when a restless soul tries to enter a body not yet born', Jabo explains to Jenny. Whether he refers to the child's soul or Femi's is unclear, though the word 'restless' suggests the latter and might indicate that Femi is trying to possess Billie's child, as he later possesses Billie herself. 'Billie is my child', Jenny responds, shifting focus from the unborn child to her own daughter. 'If the sickly one survives, the child dies', Jabo concludes cryptically. Since 'child' now refers to Billie, his statement seems to indicate that if her baby survives, she will die, which is in fact what occurs; thus, mother and child are doubled. Yet, after her energetic dance with Jabo, Billie is 'the sickly one' who lies on a couch while Jenny tells her, 'You're in no condition for all that dancing'. Thus, 'the sickly one' and 'the child' – that is, Billie and her child – are redoubled.

To make relations among these characters even more complex, mother and child are again doubled when Billie and Jenny, both of whom are sexually involved with Memphis, receive a child from him, either directly

Figure 8   Memphis (Wally Taylor) and Jenny (Marlene Clark) watch Billie (Avis McCarther) in *Lord Shango* (1975). Bryanston Pictures/Photofest

or indirectly. At the outset of the film, Jenny hopes to conceive a baby with Memphis, who has suggested that her baptism might facilitate their becoming parents. After the ceremony, some of their discussion of conception occurs as they look into a mirror, their own duplication suggesting the many other doubles involved in their having a child. Memphis reassures Jenny that she will conceive 'if it's the Lord's will' and that 'He'll answer [their] prayers'. Jenny, angry that her baptism has resulted in death rather than (re)birth, tells him, 'All we got to show for it is one dead boy!'. Yet, in a very circuitous fashion, the ritual she undergoes does result in her gaining the child she has wished for, though not, as she caustically says to Memphis, 'When your Lord touches me where you say he'll do the most good'. Indeed, whether the Lord worshipped by Memphis or Lord Shango is responsible for Jenny's ultimately gaining a child is uncertain. Standing before the head priest of the Yoruba, Jenny asks Banjokoji, an idol representing Shango, for 'a child', not specifying whether she hopes to conceive a child or wants Billie to return to her. The priest himself clarifies, asking Banjokoji to 'bring back her child so she may embrace her again', thereby seeming to demonstrate preternatural knowledge of Jenny's situation. If Shango does return Billie to Jenny, he does so because she provides him with her baptism medallion; thus, her baptism not only leads to Femi's death, Billie's pregnancy and her own surrogate parenthood, but also provides the means by which this last result becomes possible. That said, the Lord may be doing more than simply providing an object of sacrifice to Lord Shango. 'That boy provoked God, and he was struck down by the sword of the Heavenly Ghost', Memphis avers. If so, then Femi's death and its consequences for Jenny are attributable not to Shango, but to the Christian God.

These two deities, together with their respective religions, function as yet another pair of doppelgängers in *Lord Shango*. The Baptist Church is doubled by the ceremonial space of the Yoruba village; Reverend Slater, by Shango's priest; the church choir, by the African drummers. Likewise, Femi's funeral is duplicated by the funerals for Davis and Tibbles. 'Your death was that of a warrior who died for Shango', the Yoruba priest declares of Femi. Similarly, Slater proclaims that 'Brother Davis served our merciful Jesus well'. How these Yoruba and Christian funerals depict the afterlife differs considerably, however. The priest says to Femi's corpse, 'It is now your duty in spirit to protect your loved ones'. As events amply demonstrate, Femi's spirit is still quite active in the material world. In contrast, Slater says that Davis 'has found his rightful place in the kingdom of heaven' and makes no mention of his intervening in earthly affairs. Femi's spirit appears to believe that his duty to protect Billie involves possessing her, together with Jabo and even Memphis, who claims that he is 'overcome by something' when he has sex with Billie, and whose claim is supported when Billie tells Jenny, 'It's Femi's baby. It was like being with Femi'. If Femi's spirit is indeed responsible for impregnating Billie, then her conception doubles that of the Virgin Mary through the Holy Spirit, and it evokes Jenny's comment to Memphis about the Lord touching her. This notion of divine conception seems to be in Jenny's mind when she creates a ritual that involves having sex with Jabo, whom she calls 'my Lord' as if anticipating his possession by Lord Shango. In effect, Jenny does eventually have a child with Jabo, and one that might have been conceived through spiritual possession, though this outcome is achieved by their taking Billie and Femi's child. This child replaces the one Jabo lost, just as Jenny replaces his late wife; thus, by serving as a vessel for Femi and Shango, Jabo earns restitution for the sacrifice of his family.

Such sacrifice is an additional way in which Christianity and the Yoruba religion double each other. 'The price of life is sacrifice', Jabo tells Memphis, and Slater agrees. 'He ain't tellin' you wrong', he says to Memphis, 'Didn't our Lord offer his only begotten Son?'. Yet the frequency and efficacy of sacrifice are points of difference between the two faiths. Only one Christian, Memphis, makes a sacrifice, which is rewarded not by the Christian God but by a Yoruba one, since sacrificing his freedom and marrying Billie may be why Jabo/Shango spares his life. In contrast, both Jenny and Billie make sacrifices to Shango, which yield immediate results. The Yoruba religion is likewise proven to be more potent than its Christian counterpart when Slater and his choir are unable to exorcise Femi, who is drawn rather than driven out of Billie's body by Jabo/Shango.

In favouring the Yoruba religion, *Lord Shango* problematises the notion of the evil spirit. Jenny goes so far as to shout at Memphis, 'Your God is the Devil!'. While the film stops well short of such an extreme conflation, it does depict the Christian God as largely absent and Femi and Shango as active and benevolent, though unforgiving. Moreover, it demonstrates how the Yoruba religion empowers women. When Jenny and Billie leave the Baptist Church, they gain access to the power of Shango and control over their destinies. That these women take their fates into their own hands is signified and emphasised by a scene in which Jenny, knitting a blanket for her grandchild, calls to mind both Shango and the Fates of Greek mythology. As she knits, drums pound and three horizontal lines, the Abaja tribal marks, appear on her cheeks. Crosscut with her knitting are life-or-death scenes of Memphis and Billie. In the former, Jabo/Shango saves Memphis from a near-fatal fall. In the latter, Billie prepares to join Femi in the afterlife. At the moment when Memphis lives and Billie chooses to die, Jenny draws out and cuts a thread, evoking Lachesis and Atropos. Her knitting needles double the drumsticks that Jabo carries as a reminder of the pact he made with Shango, and both sets of twin phallic symbols represent the potency and creative capacity of 'the god of fertility'.[46] They also duplicate the double-headed oshe (battle axe) closely associated with Shango. As Robert Plant Amstrong observes, 'Doubleness is a basal dynamic of the Yoruba consciousness', and 'the *sine qua non* of the *oshe Shango* is doubleness', for the 'twinned celts' of the baton represent what 'the Yoruba believe to be the operative principle of thunder', its repetitive quality.[47] While the drumsticks figure the family Jabo has lost through his own sacrifice, the knitting needles are linked with the one that he and Jenny gain through the sacrifices of others. 'This is all I have left of my family', Jabo tells Jenny and Billie, before driving the drumsticks into Femi's grave and compelling the man's spirit to give Billie a sign of his intent to intervene on her behalf. This sign consists of the thunder and lightning associated with Shango's sexual energy,[48] together with mist that rises from the grave. These indications of life from death, called forth after the drumsticks penetrate the earth, render Femi's grave a womb/tomb from which his spirit emerges to claim Billie, while leaving her child for Jenny and Jabo. Like Jabo's drumsticks, Jenny's knitting needles draw life from death and are at work while Billie dies and her baby is born. In the film's final scene, Jenny carries this baby, wrapped in its newly knitted blanket, as she walks away with Jabo. Both are dressed in tribal garments. Though the gospel song playing on the soundtrack celebrates the Lord, whether it refers to the Christian God or Lord Shango is left to the viewers to determine.

The Return of the Repressed: *J. D.'s Revenge*

J. D.'s Revenge begins with a flashback to New Orleans in 1942. Betty Jo (Alice Jubert) is married to Elija Bliss (Louis Gossett Jr) but having an affair with his brother, Theotis (Fred Pinkard), who is the father of her infant daughter, Roberta. Betty Jo and Theotis argue while standing among the hanging carcasses of cows in the meat-packing plant where her brother, the hustler and womaniser J. D. Walker (David McKnight), conducts his wartime business in black-market beef. After Betty Jo threatens to tell Elija that Theotis is Roberta's father, he slits her throat and flees. J. D., who has overheard their argument while approaching them, discovers her body. Elija then finds him standing over Betty Jo, his left hand covered in her blood and his right one holding a switchblade. Elija accuses J. D. of murder. Theotis returns to the scene of his crime, takes the opportunity to frame J. D., and shoots him. The action advances to 1976, when Isaac Hendrix (Glynn Turman) is studying law, driving a taxi and living with his girlfriend, Christella (Joan Pringle). While participating in the nightclub act of the hypnotist Sara Divine (Jo Anne Meredith), Isaac is possessed by the spirit of J. D. Over time, he not only begins speaking in the other man's voice, but also styling his hair, dressing and acting like him. Isaac/J. D. verbally and physically abuses Christella, who leaves and returns to him. Meanwhile, Carl (Julian Christopher), Christella's ex-husband and a detective, investigates Isaac and discovers the history of J. D., Betty Jo and the Bliss brothers. Isaac/J. D. learns that Elija and Theotis run a popular church where the former preaches. Having ingratiated himself with the evangelist and become involved in a quasi-incestuous relationship with the adult Roberta (Alice Jubert), J. D.'s niece, Isaac/J. D. reveals himself to Elija and arranges for a confrontation with Theotis in the meat-packing plant. Theotis is accompanied there by Elija and followed by Roberta. After Isaac/J. D. tells them that Theotis impregnated and murdered Betty Jo, the three struggle over a gun that Theotis is carrying, which discharges and kills him. J. D. then relinquishes the body of Isaac, who resumes the life that he led before becoming possessed.

Possession in *J. D.'s Revenge*, as in *Abby*, complicates the gender expression of the possessed. Isaac's conventional masculinity is established in the first scene of the film, which depicts him breaking up a fight on a football field. It is compromised when J. D.'s spirit enters Isaac, whom Elija later describes as a yonic 'vessel' for the gangster, during Sara Divine's gender-bending show. Directed by the hypnotist, Isaac and three other men begin to undress onstage. One removes his trousers, causing Sara to ask whether he is 'a stripper in drag'. Eliding the possibility of a male stripper, her question indicates how the men's performance evokes and inverts that of the topless women whom Isaac and Christella, together with their married friends Tony (Carl W. Crudup) and Phyllis (Stephanie Faulkner), watch dancing at another nightclub earlier in the evening. While Christella and Phyllis view these half-nude men with surprise and amusement, Tony is nonplussed by how their behaviour transgresses conventional gender roles. As Sara's act continues and J. D.'s spirit starts to affect Isaac, he becomes wholly passive and open to psychic influence. Onstage, he envisions a cow's throat being cut and Betty Jo's own throat being slit by Theotis. Later, he sees J. D. having rough sex, slapping a woman, cutting meat, arguing with and shaking Betty Jo, and staring at his hand covered in her blood. In one especially lurid vision, Betty Jo's body hangs from a meat hook, blood pouring from it. The link between abusing and killing women and butchering meat, which is established and stressed in the film's opening scene and reinforced in all of Isaac's visions, exemplifies what Carol J. Adams provocatively describes as the 'overlap of cultural images of sexual violence against women and the fragmentation and dismemberment of nature and the body', while literalising the 'metaphoric sexual butchering' of women that 'recurs in literature and movies'.[49] These associations further feminise Isaac, whose biblical namesake is very nearly butchered. Moreover, just as the Isaac of the Bible is the child of Sarah, so too the Isaac/J. D. of *J. D.'s Revenge* is the figurative son of Sara, whose hypnosis makes possible his dual existence. Although the other men in her act return to normal, Isaac, having been psychically penetrated and feminised by both the hypnotist and J. D., is troubled by recurring visions and suffers from a debilitating headache that continues until he and Christella return home and go to bed. In yet another inversion of gender stereotypes that aligns with his shifting identity, when she attempts to initiate sex, he declines. 'What's happened to my lover man?', she wonders.

That he has been replaced by J. D. becomes obvious during subsequent encounters between Isaac and Christella, wherein Isaac/J. D.'s virility is not only restored, but also exaggerated and distorted to the point of becoming monstrous and threatening. In one bedroom scene, having experienced more visions, Isaac suffers from another headache. Christella, no longer expecting sex, suggests that he sleep. After going into the bathroom for some aspirin, Isaac sees J. D. rather than himself in the mirror, the gangster's face contorted with lust and made even more frightful by an ugly scar that runs along his right cheek. When Isaac returns to Christella, the other man's spirit has taken over. 'What happened to your headache?', she enquires, as his hands close around her neck and he begins aggressive foreplay, followed by even more forceful sex. By turns puzzled, aroused and disturbed, she finally asks him to stop. He ignores her, and the scene ends with her staring at him in concern and confusion. This initial instance of sexual violence ominously foreshadows two brutal attacks on Christella. In the first, Isaac/J. D. insults and hits her, furious at being spoken to as if he were 'sissified' and a 'wimp', and literally throws her out of their apartment. When Isaac's personality temporarily resurfaces, he apologises to Christella and coaxes her to return home, where he is again possessed by J. D. and attempts to rape her. After she escapes from Isaac/J. D. by hitting him with a vase, he mutters to himself, 'Get her! Punch her!', before giving up on his assault and heading to a nightclub, where he seduces another woman.

This second attack on Christella is rendered more complex by its *mise en scène*, which reinforces the uncanny doubling of Isaac and J. D. After Christella returns to the apartment that she once more shares with Isaac, the camera moves from her to a medium shot of a menacing African Mardi Gras mask hanging on the wall. This shot is accompanied by a startling orchestral stab, which is followed by a few seconds of funk music that plays while the camera, having lingered on the mask for a moment, pans to another medium shot of a shirtless Isaac/J. D. as he steps into the living room. The extradiegetic music first signals that viewers ought to be alarmed by what the mask says about the man, then suggests that he has a newfound hipness, either despite or because of the revelation that his hair is now styled in a conk – that is, relaxed with chemicals and brushed back in a fashion popular among African American men during J. D.'s heyday in the 1940s. By the 1970s, the conk had been replaced by the Afro, a natural hairstyle associated with Black pride.[50] Both the mask and the conk call attention to how the dynamics of possession are informed by the involved and uncanny relationship between surface and depth, object and subject. Rather than remaining apart from and in tension with each other, these pairs gradually come into alignment as Isaac/J. D.'s appearance is coordinated with his essence, and as he and his doppelgänger become one. He not only changes his hairstyle from a short Afro to a conk, but also trades his cab-driving outfit of casual clothing and a leather cap for a suit and a fedora. Although other characters are surprised by his uncannily outmoded appearance, which looks unfamiliar on a young man, they nonetheless take him seriously. 'You're really somethin' else', the woman he seduces tells him, more perceptively than she realises, before bringing him home for what she describes as the best sex of her life. Similarly, Elija is struck dumb in the middle of a fiery sermon when Isaac/J. D. enters his church, recognising the gangster within the law student even before J. D. speaks through Isaac.

Deep significance is likewise inscribed on the surface of the Mardi Gras mask. As Willie J. Harrell Jr explains, when considering 'African

American Mardi Gras mask and costume traditions', the 'importance of these performances should not be placed so much on the act of disguising (the masker) as on the act of revealing (the representation)'.[51] In other words, the primary function of the mask is not to hide the one who wears it, but to display what or whom the wearer represents. This insight aligns with Eve Kosofsky Sedgwick's observation that in classical Gothic novels surfaces are as meaningful as depths, and that, for instance, 'the veil that conceals and inhibits sexuality comes by the same gesture to represent it, both as a metonym of the thing covered and as a metaphor for the system of prohibitions by which sexual desire is enhanced and specified'.[52] The Mardi Gras mask works in much the same fashion as the Gothic veil. Hideous and frightening, it serves not only as a metonym for J. D.'s scarred, scowling visage, but also as a metaphor for the deeply repressed belligerence and misogyny that his possession of Isaac brings to the surface. Furthermore, it replicates and represents Isaac's own face, which J. D. wears like a mask, thereby causing viewers to wonder about the extent to which the former's personality aligns with the latter's.

Indeed, J. D. is revealed to be not an entity wholly foreign to Isaac, but rather his uncanny alter ego, a Hyde to his Jekyll, who emerges from repression. 'You've always seemed to be, you know, sorta repressed', Tony explains to him. Isaac's repression manifests itself in self-denial. In a twist on the inhibitive practices of Utterson, who avoids the theatre and '[drinks] gin when he [is] alone, to mortify a taste for vintages',[53] Isaac must be persuaded to go out on the town and drinks beer rather than gin, presumably to avoid becoming intoxicated and losing control of himself. Tony, who works in a hospital and enjoys drinking gin, asks his friend, 'When are you gonna learn that it's medically proven that good gin cleanses your soul out?'. Isaac responds to his joke, which recommends consuming liquor as a means of catharsis, by denying its aggressive, Freudian implication that his spirit is somehow corrupted. 'Listen, man, ain't nothin' wrong with my soul', he asserts. Whereas Tony stops short of punningly associating the word *spirit* with both soul and alcohol, Christella confuses these two types of spirits, both of which are interchangeable insofar as they eliminate inhibitions, when Isaac comes home under the influence of J. D. rather than that of alcohol. 'You're drunk!', she exclaims, having observed his unusual behaviour and not realising that he is now entirely possessed. That Christella, not Isaac, is the one who drinks is indicated by the nearly empty wine bottle sitting near her – which he picks up and tips back as if to drink from, only to set down again because, in thrall to J. D., he does not require its liberating agency. Likewise, though Christella tells Isaac, 'What you need is a little wine to kinda loosen you up and get rid of all that tension', he finds relief from his excruciating headache only when he succumbs to J. D. and initiates rough sex with her.

Their encounter at once delights and disturbs Christella, whose ambivalence suggests that she may be repressing submissive and even masochistic inclinations, and that her own alter ego is awakened by the emergence of Isaac's. This interpretation is supported by Christella's suggestive exchange with Carl, her ex-husband. After she minimises the conspicuous bruise that Isaac's slap has left on her cheek, and unconvincingly asserts that her boyfriend 'isn't dangerous', Carl says, 'I thought you didn't like violent cats. I thought that turned your stomach. I don't understand you'. She retorts, 'Now let's not start in on that, Carl, because it wasn't about that'. Though Christella's referent is ambiguous, she and Carl seem to allude to an incident in their past, likely one that contributed to the dissolution of their marriage, in which she objected to his violent treatment of her. Carl's propensity towards violence, which is simultaneously inhibited and enabled by his career in law enforcement, is amply demonstrated by his threat to 'blow [Isaac's] goddamn brains away'. Both Carl and Isaac may well be drawn to legal professions in order to mask and manage their belligerent tendencies. Christella's becoming romantically involved with these two potentially aggressive men demonstrates her compulsion to repeat past traumatic experiences, probably in an unconscious attempt to restage and master paternal abuse from her childhood. That Isaac/J. D. repeatedly calls himself 'Daddy' and promises, 'Daddy ain't gonna hurt you, baby', before he assaults her indicates as much. Both the repressed desires that underlie Christella's repetition compulsion and the compulsion itself are amplified by and akin to Isaac's possession, for, as Freud notes, when 'the manifestations of a compulsion to repeat . . . act in opposition to the pleasure principle', they 'give the appearance of some "daemonic" force at work'.[54] Since his motivations and hers are so closely entwined, the boundary between the supernatural and the psychological is somewhat blurred in *J. D.'s Revenge*, which, like *Jekyll and Hyde*, suggests a difference in degree rather than in kind between the two categories. Both texts also demonstrate how pervasive repression enables normative interpersonal relations, and how everyone harbours an alter ego who, if freed, would tear the social fabric to pieces.

Moreover, both the novella and the film explore how men in the legal and medical professions cope with this ubiquitous doppelgänger, once he is released and particularised. Isaac, a law student, is chosen by J. D. not only because he has a propensity towards violence, but also because, as an evolving agent of justice, he can be shaped into an appropriate means of punishing Theotis. Carl serves as an Utterson-like figure who, in hunting and seeking to eliminate another man's alter ego, fosters his own. A doctor whom Isaac consults about his headaches fails, like Lanyon, to appreciate the transcendental nature of his affliction and advises him to relax. Another medical man, Tony, construes his friend's possession in purely psychological terms and, in keeping with his role as an opponent of repression and a champion for expression, praises him for '[letting] it all out' and '[letting] off some steam'. He goes so far as to assure Isaac, 'I think it's a good thing to go upside of a woman's head when she starts handing you lip', and claims, 'believe it or not, they like that'. Tony's assertion that men ought to dominate and abuse women, and that women enjoy mistreatment, is more disturbing and less comprehensible than Isaac's being compelled to indulge in such domination and abuse. Even when possessed by J. D. and mistreating Christella, Isaac is agonised and struggles against the spirit. Later, though he has no memory of physically and verbally hurting Christella, he nonetheless regrets his actions and rejects his friend's pernicious interpretation of them.

The anger and misogyny that J. D. unleashes, Isaac resists and Tony rationalises emerged swiftly and dramatically in the United States after the 1965 release of *The Negro Family*, by Daniel Patrick Moynihan. As noted in Chapter 3, the Moynihan Report traced the challenges facing disadvantaged members of the Black community to the inversion of conventional gender roles and the ascendancy of women. Benita Roth explains that the report 'was seized upon by many Black male activists as both a manifestation of white racism and proof that Black women out of their traditional place were abetting that racism'.[55] Roderick A. Ferguson likewise observes that 'black nationalist groups . . . agreed with Moynihan's thesis about the emasculating effects of black women and the need for black men to resume their role as patriarchs'.[56] In her controversial book, *Black Macho and the Myth of the Superwoman* (1978), Michele Wallace contends that the Moynihan Report '[loosened] the black man's tongue' and enabled him to speak openly against 'the employed black woman' who had been implicated in his oppression.[57] 'This report did not create hostility. It merely helped to bring the hostility to the surface. The result was a brain-shattering explosion upon the heads of black women, the accumulation of over three hundred years of rage'.[58] This return of repressed rage, together with the involvement of Black women in second-wave feminism, catalysed and fuelled a heated debate about gender roles and responsibilities among African Americans that continued throughout the 1970s. The parameters of this debate are drawn in *The Black Woman: An Anthology* (1970), edited by Toni Cade Bambara. In 'Dear Black Man', Fran Sanders writes, 'Don't approach me as you would an enemy. I am on your side and have always been'.[59] In 'Is the Black Male Castrated?', Jean Carey Bond and Patricia Peery take issue with 'Moynihan and his gang', who erroneously 'postulate that Black society is matriarchal, and that Black women have been the primary castrating force in the demise of Black manhood'.[60] In fact, the authors contend, 'many Black women must bear a heavy burden of male frustration and rage through physical abuse [and] desertion'.[61] This burden is certainly borne by Christella. In keeping with the implications of her name, she sacrifices herself for Isaac by arguing on his behalf with a sceptical Carl, who believes him to be not possessed but 'a maniac', and by offering him forgiveness, love and support even after he has mistreated and neglected her.

The alignment between Christella's name and behaviour exemplifies how *J. D.'s Revenge* functions as a religious allegory that first questions and then seems to affirm the integrity and efficacy of Christianity. Three of the five characters with biblical names are involved in criminal or illicit activity: Enoch is a pimp who runs numbers, while Theotis and Elija direct a religious racket. Although they appear to have risen from what Carl's superior in the police department suggestively terms 'the underworld' to respectable positions as co-leaders of a church, a private conversation between the two reveals at least one of them to be an avaricious charlatan. When Elija tells his brother, 'I'll tend to spiritual matters, and you run the organization', Theotis responds with scorn. 'You're just selling cheap, feel-good thrills to a bunch of suckers who are looking for the second coming of Jesus', he says, 'Just keep in mind what you really do, Elija, and I'll keep the show running'. His use of the term *show* links Elija's preaching with Sara Divine's nightclub act – which, since it actually opens Isaac to J. D.'s spirit, is demonstrably more effective than the sermons in which Elija merely describes how the Holy Spirit enters 'these vessels we call ourselves'. Elija's name belies his true identity as a false prophet, while his brother's, Theotis, suggests self-exaltation by modifying the word '*theosis*', which means 'deification'. Their church is the latest swindle in a series. Once a crooked boxer who threw fights and 'took dives whenever [Theotis] told him to', Elija now embellishes his sermons with terminology from their previous con game and speaks fervently of 'demons goin' down for the final count'. He is accused of being 'a fake and a phony' and not 'even a decent fighter' by a man attending one of his church services, who proves his point by knocking the preacher to the ground with a punch to his jaw.

Yet while Theotis, in an instance of projection, thinks Isaac/J. D. is 'some hustler running a game', Elija '[starts] to believe [his] own jive sermons', as his brother notes derisively. 'I've come to save your soul, J. D.', he declares with sincerity, fingering a crucifix, when he and his brother confront their resurrected adversary. Elija's clerical prowess is called into question when J. D.'s spirit is released not by an exorcism, but by a gunshot that kills the object of his revenge. Nevertheless, Elija's conclusion that Isaac has served as 'a vessel for God's justice' seems correct. Notably, J. D. himself does not punish his nemesis. Elija exhorts him to 'leave vengeance to the Lord' and he does so, watching while Roberta or Elija kills Theotis, either accidentally or by heavenly design. The latter explanation seems more likely, for Sara Divine's surname, though certainly contrived for the stage, still suggests that God sets the wheels of justice in motion by resurrecting J. D., who introduces himself to the woman in the nightclub as 'the water walker' and likens himself to Jesus. Although the gangster is hardly Christlike, his rising from the dead at least problematises Theotis's claim that the second coming is a scam.

Tricksters Matching Wits: *Petey Wheatstraw*

The horror-comedy *Petey Wheatstraw* begins with the birth of its eponymous protagonist, who improbably comes into the world as a sassy six-year-old boy (Clifford Roquemore II). The adult Petey (Rudy Ray Moore), a successful comedian, books a series of shows in Los Angeles. Meanwhile, his rivals, Leroy (Leroy Daniels) and Skillet (Ernest Mayhand), borrow money from the mobster Mr White (George Mireless) to finance their own comedy shows, which they belatedly realise are scheduled to overlap with Petey's. After they fail to convince Petey to delay his performances, they have their henchmen gun him down. Lucifer (G. Tito Shaw) appears and offers to resurrect him, provided that Petey agrees to marry his hideous daughter (Ebony Wright) and give him a grandson. The two strike a bargain, and the Devil equips Petey with a magical cane, which he uses both to help those in his community and to humiliate Leroy and Skillet. In an ill-advised attempt to deceive Lucifer, Petey and his friends disguise an incapacitated man as the comedian and offer him to the demons tasked with taking Petey to hell. After this man escapes, Lucifer's minions pursue and fight Petey and his allies. Ultimately, the comedian uses the Devil's own cane to defeat him. He then breaks the cane in two and enters what he believes to be a car full of his friends, which in fact carries Leroy and Skillet, now demons, together with Lucifer and his daughter, who removes her veil and exposes her ugliness while Petey screams.

Petey Wheatstraw plays for laughs the uncanny doubling between possessor and possessed, as the Devil and Petey mirror each other. Although Petey retains a degree of agency and autonomy, he is diabolically possessed insofar as his agreement obliges him to descend into hell and remain forever with the Devil and his daughter, whose attraction to a man so like her father might suggest an unresolved Electra complex. Both Lucifer and Petey are tricksters, and the story of their matching wits is in keeping with the enduring tradition of Black folktales.[62] Zora Neale Hurston's biographer Robert Hemenway explains that 'the devil in black folklore is not the terror he is in European folklore. Rather, he is a powerful trickster'.[63] As Hurston herself notes, in African American folktales 'the devil always [outsmarts] God' and, in turn, the ingenious folk heroes Jack or John '[outsmart] the devil'.[64] Fully cognisant of Lucifer's reputation as a trickster, Petey is initially wary of entering into an agreement with him. 'You always wind up on top', he tells his potential father-in-law. Yet Petey also knows that this diabolical trickster can himself be tricked, and he cites 'that Daniel Webster trick' as an example of a human being who outwits the fiend. Petey alludes to Stephen Vincent Benét's short story, 'The Devil and Daniel Webster' (1936), in which the expert orator persuades a jury of the damned to free Jabez Stone from a diabolical contract, before kicking Satan out of New Hampshire. Inspired by Webster's success and confident in what he believes to be his own superior abilities as a trickster, Petey strikes a deal with the Devil under the naïve assumption that he will eventually be able to extricate himself from it. 'I can figure out a way to keep from marrying the Devil's daughter', he assures his doubtful friends.

Petey's stratagem, which involves compelling a drunk and drugged man to wear a mask that replicates his own face, exemplifies the duplicity (both the deceit and the duplication) on which the plot of *Petey Wheatstraw* turns. Petey and his adversary the Devil are literally and figuratively two-faced. 'There you lay and here you stand', Petey's friend Jimmy observes, as the camera cuts between Petey and the masked drunk, whose prone form doubles not only the comedian standing above him, but also Petey's corpse as it lies on a pavement before being reanimated by Lucifer. Likewise doubled, the Devil appears as both a well-dressed man and a goat-like monster in a red jumpsuit and a black cape, which latter outfit resembles the black-and-red clothing worn by the resurrected Petey. These doubles are redoubled when images of Petey and Lucifer are superimposed, as the former uses the latter's magic cane to wreck the nightclub where Leroy and Skillet stage their show. The phallic properties of this cane are made obvious during its initial activation, when a trembling Petey holds it in front of his crotch as it becomes erect. Intoxicated by its supernatural potency, he declares, 'I've got [the Devil's] cane, and that makes me just as powerful as he', thereby establishing yet another link between these doppelgängers (see Figure 9).

Handed down from the fiend that Petey calls 'Father' to the man that Lucifer calls 'Son', this patrimonial cane exemplifies how *Petey Wheatstraw* reinforces patriarchal norms while marginalising and caricaturing women. 'All you have to do is wield the cane, Petey, and my power is yours', Lucifer promises his prospective son-in-law. His daughter, like his cane, is to be passed to Petey so that Lucifer, who has no son, can obtain a grandson and extend his paternal line. Notably, whereas the cane and its patriarchal power are merely loaned to Petey, the Devil's daughter is his forever. 'Just marry her, so I can rest!', Lucifer urges him. Petey's resurrection, revenge and borrowed power amount to a diabolical dowry from an exhausted father who is desperate to rid himself of a daughter so hideous that she is constantly veiled, even when alone with him in hell. Her veil not only conceals her ugliness, but also underscores her primary identity and role as a bride, which is further emphasised by a distorted version of Wagner's 'Bridal Chorus' that plays when she is on-screen. Her secondary function as her father's daughter is indicated by the fact that she is unnamed and referred to only as 'my pet' and 'my dear' by Lucifer. The woman's mother is never shown or even mentioned, though the Devil's regret at not having enjoyed a stag party indicates that he might be married. If so, his wife is in no position to object to his being waited on by an attractive demoness while having a bath. Like Lucifer, Petey appreciates feminine beauty. He tries to break his deal with the Devil not because he fears going to hell, but because he is horrified by the prospect of marrying an ugly woman. Viewed from a different perspective, Petey's marrying and settling down means his literally and figuratively being condemned to hell. On earth, he is free to play the field and date at least two women, Sheila (uncredited) and Nell (Ebony Wright). The former

Figure 9 Petey (Rudy Ray Moore) holds the Devil's cane in *Petey Wheatstraw* (1977). Generation International Pictures/Photofest

is possessive and jealous; the latter, like the Devil's daughter, erotically voracious yet sex-starved.

Other women in the film are depicted as either sex objects or shrews. The former category includes the bevy of female demons whom Petey exhausts in a fast-motion orgy during his stag party in a funeral home, which humorously reworks the long-standing Gothic association between Eros and Thanatos. Foremost in the latter group is an angry, knife-wielding woman whose cheating husband Petey uses his magic cane to transform from 'a damn dog' into an actual canine. The Devil's daughter likewise calls Petey a 'dirty dog' after he abandons her, though she literally enjoys the last laugh when, in one of the film's many uncanny duplications, Petey the trickster is tricked into entering a car that doubles his friend Jimmy's Cadillac. There his jilted bride, howling with glee, unveils and declares, 'Now you may kiss the bride!'. Petey literally and figuratively puts himself in this situation, having first created an Oedipal conflict with Lucifer by refusing to return his cane and then, believing that he has vanquished his foe, breaking the cane, thereby leaving himself castrated and impotent.

That Petey opposes the Devil with his own power rather than God's demonstrates the absence of the heavenly in *Petey Wheatstraw*. Indeed, the divine functions only as an opposing term to the diabolical. Fretting over Petey's plan to trick the Devil, Nell warns, 'If you cross him, he's gonna be mad as hell. I mean, heaven'. Likewise, when Lucifer's daughter first fixes her lascivious gaze on Petey, she growls, 'He's divinely sexy'. In a world that seems to be given over to the Devil, terms associated with God have come to indicate transgression. Moreover, the only scene in the film that features a church is replete with death. After Leroy and Skillet's main henchman, Scarface Willie (Marvin Jones), accidentally shoots and kills Larry (Bryan L. Roquemore), the little brother of Petey's friend Ted (Ted Clemmons), the boy's funeral is held at the Mount Chapel Baptist Church. As the mourners leave the church, Scarface Willie directs one of his fellow gangsters to mow all of them down with a submachine gun in order to kill Petey. Moments before this massacre occurs, the preacher intones, 'The Lord giveth, and the Lord taketh away'. In fact, it is the Devil, not the Lord, who gives life back to Petey and the other mourners, though he is not involved in their deaths. 'Are you responsible for all this madness?', Petey asks Lucifer, who responds, 'In most cases I am, but in this particular instance I happened to walk [in] upon this disaster'. The Devil's resurrecting the slain congregation is but one example of how the power of evil may be used for good. During one remarkable and extended sequence, Petey uses Lucifer's magic cane to benefit those living in a Black neighbourhood. In addition to turning the cheating husband into a dog, he saves a boy from being run over, slims down an overweight woman, replaces a family's broken-down car with a brand-new one, and causes cash to rain onto the sidewalk. As Petey joyously performs his good deeds, the song 'Ghetto St. U.S.A.' plays on the soundtrack, blending the infernal and the celestial. The lyric describes the ghetto as a hellish place 'down here', where 'people [are] sleepin'' out in the streets' and children '[walk] around hungry, with no shoes on their feet'. Yet, drawing on how Exodus 3: 8 characterises the Promised Land, it also describes 'streets of milk and honey' whose residents are 'looking for a blessing', which Petey paradoxically delivers to them by diabolical means, thereby himself conflating the hellish and the heavenly.

By depicting these ultimate opposites as doubles, *Petey Wheatstraw* joins *J. D.'s Revenge*, *Lord Shango* and *Abby* in revealing the fundamentally uncanny nature of both the evil spirit and religion itself. By showing how a womaniser is possessed, body and soul, by the Devil and his daughter, the film also aligns with *Sugar Hill* and *The House on Skull Mountain* in exploring (the loss of) autonomy and the (dis)empowerment of women. Although these issues are treated with less sophistication by *Petey Wheatstraw* than by its predecessors, the film's broad comedy enables it to approach them more directly. For example, the figurative link in *Lord Shango* between man and dog as objects of (propitiatory) sacrifice is literalised when Petey transforms the philandering husband into a puppy for his vengeful wife. Likewise, though the cane imbued with diabolical power that Lucifer loans to Petey recalls the one transferred from Baron Samedi to Sugar Hill, in Petey's hands this quintessential phallic symbol becomes both obscene and absurd, its fetishistic phallocentrism exposed and parodied.

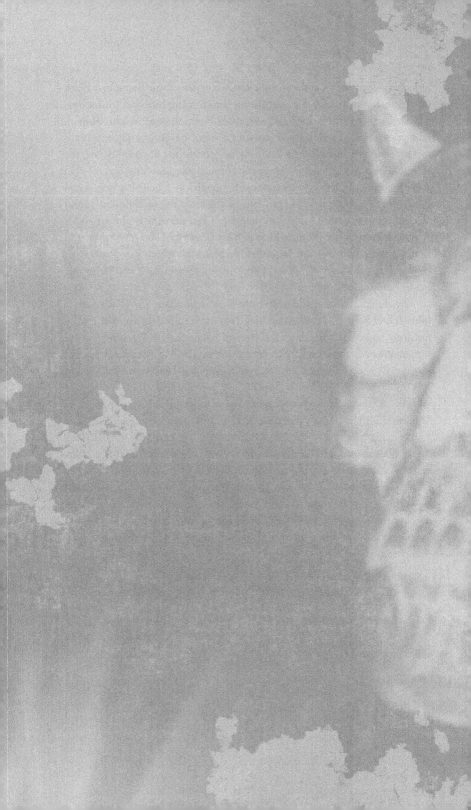

Conclusion
The Legacy of the Blaxploitation Horror Film

PETEY WHEATSTRAW, the last noteworthy Blaxploitation horror film, was released in 1977. By this point, both sociocultural and commercial factors were bringing the Blaxploitation genre to an end. 'Blaxploitation came to a speedy demise', Ed Guerrero observes, when 'black critical reaction to the violent, drug-dealing pimps and gangsters of Blaxploitation formula sharpened, and Hollywood became less economically dependent on the genre for short-term profit', having 'realized that it did not need an exclusively black vehicle to draw the large black audiences that had saved it from financial disaster'.[1] As Novotny Lawrence explains, concerned by the continuing and increasingly heated debate between civil rights organisations and those defending Blaxploitation films, 'major studios by 1974 shied away from producing the features'.[2] Meanwhile, blockbusters with crossover appeal such as *Jaws* (Steven Spielberg, 1975), *Star Wars* (George Lucas, 1977) and *Saturday Night Fever* (John Badham, 1977) were proving immensely popular among Black and white filmgoers alike.[3]

The end of the Blaxploitation era began a decade-long decline in the number of African Americans who featured in horror films. Robin Means Coleman points out that during the 1980s, 'in a notable reversal' from the 1970s, Black characters moved from major to minor roles, entering 'supporting relationships with (monstrous) Whites'.[4] Their marginalisation in films such as *Halloween* (John Carpenter, 1978), *Friday the 13th* (Sean S. Cunningham, 1980) and *A Nightmare on Elm Street* (Wes Craven, 1984) was in part a function of a shift in *mise en scène* from the inner city to the suburbs or the countryside, 'places viewed as inaccessible to Blacks'.[5] This view was somewhat simplistic, and the off-screen situation a bit more complex than the largely white worlds of Haddonfield, Camp Crystal Lake or Elm Street indicated. From 1970 to 1980, during what John Reid describes as 'the much-touted "suburbanization" of blacks', the number of African Americans living in the suburbs increased from 4.3 million to 6.2 million.[6] Still, in 1980 two-thirds of white Americans living in metropolitan regions were located in the suburbs, as compared with 29 per cent of African Americans, who constituted only 6.1 per cent of the suburban population.[7] That suburbs '[remained] overwhelmingly white and central cities [were] increasingly black'[8] is reflected in most mainstream horror films of the 1980s. Those set in predominantly white suburban and rural areas eliminated Black characters not only by relegating them to smaller roles, but also by killing them at a disproportionately high rate, in a move that became a cliché.[9]

During the 1980s, the presence of African Americans in horror cinema decreased sharply behind the camera as well as in front of it. Films with Black directors were obscure, low-budget productions, some of which never appeared in theatres. These included *Silent Death* (Vaughn Christion, 1983), *RuPaul's Trilogy of Terror* (John Witherspoon, 1984), *Zombie Island Massacre* (John Carter, 1984), *Black Devil Doll from Hell* (Chester Novell Turner, 1984), *Deathly Realities* (S. Torriano Berry, 1985), *Obeah* (Hugh A. Robertson, 1987) and *Tales from the QuadeaD Zone* (Chester Novell Turner, 1987). An exception proving the rule that African Americans were underrepresented in horror films of the 1980s is *Vamp* (Richard Wenk, 1986), a horror-comedy starring Grace Jones as a vampire stripper. At once underdeveloped and overdetermined, her one-dimensional character wears white face powder that evokes not only whiteface minstrelsy but also the Vodou love goddess Erzulie Freida, who is both 'Mother and Sacred Harlot'.[10] Clad in 'Egyptian regal headdresses, spiraling breastplates, and magical body paint', she figures 'the primordial Black Mother/Goddess'.[11] Yet she is silent throughout the film but for animalistic growls and screeches, and relegated to a seedy nightclub in a bad part of town, where she is discovered by slumming, would-be frat boys. Giselle Liza Anatol concludes that the 'primary lesson' of *Vamp* 'focuses attention on young white men, using the black female body as a fetishized prop: Beware of the exotic, seductive black woman'.[12] Much more three-dimensional and sympathetic is the vampire played in the next decade by Eddie Murphy in another horror-comedy, *A Vampire in Brooklyn* (Wes Craven, 1995).

Produced and co-written by Murphy, and co-starring Angela Bassett, *A Vampire in Brooklyn* is among the films that marked the return of African Americans to horror cinema in the 1990s, not only as actors but also as writers, directors and producers. At the start of this period, James Bond III followed Bill Gunn and anticipated Jordan Peele by writing, directing and starring in *Def by Temptation* (1990), an auteur project that tells the story of a young divinity student who struggles with his faith and against a beguiling succubus. Rusty Cundieff likewise worked as both writer and director on *Tales from the Hood* (1995), a horror-comedy co-written and produced by another African American, Darin Scot, and executive-produced by Spike Lee. This anthology, whose frame story underscores the lethal effects of drug abuse by positioning three pushers in a funeral home, explores how addiction, poverty, crime and racism affect the Black community of South Central Los Angeles. Cundieff and Scot created two more entries in the series, *Tales from the Hood 2* (2018) and *Tales from the Hood 3* (2020). Another significant franchise that focused on Black urban lives began with *Candyman* (Bernard Rose, 1992), which takes place in Cabrini-Green Homes, a Chicago housing project. It was followed by *Candyman: Farewell to the Flesh* (Bill Condon, 1995) and *Candyman: Day of the Dead* (Turi Meyer, 1999). The first film in a third series, *Blade* (Stephen Norrington, 1998), features Wesley Snipes as a vampire hunter. It led to *Blade II* (Guillermo del Toro, 2002) and *Blade: Trinity* (David S. Goyer, 2004). Like the *Blade* films and *A Vampire in Brooklyn*, *Fallen* (Gregory Hoblit, 1998) starred a major Black actor – in this instance, Denzel Washington as a Philadelphia detective at odds with a homicidal demon.

African Americans continued to figure prominently in horror films during the first decade of the twenty-first century. Eddie Murphy featured in a second horror-comedy, *The Haunted Mansion* (Rob Minkoff, 2003), and Will Smith led the cast of *I Am Legend* (Francis Lawrence, 2007), the tale of a man alone in a postapocalyptic world of vampiric mutants and a remake of *The Omega Man* (Boris Sagal, 1971), itself a remake of *The Last Man on Earth* (Ubaldo Ragona and Sidney Salkow, 1964). Another adaptation of a film from the 1970s, *Bones* (Ernest R. Dickerson, 2001), reimagines *J. D.'s Revenge* and pays homage to Blaxploitation horror. The work of a Black director, *Bones* features Snoop Dogg as a revivified numbers runner who seeks to punish his murderers, and Pam Grier, the star of *Scream Blacula Scream* and other Blaxploitation films,[13] as Pearl, his faithful love interest. Though a criminal, Jimmy Bones is respected by and protective of his community in 1979, when he is killed by a corrupt white policeman and a Black pusher for refusing to market crack cocaine. In 2001, his drug-ravaged neighbourhood has become a ghetto and his abandoned home a house haunted by his vindictive spirit, which has taken the form of a ravenous black dog. After a group of young people buy the house and turn it into a nightclub, Bones is resurrected and carries out his revenge. Set in an indeterminate urban landscape that could represent any inner city, *Bones* uses the eponymous character's boarded-up dwelling as a metonym for the deterioration of a once thriving African American community. Like *Candyman*, it figures the return of repressed Black rage as a vengeful spirit. Other spirits of wrath and lust are featured in *Black Devil Doll from Hell*, *Tales from the Hood*, *Def by Temptation*, *Fallen*, *A Haunted House* (Michael Tiddes, 2013), which parodies found-footage films about demonic possession and depicts the paranormal ordeals of a Black couple, and *The Alchemist Cookbook* (Joel Potrykus, 2016), whose demon is off-screen and possibly imaginary.

Together with the evil spirit, the vampire, true to its nature, has endured and proliferated in Black horror films. This classic monster is featured in *Vamp*, *A Vampire in Brooklyn*, the *Blade* series, *Queen of the Damned* (Michael Rymer, 2002), *Cryptz* (Danny Draven, 2002), *Da Sweet Blood of Jesus* (Spike Lee, 2014), *Transfiguration* (Michael O'Shea, 2016), *Vampires vs. The Bronx* (Oz Rodriguez, 2020), *The House Next Door: Meet the Blacks 2* (Deon Taylor, 2021) and *Black as Night* (Maritte Lee Go, 2021). Two of these films honour their Blaxploitation predecessors: *Da Sweet Blood of Jesus* is a fairly faithful adaptation of *Ganja & Hess*, and Deon Taylor calls the master vampire in *The House Next Door* Dr Mamuwalde, after the lead character of *Blacula* and *Scream Blacula Scream*. Indeed, Taylor is developing a remake of *Blacula*.[14] Other films in this category continue to explore the race-related concerns of their antecedents from the 1970s in thought-provoking ways. The *Blade* franchise features an African American human-vampire hybrid whose primary adversary in the first two films of the series is likewise a mixed being, a white man turned into a vampire by a bite rather than a 'pureblood' who is born as a vampire. In *Vampires vs. The Bronx*, the white vampires are intent on gentrifying – that is, vampirising – a racially and ethnically diverse neighbourhood. Likewise, though the leaders of the evil vampire coven in *Black as Night* are African Americans, they prey on the homeless and those living in a low-income housing community in New Orleans, while themselves operating from a mansion in the Garden District.

Whereas vampires have remained popular, other Gothic archetypes have become dormant, perhaps awaiting their eventual return to the screen. Neither Frankenstein's Creature nor Jekyll/Hyde have reprised their roles in Black horror films since the 1970s, despite or perhaps because of the fact that white versions of these monsters have featured in films by white directors.[15] Similarly, while Black werewolves and werewolf hunters have appeared in *Underworld* (Len Wiseman, 2003) and *Werewolves Within* (Josh Ruben, 2021), no one has created a film comparable to *The Beast Must Die*, although white directors have made a number of werewolf films since the 1970s.[16] Zombie films abound, but most feature white protagonists, some of whom confront Black antagonists and zombies. Exceptions include *Voodoo Dawn* (Steven Fierberg, 1990) and the direct-to-video *Hood of the Living Dead* (Eduardo Quiroz and Jose Quiroz, 2005), in which both the lead characters and the zombies are Black. Other very low-budget Black horror films featuring African American vampires, werewolves and zombies have been directed by John Bacchus: *Vampiyaz* (2004), *Bloodz vs. Wolvez* (2006) and *Zombiez* (2005).

As this overview indicates, except for films about evil spirits and vampires, most Black horror movies created after the heyday of Blaxploitation appear to have shifted their attention away from the classic Gothic monsters. This transition is unsurprising, given Joseph Conrad's observation that 'fashions in monsters do change',[17] but determining precisely why and how they change is challenging. One certainty is that the Gothic figures of the past assume different shapes in the present, for both trends in monsters and monsters themselves are always transforming. Thus, in many contemporary Black horror films, the emphasis on collage and (in)justice that is essential to Frankenstein's Creature is expressed not in a single monster, but rather in a monstrous narrative form. These stitched-together anthologies combine horror and humour to tell morality tales of outrageous crimes and condign punishments. Corrupt police officers and prison officials, domestic abusers, misogynists, thieves, racists and homicidal gang members suffer for their transgressions in *Tales from the Hood* and its sequels. Inspired by the first of these films, *Hood of Horror* (Stacy Title, 2006) likewise portrays immoral men and women who are punished with damnation. Taking a different approach to the Frankensteinian form, the horror-comedy *Scary Movie* (Keenen Ivory Wayans, 2000) and its four sequels use collage to bring together parodies of mainstream horror films and other types of popular culture.

Get Out (Jordan Peele, 2017) is a more direct appropriation of Frankenstein's Creature. Peele's directorial debut tells the story of Chris Washington (Daniel Kaluuya), a Black photographer, and his white girlfriend, Rose Armitage (Allison Williams). When the couple visits Rose's family, Chris eventually realises that her father, the neurosurgeon Dr Dean Armitage (Bradley Whitford) is transplanting the brains of older white people into the bodies of younger Black ones, who retain enough cerebral tissue and consciousness to remain aware of their existence and possession by an alien mind. Although Peele has cited *The Stepford Wives* (Bryan Forbes, 1975) and *Rosemary's Baby* as inspirations for *Get Out*,[18] the plot if not the quality of his sophisticated tale of body snatching and mind splicing aligns more closely with the storylines of two less celebrated horror films, *Change of Mind* (Robert Stevens, 1969) and *The Thing with Two Heads*.

In *Change of Mind*, David Rowe (Raymond St Jacques) is a white district attorney dying of cancer whose brain is transplanted by the pioneering neurologist Dr Bornear (Anthony Kramreither) into the body of an African American man killed in a car accident. When a racist white sheriff (Leslie Nielsen) is accused of murdering the Black woman with whom he was having an affair, Rowe prosecutes him. On learning that the sheriff is innocent, Rowe is compelled by his conscience to drop the charges, though doing so ends his legal career.

Change of Mind explores the connections among medicine, law and identity first drawn in Shelley's *Frankenstein*. 'And what was I?', Victor Frankenstein's composite creation wonders.[19] Likewise, immediately after Lowe's operation, a journalist asks Dr Bornear, 'What is he now, doctor: a white man with a black body, or a black man with a white brain?'. Bornear's broad-minded colleague Dr Kelman (Ron Hartmann) responds, 'A human being'. His answer is later clarified by both medical and legal professionals, who, in a victory of mind over matter, concur that Rowe maintains his identity, despite having changed bodies. Yet, striving to cope with the physical, psychological and social side effects of his operation, Rowe suffers from migraine headaches and nightmares, as he struggles to integrate not only his body and mind, but also his new identity and old life. Rowe's hybridity does, however, open his eyes to racism, which he sees and combats in both his personal and professional lives, while maintaining his commitment to serving justice in a colour-blind fashion. As the film's punning title indicates, Rowe's brain transplant enables him to occupy not only a different head, but also a different subject position. Unfortunately, his liminal subjectivity isolates him from both the Black and white worlds, and at the end of the film Rowe, like Shelley's Creature, exiles himself.

Whereas *Change of Mind* holds out at least the possibility of advancing racial integration and justice via Frankensteinian science, *The Thing with Two Heads* illustrates how American medicine and law seek to alienate Black men from themselves and others, and to make them into monsters. *Get Out* makes a similar point, albeit in much subtler and more complex ways. Like Dr Maxwell Kirshner, whose brain-transplant operation enables him to temporarily inhabit and control the body of Jack Moss, Dr Dean Armitage makes it possible for white men and women to colonise Black bodies. Both doctors' plans are thwarted by intrepid African American protagonists. Off-screen, Dr Fred Williams separates Kirshner from Moss. More dramatically, in a hunter/hunted reversal, Chris avoids having a white man's brain put into his body by impaling Armitage on the antlers of a deer mount, causing the scientist to knock over a candle and set fire to his operating room in a scene that evokes the fiery finale of *The Ghost of Frankenstein* (Erle C. Kenton, 1942). Acting as a one-man analogue for the villagers of *Frankenstein*, *The Bride of Frankenstein* and *Son of Frankenstein* (Rowland V. Lee, 1939), Chris likewise destroys, though indirectly, the two-headed monsters that Armitage has created by putting the brains of his parents into the bodies of two African American abductees. Georgina (Betty Gabriel), a housekeeper possessed by Marianne Armitage, is killed when she attacks Chris and the car that he is driving crashes into a tree. Walter (Marcus Henderson), a groundskeeper controlled by Roman Armitage, dies by his own hand after Chris awakens Walter's consciousness. While the climax of *Get Out* calls to mind the endings of other Frankensteinian films, its ingenious denouement at once evokes and subverts the conclusions of *Blackenstein* and *Dr. Black, Mr. Hyde*, both of which depict white policemen destroying Black monsters. Although racist science has been vanquished, it seems that injustice will ultimately prevail when a police car approaches Chris and a bloodied Rose. As he raises his hands and she calls for help, both they and the viewers anticipate that white cops will arrest him and rescue her. Instead, from the squad car emerges Rod Williams (Lil Rel Howery), a Black man and the best friend of Chris, with whom he drives away while Rose is left bleeding in the road.

After appropriating the story of Frankenstein's Creature, Peele signified on that of Jekyll/Hyde, a multiplicitous figure who is appropriately doubled, redoubled and further multiplied in *Us* (2019). Beginning with a life-or-death struggle between two families of doppelgängers, the film ultimately encompasses an entire nation of them. *Us* begins in 1986, when the young Adelaide 'Addy' Wilson (Madison Curry) watches a television commercial for Hands Across America. This fundraising effort for the homeless and hungry, in which people linked hands across the country, recalls the emphasis in Stevenson's *Jekyll and Hyde* on hands and handwriting as a means of distinguishing good from evil and ego from alter ego.[20] Addy later confronts her doppelgänger in a house of mirrors that references the cheval glass in Stevenson's novella, together with the mirror scenes of every film adaptation of *Jekyll and Hyde*. As an adult, Addy (Lupita Nyong'o) and her family battle their doubles, eventually realising that clones for everyone in the country, the Tethered, have emerged from subterranean facilities to kill their counterparts on the surface. *Us* thus reimagines the anxiety in *Dr. Black, Mr. Hyde* about the conflict between the upwardly mobile Black bourgeoisie and its double, the repressed and impoverished underclass, by literally placing these doppelgängers above and below ground.

Get Out and *Us* are foremost within a contemporary renaissance of Black horror cinema that might be viewed as the repetition with a difference of the original Blaxploitation horror cycle.[21] That these and many other Black horror films released in the past two decades are directed by African Americans indicates how the production of such movies has evolved since the era of Blaxploitation, when, as Jesse Algeron Rhines points out, 'Much more often than not, whites were in control behind the camera', producing, financing, directing and distributing films that '[reproduced] their own point of view'.[22] Horror stories told by Black filmmakers are now reformulating what Toni Morrison called 'American Africanism – a fabricated brew of darkness, otherness, alarm, and desire'.[23] This generation of films provides scholars with exciting opportunities and avenues for investigation that are already being pursued.[24] More importantly, as these narratives express, address and release renewed fears about some of the issues that were central to the Blaxploitation horror film, especially police brutality and persistent racial misunderstanding and inequity, they offer audiences both a means of catharsis and a measure of hope.

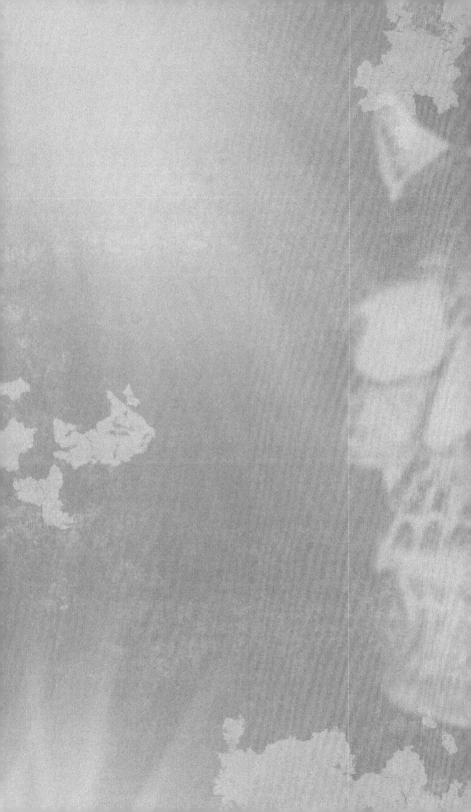

Notes

Introduction: Blaxploitation, Adaptation/Appropriation and the (Black) Gothic

1. In keeping with the current practice of many American news outlets and scholars, when referring to individuals or groups I capitalise *Black* but leave *white* in lower case. See David Bauder, 'AP Says It Will Capitalize Black but Not White', *AP News*, 20 July 2020, *httpsapnews.com/article/entertainment-cultures-race-and-ethnicity-us-news-ap-top-news-7e36c00c5af0436abc09e051261fff1f* (last accessed 20 June 2022).
2. Novotny Lawrence, *Blaxploitation Films of the 1970s: Blackness and Genre* (New York: Routledge, 2008), p. 56.
3. Eithne Kramer and Peter Krämer, 'Blaxploitation', in M. Hammond and L. R. Williams (eds), *Contemporary American Cinema* (Maidenhead: Open University Press, 2006), p. 189. Blaxploitation horror was part of an international surge of exploitation horror cinema of the 1960s and 1970s that Xavier Aldana Reyes terms 'Exploitation Gothic'. See Xavier Aldana Reyes, *Gothic Cinema* (London and New York: Routledge, 2020), pp. 185–211.
4. Lawrence, *Blaxploitation Films of the 1970s*, p. 56.
5. Jesse Algeron Rhines, *Black Film/White Money* (New Brunswick NJ: Rutgers University Press, 1996), pp. 45–6.
6. Lawrence, *Blaxploitation Films of the 1970s*, p. 95.

7. Lawrence, *Blaxploitation Films of the 1970s*, p. 95.
8. Lawrence, *Blaxploitation Films of the 1970s*, pp. 95–6.
9. Jan-Christopher Horak, 'Tough Enough: Blaxploitation and the L.A. Rebellion', in A. N. Field, J. Horak and J. N. Stewart, *L.A. Rebellion: Creating a New Black Cinema* (Oakland CA: University of California Press, 2015), p. 121.
10. Paula J. Massood, *Black City Cinema: African American Urban Experiences in Film* (Philadelphia PA: Temple University Press, 2003), p. 82.
11. Donald Bogle, *Toms, Coons, Mulattoes, Mammies, and Bucks: An Interpretive History of Blacks in American Films*, 4th edn (New York: Continuum, 2001), p. 241.
12. Bogle, *Toms, Coons, Mulattoes, Mammies, and Bucks*, pp. 241–2.
13. Bogle, *Toms, Coons, Mulattoes, Mammies, and Bucks*, p. 242.
14. Rhines, *Black Film/White Money*, p. 45.
15. Griffin, Junius, 'Black Movie Boom – Good or Bad?', *The New York Times*, 17 December 1972, *www.proquest.com/historical-newspapers/article-1-no-title/docview/119532594/se-2?accountid=12073* (last accessed 18 June 2022).
16. Lawrence, *Blaxploitation Films of the 1970s*, pp. 29–30.
17. Bogle, *Toms, Coons, Mulattoes, Mammies, and Bucks*, p. 242.
18. Mikel J. Koven, *Blaxploitation Films* (Harpenden: Pocket Essentials, 2001), p. 9.
19. See Lawrence, *Blaxploitation Films of the 1970s*, pp. 62, 69.
20. See Eithne Quinn, *A Piece of the Action: Race and Labor in Post-Civil Rights Hollywood* (New York: Columbia University Press, 2019), p. 176.
21. Allyson Nadia Field, Jan-Christopher Horak and Jacqueline Najuma Stewart, 'Introduction: Emancipating the Image: The L.A. Rebellion of Black Filmmakers', in *L.A. Rebellion: Creating a New Black Cinema*, p. 1.
22. Bruce Scivally, *Dracula FAQ: All That's Left to Know About the Count from Transylvania* (Milwaukee WI: Backbeat Books, 2015), p. 125.
23. For Crain's recollections about working on *Blacula* and *Dr. Black, Mr. Hyde*, see Paula Jai Parker, 'Paula Jai Parker and William Crain', Horror Noire: Uncut Podcast, 2020, *www.shudder.com/play/7bb2480e5670cdbd* (last accessed 30 June 2022).
24. Christopher Sieving, *Pleading the Blood: Bill Gunn's* Ganja & Hess (Bloomington IN: Indiana University Press, 2022), p. 69.
25. Sieving, *Pleading the Blood*, p. 70.
26. Sieving, *Pleading the Blood*, pp. 71–2.
27. See Leerom Medovoi, 'Theorizing Historicity, or the Many Meanings of *Blacula*', *Screen*, 39/1 (1998), 1–21; Novotny Lawrence, 'Fear of a Blaxploitation

Monster: Blackness as Generic Revision in AIP's *Blacula*', *Film International*, 7/3 (2009), 14–27; Paul R. Lehman and John Edgar Browning, 'The *Dracula* and the *Blacula* (1972) Cultural Revolution', in J. E. Browning and C. J. Picart (eds), *Draculas, Vampires, and Other Undead Forms: Essays on Gender, Race, and Culture* (Lanham: Scarecrow Press, 2009), pp. 19–36; Brooks E. Hefner, 'Rethinking *Blacula*: Ideological Critique at the Intersection of Genres', *The Journal of Popular Film and Television*, 40/2 (2012), 62–74; Morgan Woolsey, 'Hearing and Feeling the Black Vampire: Queer Affects in the Film Soundtrack', *Current Musicology*, 106 (2020), 9–26; Manthia Diawara and Phyllis R. Klotman, '*Ganja and Hess*: Vampires, Sex, and Addictions', *Black American Literature Forum*, 25/2 (1991), 299–314; Harrison M. J. Sherrod, 'The Blood of the Thing (Is the Truth of the Thing): Viral Pathogens and Uncanny Ontologies in *Ganja and Hess*', in L. Novotny and G. R. Butters Jr (eds), *Beyond Blaxploitation* (Detroit MI: Wayne State University Press, 2016), pp. 102–13; Maisha Wester, 'Re-Scripting Blaxploitation Horror: *Ganja and Hess* and the Gothic Mode', in J. Edwards and J. Höglund (eds), *B-Movie Gothic* (Edinburgh: Edinburgh University Press, 2017), pp. 32–49; Sieving, *Pleading the Blood*.

28. See Elizabeth Young, *Black Frankenstein: The Making of an American Metaphor* (New York: New York University Press, 2008), pp. 190–7; Justin Ponder, '"We Are Joined Together Temporarily": The Tragic Mulatto, Fusion Monster in Lee Frost's *The Thing with Two Heads*', *Ethnic Studies Review*, 34/1 (2011), 135–55; Chera Kee, *Not Your Average Zombie: Rehumanizing the Undead from Voodoo to Zombie Walks* (Austin TX: University of Texas Press, 2017), pp. 120–9; Christopher J. Olsen and CarrieLynn D. Reinhard, *Possessed Women, Haunted States: Cultural Tensions in Exorcism Cinema* (Lanham MD: Lexington Books, 2017), pp. 50–6.
29. See Lawrence, *Blaxploitation Films of the 1970s*, pp. 58–75.
30. See Harry M. Benshoff, 'Blaxploitation Horror Films: Generic Reappropriation or Reinscription?', *Cinema Journal*, 39/2 (2000), 31–50. See also Steven Jay Schneider, 'Possessed By Soul: Generic (Dis)Continuity in the Blaxploitation Horror Film', in X. Mendik (ed.), *Necronomicon Presents Shocking Cinema of the Seventies* (Hereford: Noir Publishing, 2002), pp. 106–20.
31. See Robin R. Means Coleman, *Horror Noire: Blacks in American Horror Films from the 1890s to Present* (New York and London: Routledge, 2011), pp. 118–44.
32. Means Coleman, *Horror Noire*, p. 12.
33. Linda Hutcheon, *A Theory of Adaptation*, 2nd edn (London and New York: Routledge, 2013), p. 9. Italics in original.

34. Kamilla Elliott, *Rethinking the Novel/Film Debate* (Cambridge: Cambridge University Press, 2003), p. 128.
35. See Simone Murray, *The Adaptation Industry: The Cultural Economy of Contemporary Literary Adaptation* (New York: Routledge, 2012), pp. 7–10.
36. Murray, *The Adaptation Industry*, p. 10.
37. Lawrence, 'Fear of a Blaxploitation Monster', 16.
38. Medovoi, 'Theorizing Historicity', 3.
39. Benshoff, 'Blaxploitation Horror Films', 43.
40. Julie Sanders, *Adaptation and Appropriation* (London: Routledge, 2006), p. 19.
41. Sanders, *Adaptation and Appropriation*, p. 26.
42. Sanders, *Adaptation and Appropriation*, p. 26.
43. Timothy Corrigan, 'Defining Adaptation', in T. M. Leitch (ed.), *The Oxford Handbook of Adaptation Studies* (Oxford: Oxford University Press, 2017), p. 26.
44. Henry Louis Gates, *The Signifying Monkey: A Theory of Afro-American Literary Criticism* (New York: Oxford University Press, 1988), p. xix.
45. Gates, *The Signifying Monkey*, p. xxvii.
46. See Gladstone Lloyd Yearwood, *Black Film as a Signifying Practice: Cinema, Narration and the African American Aesthetic Tradition* (Trenton: Africa World Press, 2000). See also Keith M. Harris, *Boys, Boyz, Bois: An Ethics of Black Masculinity in Film and Popular Media* (New York: Routledge, 2006).
47. Jonathan Munby, 'Signifyin' Cinema: Rudy Ray Moore and the Quality of Badness', *Journal for Cultural Research*, 11/3 (2007), 203–19.
48. Robin Wood, *Hollywood from Vietnam to Reagan … and Beyond*, rev. edn (New York: Columbia University Press, 2003), p. 68.
49. Charles L. Crow, *American Gothic* (Cardiff: University of Wales Press, 2009), p. 85.
50. María M. García Lorenzo, 'The Unwhitening of Discourse: The Gothic in African-American Literature', in I. Soto and V. Showers, *Western Fictions, Black Realities: Meanings of Blackness and Modernities* (East Lansing MI: Michigan State University Press, 2012), p. 49.
51. Corinna Lenhardt, *Savage Horrors: The Intrinsic Raciality of the American Gothic* (Bielefeld: Transcript, 2020), p. 16.
52. Maisha Wester, 'The Gothic in and as Race Theory', in J. E. Hogle and R. Miles (eds), *The Gothic and Theory: An Edinburgh Companion* (Edinburgh: Edinburgh University Press, 2019), pp. 53–70.
53. Maisha Wester, *African American Gothic: Screams from Shadowed Places* (New York: Palgrave Macmillan, 2012), p. 2. See also 'Black Diasporic Gothic', in M. Wester and X. Aldana Reyes (eds), *Twenty-First-Century Gothic: An*

Edinburgh Companion (Edinburgh: Edinburgh University Press, 2019), pp. 289–303.
54. Fred Botting views 'the fascination with transgression' as essential to the Gothic. Likewise, Teresa A. Goddu chararcterises it as 'obsessed with transgressing boundaries'. See Fred Botting, *Gothic* (London and New York: Routledge, 1996), p. 2. See also Teresa A. Goddu, *Gothic America: Narrative, History, and Nation* (New York: Columbia University Press, 1997), p. 5.
55. Benshoff, 'Blaxploitation Horror Films', 31, 45.
56. Wester, 'Re-Scripting Blaxploitation Horror', p. 33.
57. Wester, 'Re-Scripting Blaxploitation Horror', p. 33.
58. Wester, 'Re-Scripting Blaxploitation Horror', p. 33.
59. Wester, 'Re-Scripting Blaxploitation Horror', p. 34. Christopher Sieving refutes the notion that *Ganja & Hess* was commissioned 'to cash in on the box office success of *Blacula*', pointing out that 'Blacula was not released until August 1972, *after* filming wrapped on *Ganja & Hess*', and noting that Gunn approached the studio with his idea for the film, not vice versa. See Christopher Sieving, *Pleading the Blood*, p. 55.
60. Wester, 'Re-Scripting Blaxploitation Horror', p. 34.
61. Schneider, 'Possessed By Soul', p. 110.
62. Schneider, 'Possessed By Soul', p. 110.
63. Schneider, 'Possessed By Soul', p. 113.
64. Schneider, 'Possessed By Soul', pp. 113–14.
65. Schneider, 'Possessed By Soul', pp. 115–16.
66. Schneider, 'Possessed By Soul', pp. 116–17.
67. Schneider, 'Possessed By Soul', pp. 117–19. For an extended discussion of interracial relationships in (Blaxploitation) horror movies, see also Steven Jay Schneider, 'Mixed Blood Couples: Monsters and Miscegenation in U. S. Horror Cinema', in R. B. Anolik and D. L. Howard (eds), *The Gothic Other: Racial and Social Constructions in the Literary Imagination* (Jefferson NC: McFarland & Co., 2004), pp. 79–84.
68. Peter Hutchings, *The Horror Film* (London and New York: Routledge, 2004), p. 115.
69. Hutchings, *The Horror Film*, p. 115.
70. Ewan Kirkland, *Videogames and the Gothic* (London and New York: Routledge, 2021), p. 11.

1 Queer Bloodlines: The Vampire

1. Walter Bernhart and Werner Wolf, *Framing Borders in Literature and Other Media* (Amsterdam: Rodopi, 2006), p. 3.
2. Bram Stoker, *Dracula*, ed. Roger Luckhurst (Oxford: Oxford University Press, 2020), p. 4.
3. Stoker, *Dracula*, p. 351.
4. Gérard Genette, *Palimpsests: Literature in the Second Degree* (Lincoln NE: University of Nebraska Press, 1997), p. 5.
5. Julia Kristeva, 'Word, Dialog and Novel', in T. Moi (ed.), *The Kristeva Reader* (New York: Columbia University Press, 1986), p. 37.
6. See Lyndon W. Joslin, *Count Dracula Goes to the Movies: Stoker's Novel Adapted*, 3rd edn (Jefferson NC: McFarland & Co., 2017), p. 3.
7. See Julia Kristeva, 'Revolution in Poetic Language', in T. Moi (ed.), *The Kristeva Reader*, pp. 120–2.
8. See Mikhail Bakhtin, *The Dialogic Imagination: Four Essays*, ed. Michael Holquist, trans. Caryl Emerson and Michael Holquist (Austin TX: University of Texas Press, 1981 (2008)), p. 429.
9. Julia Kristeva, *Desire in Language: A Semiotic Approach to Literature and Art* (New York: Columbia University Press, 1980), p. 36. Italics in original.
10. John William Polidori, *The Vampyre*, in R. Morrison and C. Baldick (eds), The Vampyre *and Other Tales of the Macabre* (Oxford: Oxford University Press, 1997), p. 23.
11. Carol A. Senf, *The Vampire in Nineteenth-Century English Literature* (Bowling Green OH: Bowling Green State University Popular Press, 1988), p. 43.
12. Michel Foucault, *Power/Knowledge: Selected Interviews and Other Writings, 1972–1977*, ed. Colin Gordon, trans. Colin Gordon, Leo Marshall, John Mepham and Kate Soper (New York: Pantheon Books, 1980), p. 223.
13. See D. L. Macdonald, *Poor Polidori: A Critical Biography of the Author of* The Vampyre (Toronto: University of Toronto Press, 2016), p. 98.
14. See Fiona MacCarthy, *Byron: Life and Legend* (New York: Farrar, Straus and Giroux, 2002), pp. xii–xiii, 58–9, 126–7. See also Louis Crompton, *Byron and Greek Love: Homophobia in 19th-Century England* (Berkeley CA: University of California Press, 1985).
15. George Haggerty, *Men in Love: Masculinity and Sexuality in the Eighteenth Century* (New York: Columbia University Press, 1999), p. 4.
16. Eve Kosofsky Sedgwick, *Between Men: English Literature and Male Homosocial Desire* (New York: Columbia University Press, 2015), p. 94.

17. Max Fincher, *Queering Gothic in the Romantic Age: The Penetrating Eye* (Basingstoke: Palgrave Macmillan, 2007), p 138.
18. Polidori, *The Vampyre*, p. 4.
19. Stephen Donaldson and Wayne R. Dynes, *History of Homosexuality in Europe and America* (New York: Garland, 1992), p. 299.
20. George P. Putnam (ed.), *Hand-book of Chronology and History: The World's Progress, a Dictionary of Dates: With Tabular Views of General History, and a Historical Chart*, 6th edn (New York: George P. Putnam, 1852), p. 425.
21. Sedgwick, *Between Men*, p. 21. Ken Gelder sees this triangle at work in *The Vampyre* and *Carmilla*. See *Reading the Vampire* (London: Routledge, 1994), pp. 59–60.
22. Polidori, *The Vampyre*, pp. 17, 21, 22, 23.
23. Polidori, *The Vampyre*, p. 12.
24. Polidori, *The Vampyre*, pp. 22–3.
25. Polidori, *The Vampyre*, p. 241.
26. Polidori, *The Vampyre*, p. 241n.
27. Joseph Sheridan Le Fanu, *Carmilla: A Critical Edition*, ed. Kathleen Costello-Sullivan (Syracuse NY: Syracuse University Press, 2013), p. 5.
28. Le Fanu, *Carmilla*, pp. 72, 22.
29. Le Fanu, *Carmilla*, p. 31.
30. Le Fanu, *Carmilla*, pp. 16, 46. Carmilla is 'infantile as well as maternal'. See William Veeder, 'Carmilla: The Arts of Repression', *Texas Studies in Literature and Language*, 22/2 (1980), 215.
31. For queerness in *Carmilla*, see Ardel Thomas, *Queer Others in Victorian Gothic: Transgressing Monstrosity* (Cardiff: University of Wales Press, 2012), pp. 100–7; Amy Leal, 'Unnameable Desires in Le Fanu's *Carmilla*', *Names*, 55/1 (2007), 37–52; Adrienne Antrim Major, 'Other Love: Le Fanu's *Carmilla* as Lesbian Gothic', in R. Bienstock Anolik (ed.), *Horrifying Sex: Essays on Sexual Difference in Gothic Literature* (Jefferson NC: McFarland & Co., 2007), pp. 151–66.
32. Le Fanu, *Carmilla*, p. 5.
33. Le Fanu, *Carmilla*, p. 29.
34. Le Fanu, *Carmilla*, p. 52.
35. Le Fanu, *Carmilla*, p. 53.
36. Le Fanu, *Carmilla*, p. 4.
37. Sigmund Freud, 'Jokes and their Relation to the Unconscious' (1905), in James Strachey (ed.), *The Standard Edition of the Complete Psychological Works of Sigmund Freud*, vol. 8 (London: Hogarth Press and the Institute of Psycho-Analysis, 1960 (1981)), p. 105.

38. Le Fanu, *Carmilla*, p. 66.
39. Le Fanu, *Carmilla*, p. 66.
40. Le Fanu, *Carmilla*, pp. 4, 70.
41. Bram Stoker, *Dracula*, ed. Roger Luckhurst (Oxford: Oxford University Press, 2011 (2020)), p. 31.
42. Stoker, *Dracula*, p. 30.
43. Stoker, *Dracula*, pp. 344, 30.
44. Stoker, *Dracula*, p. 224.
45. Stoker, *Dracula*, pp. 24, 23.
46. Stoker, *Dracula*, p. 24.
47. Sigmund Freud, 'Character and Anal Erotism' (1908), in James Strachey (ed.), *The Standard Edition of the Complete Psychological Works of Sigmund Freud*, vol. 9 (London: Hogarth Press and the Institute of Psycho-Analysis, 1959 (1981)), pp. 169, 175.
48. Sigmund Freud, *The Complete Letters of Sigmund Freud to Wilhelm Fliess, 1887–1904*, ed. J. Moussaief Masson (Cambridge MA: Belknap Press of Harvard University Press, 1985), p. 227.
49. Freud, 'Character and Anal Erotism', p. 174.
50. Stoker, *Dracula*, p. 223.
51. Stoker, *Dracula*, p. 79.
52. Stoker, *Dracula*, pp. 47, 36.
53. Stoker, *Dracula*, p. 279.
54. Kristeva explains that excrement and corpses, together with their attendant odours, are powerful and closely related instantiations of the abject. 'The corpse . . . is cesspool', she writes, 'the most sickening of wastes'. See Julia Kristeva, *Powers of Horror: An Essay on Abjection*, trans. Leon S. Roudiez (New York: Columbia University Press, 1982), p. 3.
55. Stoker, *Dracula*, p. 233.
56. Sigmund Freud, 'Three Essays on the Theory of Sexuality' (1905), in James Strachey (ed.), *The Standard Edition of the Complete Psychological Works of Sigmund Freud*, vol. 7 (London: Hogarth Press and the Institute of Psycho-Analysis, 1953 (1981)), p. 198.
57. See Freud, 'Three Essays on the Theory of Sexuality', p. 199.
58. Stoker, *Dracula*, p. 41.
59. Ellis Hanson, 'Undead', in D. Fuss (ed.), *Inside/Out: Lesbian Theories, Gay Theories* (New York: Routledge, 1991), p. 336.
60. Stoker, *Dracula*, p. 29.
61. Johann Wolfgang von Goethe, *Faust*, trans. Walter Kaufmann (New York: Anchor Books, 1961 (1990)), p. 171.

62. See Sigmund Freud, 'Notes Upon a Case of Obsessional Neurosis' (1909), in James Strachey (ed.), *The Standard Edition of the Complete Psychological Works of Sigmund Freud*, vol. 10 (London: Hogarth Press and the Institute of Psycho-Analysis, 1955 (1981)), p. 166.
63. Stoker, *Dracula*, p. 45.
64. Stoker, *Dracula*, p. 37.
65. Freud, 'Three Essays on the Theory of Sexuality', p. 186.
66. Stoker, *Dracula*, p. 53.
67. Stoker, *Dracula*, pp. 47, 102.
68. Freud, 'Three Essays on the Theory of Sexuality', p. 199.
69. Stoker, *Dracula*, p. 97.
70. Stoker, *Dracula*, pp. 95, 250, 101, 109.
71. Stoker, *Dracula*, pp. 260, 97.
72. Stoker, *Dracula*, p. 260.
73. Stoker, *Dracula*, p. 260.
74. See Christopher Craft, '"Kiss Me with Those Red Lips": Gender and Inversion in Bram Stoker's *Dracula*', *Representations*, 8 (1984), 107–33.
75. See Daniel Lapin, *The Vampire, Dracula and Incest* (San Francisco CA: Gargoyle Press, 1995); and Phyllis Roth, 'Suddenly Sexual Women in Bram Stoker's *Dracula*', *Literature and Psychology*, 27 (1977), 113–21.
76. Stoker, *Dracula*, p. 20.
77. Stoker, *Dracula*, p. 39.
78. Stoker, *Dracula*, p. 58.
79. Stoker, *Dracula*, pp. 143, 149, 150.
80. Stoker, *Dracula*, p. 53.
81. Stoker, *Dracula*, p. 218.
82. Stoker, *Dracula*, p. 219.
83. Kathleen P. Long, *Gender and Scientific Discourse in Early Modern Culture* (Farnham: Ashgate, 2010), p. 7.
84. Stoker, *Dracula*, p. 351.
85. Stoker, *Dracula*, p. 351.
86. Stoker, *Dracula*, p. 37.
87. Stoker, *Dracula*, p. 384, n. 200.
88. Stoker, *Dracula*, p. 344.
89. See Sedgwick, *Between Men*, pp. 83–96.
90. In the unconscious, fur 'symbolises pubic hair and particularly women's pubic hair'. See Anthony Easthope, *The Unconscious* (London: Routledge, 1999), p. 3. Likewise, in dreams 'fur stands for the pubic hair'. See Sigmund Freud, 'The Interpretation of Dreams (First Part)' (1900), in James Strachey (ed.),

The Standard Edition of the Complete Psychological Works of Sigmund Freud, vol. 4 (London: Hogarth Press and the Institute of Psycho-Analysis, 1953 (1971)), p. 86.

91. For analyses of degeneration in *Dracula*, see Charles S. Blinderman, 'Vampurella: Darwin and Count Dracula', *The Massachusetts Review*, 21/2 (1980), 411–28; Ernest Fontana, 'Lombroso's Criminal Man and Stoker's *Dracula*', in Margaret L. Carter (ed.), *Dracula: The Vampire and the Critics* (Ann Arbor MI: UMI Research Press, 1988), pp. 159–65; Daniel Pick, '"Terrors of the night": *Dracula* and "Degeneration" in the Late Nineteenth Century', *Critical Quarterly*, 30/4 (1988), 71–87; Kathleen L. Spencer, 'Purity and Danger: *Dracula*, the Urban Gothic, and the Late Victorian Degeneracy Crisis', *ELH*, 59/1 (1992), 197–225; David Glover, *Vampires, Mummies, and Liberals: Bram Stoker and the Politics of Popular Fiction* (Durham NC: Duke University Press, 1996), pp. 65–70.
92. William M. Greenslade, *Degeneration, Culture, and the Novel, 1880–1940* (Cambridge: Cambridge University Press, 1994), p. 72.
93. Stoker, *Dracula*, p. 317.
94. Cesare Lombroso, *Criminal Man*, trans. Mary Gibson and Nicole Hahn Rafter (Durham NC: Duke University Press, 2006), p. 1.
95. Max Nordau, *Degeneration* (Lincoln NE: University of Nebraska Press, 1895 (1993)), p. 15.
96. Stephen Arata, *Fictions of Loss in the Victorian* Fin de Siècle (Cambridge: Cambridge University Press, 1996), p. 2.
97. Greenslade, *Degeneration*, p. 23.
98. Glover, *Vampires, Mummies, and Liberals*, p. 67.
99. See Jordan Blair Woods, 'The Birth of Modern Criminology and Gendered Constructions of Homosexual Criminal Identity', *Journal of Homosexuality*, 62/2 (2015), 138–40.
100. David J. Skal mentions 'Renfield's tragic, unrequited love for the Count', and Harry M. Benshoff considers Renfield and Dracula a queer couple. See Skal, *Hollywood Gothic: The Tangled Web of Dracula from Novel to Stage to Screen*, rev. edn (New York: Faber and Faber, 2004), pp. 198–9; and Harry M. Benshoff, *Monsters in the Closet: Homosexuality and the Horror Film* (Manchester: Manchester University Press, 1997), p. 48.
101. Jeffrey Ogbonna Green Ogbar, *Black Power: Radical Politics and African American Identity* (Baltimore MD: Johns Hopkins University Press, 2019), pp. 2, 94.
102. Tom Adam Davies, *Mainstreaming Black Power* (Oakland CA: University of California Press, 2017), p. 92.

103. Katherine McFarland Bruce, *Pride Parades: How a Parade Changed the World* (New York: New York University Press, 2016), p. 218.
104. Simon Dickel, *Black/Gay: The Harlem Renaissance, the Protest Era, and Constructions of Black Gay Identity in the 1980s and 90s* (Münster: LIT Verlag, 2011), p. 5.
105. David Carter, S*tonewall: The Riots that Sparked the Gay Revolution*, 2nd edn (New York: St Martin's Griffin, 2010), pp. 1, 16.
106. Lillian Faderman and Stuart Timmons, *Gay L.A.: A History of Sexual Outlaws, Power Politics, and Lipstick Lesbians* (Berkeley CA: University of California Press, 2009), p. 192.
107. Roderick A. Ferguson, *One-Dimensional Queer* (Cambridge: Polity Press, 2019), p. 23.
108. Carter, *Stonewall*, p. 145.
109. Carter, *Stonewall*, p. 117.
110. See Jim Downs, *Stand by Me: The Forgotten History of Gay Liberation* (New York: Basic Books, 2016), pp. 171–2, 183–5. See also Faderman and Timmons, *Gay L.A.*, pp. 236, 237.
111. See Martin Summers, '"This Immoral Practice": The Prehistory of Homophobia in Black Nationalist Thought', in T. P. Lester (ed.), *Gender Nonconformity, Race, and Sexuality: Charting the Connections* (Madison WI: University of Wisconsin Press, 2002), pp. 21–43. See also Cheryl Clarke, 'The Failure to Transform: Homophobia in the Black Community', in E. Brandt (ed.), *Dangerous Liaisons: Blacks, Gays, and the Struggle for Equality* (New York: The New Press, 1999), pp. 31–44.
112. Timothy Stewart-Winter, 'Queer Law and Order: Sex, Criminality, and Policing in the Late Twentieth-Century United States', *The Journal of American History*, 102/1 (2015), 61–72.
113. Downs, *Stand by Me*, p. 66.
114. Ogbar, *Black Power*, p. 102.
115. Huey P. Newton, 'The Women's Liberation and Gay Liberation Movements: August 15, 1970', in D. Hilliard and D. Weise (eds), *The Huey P. Newton Reader* (New York: Seven Stories Press, 2002), p. 158.
116. Before Stonewall, there were uprisings against police harassment in Los Angeles and San Francisco. See Ardel Haefele-Thomas, Thatcher Combs, and Cameron Rains, *Introduction to Transgender Studies* (New York: Harrington Park Press, 2019), pp. 139–41, 144–5. In 1967, a police raid at the Black Cat Tavern in Los Angeles led to a series of protests. In 1975, the anti-gay Chief of Police for the LAPD, Ed Davis, used 105 police officers, dozens of squad cards, helicopters and a bus to raid a private party to benefit the Gay

Community Services Center held at the Mark IV bathhouse. See Faderman and Timmons, *Gay L.A.*, pp. 156–7, 216–18.
117. Charles R. Epp, *Making Rights Real: Activists, Bureaucrats, and the Creation of the Legalistic State* (Chicago IL: University of Chicago Press, 2010), pp. 74–5.
118. Joshua Bloom and Waldo E. Martin, *Black Against Empire: The History and Politics of the Black Panther Party* (Oakland CA: University of California Press, 2016), p. 71. Italics in original.
119. Chuck Stewart, *Lesbian, Gay, Bisexual, and Transgender Americans at Risk: Problems and Solutions* (Santa Barbara CA: Praeger, 2018), p. xxix.
120. Gerald Martinez, Diana Martinez and Andres Chavez, *What It Is … What It Was! The Black Film Explosion of the '70s in Words and Pictures* (New York: Hyperion, 1998), p. 42. Marshall's link between vampirism and slavery was actually made more than a century earlier. See Uriah Derick D'Arcy, *The Black Vampyre: A Legend of St. Domingo* (Edinburgh: Gothic World Literature Editions, 1819 (2020)).
121. Martinez, Martinez and Chavez, *What It Is … What It Was!*, p. 43.
122. Susan Sontag, 'Notes on "Camp"', in *A Susan Sontag Reader* (New York: Farrar, Straus, Giroux, 1982), pp. 106, 109.
123. Robert Miles, 'Ann Radcliffe and Matthew Lewis', in D. Punter (ed.), *A New Companion to the Gothic* (Hoboken NJ: Wiley-Blackwell, 2011), p. 97.
124. William Hughes and Andrew Smith, 'Introduction: Queering the Gothic', in W. Hughes and A. Smith (eds), *Queering the Gothic* (Manchester: Manchester University Press, 2009), p. 3.
125. Kevin J. Mumford, *Not Straight, Not White: Black Gay Men from the March on Washington to the AIDS Crisis* (Chapel Hill NC: The University of North Carolina Press, 2016), p. 71.
126. Mumford, *Not Straight, Not White*, p. 71.
127. Yvonne D. Sims, *Women of Blaxploitation: How the Black Action Film Heroine Changed American Popular Culture* (Jefferson NC: McFarland & Co., 2006), p. 43.
128. Martinez, Martinez and Chavez, *What It Is … What It Was!*, p. 42.
129. Amy Abugo Ongiri, *Spectacular Blackness: The Cultural Politics of the Black Power Movement and the Search for a Black Aesthetic* (Charlottesville VA: University of Virginia Press, 2010), p. 168.
130. Harry M. Benshoff, 'Blaxploitation Horror Films: Generic Reappropriation or Reinscription?', *Cinema Journal*, 39/2 (2000), 32.
131. Brooks E. Hefner argues that in *Blacula* queer men and African Americans form a 'coalition of the oppressed'. See 'Rethinking *Blacula*: Ideological

Critique at the Intersection of Genres', *The Journal of Popular Film and Television*, 40/2 (2012), 64–6.
132. See Karen Stollznow, *On the Offensive: Prejudice in Language Past and Present* (Cambridge: Cambridge University Press, 2020), p. 24.
133. For an analysis of the music in *Blacula* and *Ganja & Hess*, see Morgan Woolsey, 'Hearing and Feeling the Black Vampire: Queer Affects in the Film Soundtrack', *Current Musicology*, 106 (2020), 9–26.
134. While Leerom Medovoi also sees a connection between queer men and sexually transgressive women in *Blacula*, he claims that Bobby 'comes to embody the loss of African pride and a degeneration into modern sexual decadence', and that 'Blacula's subsequent victims, an uppity woman taxi-driver and a promiscuously dressed woman photographer, also seem associated with a sexually coded post-slavery loss of black male honour that must be avenged'. See 'Theorizing Historicity, or the Many Meanings of *Blacula*', *Screen*, 39/1 (1998), 7–8.
135. See Curtis J. Austin and Elbert 'Big Man' Howard, *Up Against the Wall: Violence in the Making and Unmaking of the Black Panther Party* (Fayetteville AR: University of Arkansas Press, 2006), pp. 253–4, 258. See also Orissa Arend, *Showdown in Desire: The Black Panthers Take a Stand in New Orleans* (Fayetteville AR: University of Arkansas Press, 2009), pp. 29–38.
136. See John D'Emilio, *Sexual Politics, Sexual Communities: The Making of a Homosexual Minority in the United States, 1940–1970*, 2nd edn (Chicago IL: University of Chicago Press, 1998), pp. 141, 230–1. See also Marc Stein, *Rethinking the Gay and Lesbian Movement* (New York: Routledge, 2012), p. 102.
137. See Anna Lvovsky, 'Cruising in Plain View: Clandestine Surveillance and the Unique Insights of Antihomosexual Policing', *Journal of Urban History*, 46/5 (2020), 980–1001.
138. Seth Dowland, *Family Values and the Rise of the Christian Right* (Philadelphia PA: University of Pennsylvania Press, 2015), p. 161.
139. Discussing this exchange, Joe Wlodarz observes that it 'points to white anxieties about the expansion of gay *and* black visibility in the 1970s' (italics in original). See 'Beyond the Black Macho: Queer Blaxploitation', *The Velvet Light Trap*, 53 (2004), 15.
140. Lee Edelman, *Homographesis: Essays in Gay Literary and Cultural Theory* (New York: Routledge, 1994), p. 87.
141. Daniel HoSang and Joseph E. Lowndes, *Producers, Parasites, Patriots: Race and the New Right-Wing Politics of Precarity* (Minneapolis MN: The University of Minnesota Press, 2019), p. 27.

142. Valerie Rohy, *Lost Causes: Narrative, Etiology, and Queer Theory* (New York: Oxford University Press, 2015), pp. 2, 31.
143. Leigh W. Rutledge, *The Gay Decades: From Stonewall to the Present: The People and Events That Shaped Gay Lives* (New York: Plume, 1992), p. 103.
144. Jennifer Nelson, *Women of Color and the Reproductive Rights Movement* (New York: New York University Press, 2003), p. 92.
145. Nelson, *Women of Color*, p. 4.
146. Nelson, *Women of Color*, p. 19.
147. See Bill Stanford Pincheon, 'Mask Maker, Mask Maker: The Black Gay Subject in 1970s Popular Culture', *Sexuality & Culture*, 5/1 (2001), 54.
148. A sense of 'powerful black masculinity [was] associated with the hustler/pimp', and Blaxploitation films promoted the 'glamorization of the black urban pimp or mack's masculine persona'. See Stephane Dunn, *'Baad Bitches' and Sassy Supermamas: Black Power Action Films* (Urbana IL: University of Illinois Press, 2008), pp. 98, 2.
149. In the 1960s and 1970s, 'the Afro or natural style came to symbolize collective identities rooted in Black Pride'. See Ashley R. Garrin and Sara B. Marcketti, 'The Impact of Hair on African American Women's Collective Identity Formation', *Clothing and Textiles Research Journal*, 36/2 (2018), 107.
150. For other perspectives on *Ganja & Hess*, see Harrison M. J. Sherrod, 'The Blood of the Thing (Is the Truth of the Thing): Viral Pathogens and Uncanny Ontologies in *Ganja and Hess*', in L. Novotny and G. R. Butters Jr (eds), *Beyond Blaxploitation* (Detroit MI: Wayne State University Press, 2016), pp. 102–13; Maisha Wester, 'Re-Scripting Blaxploitation Horror: *Ganja and Hess* and the Gothic Mode', in J. Edwards and J. Höglund (eds), *B-Movie Gothic* (Edinburgh: Edinburgh University Press, 2017), pp. 32–49; Christopher Sieving, *Pleading the Blood: Bill Gunn's* Ganja & Hess (Bloomington IN: Indiana University Press, 2022).
151. See Manthia Diawara and Phyllis R. Klotman, '*Ganja and Hess*: Vampires, Sex, and Addictions', *Black American Literature Forum*, 25/2 (1991), 299–314.
152. Diawara and Klotman, '*Ganja and Hess*', 307.
153. Diawara and Klotman, '*Ganja and Hess*', 314.
154. Albert J. Raboteau, *African-American Religion* (New York: Oxford University Press, 1999), p. 120.
155. Mark L. Chapman, *Christianity on Trial: African-American Religious Thought Before and After Black Power* (Eugene OR: Wipf and Stock Publishers, 1996), p. 70.
156. James H. Cone, *Black Theology and Black Power* (Maryknoll NY: Orbis Books, 1969 (2018)), p. 61.

157. Cone, *Black Theology*, p. 62. Italics in original.
158. Chapman, *Christianity on Trial*, p. 97.
159. Chapman, *Christianity on Trial*, p. 98.
160. Chapman, *Christianity on Trial*, p. 98.

2 Making Monsters: Frankenstein's Creature

1. Mary Wollstonecraft Shelley, *Frankenstein; or, The Modern Prometheus*, eds. D. L. Macdonald and Kathleen Scherf, 3rd edn (Peterborough ON: Broadview Press, 2012), p. 81.
2. Shelley, *Frankenstein*, p. 80.
3. Shelley, *Frankenstein*, p. 136.
4. See Scarlett Higgins, *Collage and Literature: The Persistence of Vision* (New York: Routledge, 2019), pp. 5–9.
5. Dennis R. Perry, 'The Recombinant Mystery of Frankenstein: Experiments in Film Adaptation', in T. M. Leitch (ed.), *The Oxford Handbook of Adaptation Studies* (Oxford: Oxford University Press, 2017), p. 138.
6. Shelley, *Frankenstein*, p. 83.
7. Scarlett Higgins, *Collage and Literature*, p. 3.
8. David Ketterer provides an overview of this topic in 'The Doppelgänger Theme', a section of his essay entitled 'Thematic Anatomy: Intrinsic Structures', in H. Bloom (ed.), *Frankenstein* (Philadelphia PA: Chelsea House, 2004), pp. 33–54. See pp. 44–53.
9. Perry, 'The Recombinant Mystery of Frankenstein', p. 139.
10. Shelley, *Frankenstein*, p. 84.
11. Shelley, *Frankenstein*, p. 83.
12. Shelley, *Frankenstein*, p. 144.
13. Shelley, *Frankenstein*, p. 100. The Creature is 'manifestly a product, or aspect, of his maker's psyche'. See Christopher Small, *Mary Shelley's* Frankenstein: *Tracing the Myth* (Pittsburgh PA: University of Pittsburgh Press, 1973), p. 214.
14. Shelley, *Frankenstein*, p. 80.
15. Shelley, *Frankenstein*, p. 81.
16. Shelley, *Frankenstein*, pp. 143, 158.
17. Shelley, *Frankenstein*, pp. 156, 175.
18. Shelley, *Frankenstein*, p. 119.
19. Shelley, *Frankenstein*, p. 99. Italics in original.
20. Shelley, *Frankenstein*, p. 107.
21. Shelley, *Frankenstein*, p. 96.

22. Shelley, *Frankenstein*, p. 109.
23. Shelley, *Frankenstein*, p. 183.
24. Shelley, *Frankenstein*, p. 171.
25. Shelley, *Frankenstein*, p. 108.
26. Shelley, *Frankenstein*, p. 103.
27. Shelley, *Frankenstein*, p. 201.
28. Shelley, *Frankenstein*, p. 201.
29. Shelley, *Frankenstein*, p. 220.
30. Shelley, *Frankenstein*, p. 152.
31. Shelley, *Frankenstein*, pp. 157, 159.
32. Shelley, *Frankenstein*, p. 22.
33. Balderston also adapted Hamilton Deane's *Dracula* (1924) for Broadway. For information about Webling's and Balderston's plays, see Steven Earl Forry, *Hideous Progenies: Dramatizations of* Frankenstein *from Mary Shelley to the Present* (Philadelphia PA: University of Pennsylvania Press, 1990), pp. 91–100.
34. For Milton as a father figure to male Romantic poets, see Harold Bloom, *The Anxiety of Influence: A Theory of Poetry* (Oxford: Oxford University Press, 1975). For how Mary Shelley and other women writers viewed him, see Sandra M. Gilbert and Susan Gubar, *The Madwoman in the Attic: The Woman Writer and the Nineteenth-Century Literary Imagination* (New Haven CT: Yale University Press, 1979).
35. Shelley, *Frankenstein*, p. 47.
36. Carl Laemmle Sr explained to journalists that his son produced *Dracula* and *Frankenstein* despite his own resistance to horror films. 'I said to Junior, "I don't believe in horror pictures. It's morbid. None of our officers are for [*Dracula*]. People don't want that sort of thing". Only Junior wanted it. Only Junior stood out for it.' See Jon Towlson, *The Turn to Gruesomeness in American Horror Films, 1931–1936* (Jefferson NC: McFarland & Co., 2016), p. 41.
37. William Shakespeare, *Richard III*, ed. Barbara A. Mowat and Paul Werstine (New York: Washington Square Press, 1996), i.1.30.
38. For Horace Walpole's analysis of the role played by comedic servants in Gothic fiction, see *The Castle of Otranto: A Gothic Story*, ed. Nick Groom (Oxford: Oxford University Press, 2014), pp. 10–12.
39. Sarah Tarlow and Emma Battell Lowman, *Harnessing the Power of the Criminal Corpse* (Basingstoke: Palgrave Macmillan, 2018), p. 6, *https://doi.org/10.1007/978-3-319-77908-9_3* (last accessed 12 January 2023).
40. Tarlow and Battell Lowman, p. 7. The Murder Act was a British law, and both Shelley's novel and Whale's film occur in Switzerland and Germany. The Act nevertheless informs the many iterations of *Frankenstein*.

41. See Susan Tyler Hitchcock, *Frankenstein: A Cultural History* (New York and London: W. W. Norton, 2007), pp. 158–9.
42. The opening intertitle for the sequel, *The Revenge of Frankenstein* (Terence Fisher, 1958), reads, 'In the year 1860, Baron Frankenstein was condemned to death for the brutal murders committed by the monster he had created'. This frame revises the plot of the original film, in which the Creature dissolves in a vat of acid and Frankenstein's story is met with disbelief.
43. Shelley, *Frankenstein*, p. 81.
44. See Tarlow and Battell Lowman, *Harnessing the Power of the Criminal Corpse*, pp. 16–18.
45. See Harvey Rachlin, *Scandals, Vandals, and da Vincis: A Gallery of Remarkable Art Tales* (New York: Penguin, 2007), pp. 66–7.
46. For a study of the relationship between the Anatomy Act and *Frankenstein*, see Tim Marshall, *Murdering to Dissect: Grave-robbing,* Frankenstein *and the Anatomy Literature* (Manchester: Manchester University Press, 1995).
47. Although the Murder and Anatomy Acts were British laws, and *The Curse of Frankenstein* is set in Switzerland, in 1860 both graverobbing and murdering to dissect were far less common across Europe than in the eighteenth century.
48. David Garland, *Peculiar Institution: America's Death Penalty in an Age of Abolition* (Cambridge MA: Belknap Press of Harvard University Press, 2010), p. 226.
49. See Michael J. Klarman, *From Jim Crow to Civil Rights: The Supreme Court and the Struggle for Racial Equality* (New York: Oxford University Press, 2004), pp. 117–18, 166–7. See also Michael L. Radelet, Hugo Adam Bedau and Constance E. Putnam, *In Spite of Innocence: Erroneous Convictions in Capital Cases* (Boston MA: Northeastern University Press, 1992), pp. 102–18.
50. Radelet, Bedau and Putnam, *In Spite of Innocence*, p. 326.
51. A related film about an incarcerated Black man who becomes a monster is *Welcome Home Brother Charles* (Jamaa Fanaka, 1975). Drawing on Blaxploitation, horror and parody to depict racist policing, together with fears of miscegenation and Black male potency, it tells the story of a man whose genitals are irradiated when a policeman attempts to castrate him. After his release from prison, empowered with a penis that can grow to enormous lengths and strangle his enemies, he takes revenge on those who wrongfully imprisoned him. See Jan-Christopher Horak, 'Tough Enough: Blaxploitation and the L.A. Rebellion', in A. N. Field, J. Horak and J. N. Stewart, *L.A. Rebellion: Creating a New Black Cinema* (Oakland CA: University of California Press, 2015), pp. 126–30.
52. See Susan Reverby, *Examining Tuskegee: The Infamous Syphilis Study and Its Legacy* (Chapel Hill NC: University of North Carolina Press, 2009).

53. Allen M. Hornblum, *Acres of Skin: Human Experiments at Holmesburg Prison: A Story of Abuse and Exploitation in the Name of Medical Science* (New York: Routledge, 1998), p. 37.
54. Harriet A. Washington, *Medical Apartheid: The Dark History of Medical Experimentation on Black Americans from Colonial Times to the Present* (New York: Anchor Books, 2008), p. 257.
55. Hornblum, *Acres of Skin*, p. 120.
56. Hornblum, *Acres of Skin*, pp. 172–4.
57. See Hornblum, *Acres of Skin*, pp. 64, 69, 122–4, and Washington, *Medical Apartheid*, pp. 262–3.
58. Washington, *Medical Apartheid*, p. 259.
59. Hornblum, *Acres of Skin*, p. 62.
60. James H. Jones, *Bad Blood: The Tuskegee Syphilis Experiment*, new edn (New York: Free Press, 1993), p. 196.
61. Hornblum, *Acres of Skin*, p. 27.
62. For a reading of this monster as a 'tragic mulatto', see Justin Ponder, '"We Are Joined Together Temporarily": The Tragic Mulatto, Fusion Monster in Lee Frost's *The Thing with Two Heads*', *Ethnic Studies Review*, 34/1 (2011), 135–55.
63. Stokely Carmichael, 'Black Power', in Richard W. Leeman and Bernard K. Duffy (eds), *The Will of a People: A Critical Anthology of Great African American Speeches* (Carbondale IL: Southern Illinois University Press, 2012), pp. 305, 308.
64. Carmichael, 'Black Power', pp. 308, 310.
65. Carmichael, 'Black Power', p. 310.
66. Elizabeth Young, *Black Frankenstein: The Making of an American Metaphor* (New York: New York University Press, 2008), p. 190.
67. See Howard L. Malchow, *Gothic Images of Race in Nineteenth-Century Britain* (Stanford CA: Stanford University Press, 1996), pp. 9–40.
68. Suzanne Gordon, *The Battle for Veterans' Healthcare: Dispatches from the Frontlines of Policy Making and Patient Care* (Ithaca NY: Cornell Publishing, 2017), p. 11.
69. Suzanne Gordon, *Wounds of War: How the VA Delivers Health, Healing, and Hope to the Nation's Veterans* (Ithaca NY: ILR Press, 2018), p. 27.
70. Ron Kovic, *Born on the Fourth of July: A True Story of Innocence Lost and Courage Found* (New York: Pocket Books, 1977), p. 130.
71. Gregory W. Mank, *The Very Witching Time of Night: Dark Alleys of Classic Horror Cinema* (Jefferson NC: McFarland & Company, 2014), p. 401.
72. As Elizabeth Young notes, 'The camera's sympathy is with Turner throughout the scene, as in several low-angle shots that emphasize the grotesquerie of the orderly's face'. See *Black Frankenstein*, p. 191. For Young's perceptive analysis of *Blackenstein*, see pp. 190–7.

73. The number of 'genitourinary injuries [involving] the external genitalia . . . rose remarkably during the Vietnam Conflict, owing to the prevalence of "booby-trap" land mine devices employed in that war'. See Cesare George, Luke G. Tedeschi and William G. Eckert, *Forensic Medicine: A Study in Trauma and Environmental Hazards* (Philadelphia PA: Saunders, 1977), p. 239.
74. Sigmund Freud, 'The Uncanny' (1919), in James Strachey (ed.), *The Standard Edition of the Complete Psychological Works of Sigmund Freud*, vol. 17 (London: Hogarth Press and the Institute of Psycho-Analysis, 1955 (1981)), p. 231.
75. Herman Graham III, *The Brothers' Vietnam War: Black Power, Manhood, and the Military Experience* (Gainesville FL: University Press of Florida, 2003), p. 45.
76. Whitney Young, 'When the Negroes in Vietnam Come Home', *Harper's Magazine*, 234 (1967), 63.
77. James E. Westheider, *Fighting on Two Fronts: African Americans and the Vietnam War* (New York: New York University Press, 1997), p. 85.
78. Jonathan F. Borus, 'The Reentry Transition of the Vietnam Veteran', *Armed Forces and Society*, 2/1 (1975), 105.
79. Peter G. Bourne, 'The Viet Nam Veteran', in *The Vietnam Veteran in Contemporary Society: Collected Materials Pertaining to the Young Veterans* (Washington DC: US Government Printing Office, 1972), p. 224.
80. James M. Fendrich, 'The Returning Black Vietnam-Era Veteran', *Social Service Review*, 46/1 (1972), 67.
81. Fendrich, 'The Returning Black Vietnam-Era Veteran', 60.
82. 'Veteran-Related Job Programs Detailed', *Commanders Digest*, 12/24 (1972), 14.
83. Young, *Black Frankenstein*, p. 197.
84. Bénédicte Boisseron, *Afro-Dog: Blackness and the Animal Question* (New York: Columbia University Press, 2018), p. ix.
85. Donald Bogle, *Toms, Coons, Mulattoes, Mammies, and Bucks: An Interpretive History of Blacks in American Films*, 4th edn (New York: Continuum, 2001), p. 13.

3 Beyond 'the animal within': Jekyll/Hyde and the Werewolf

1. Robert Louis Stevenson, *Strange Case of Dr Jekyll and Mr Hyde*, ed. Martin A. Danahay, 3rd edn (Peterborough ON: Broadview Press, 2015), p. 76.
2. Stevenson, *Strange Case*, p. 79.
3. For deconstructive approaches to *Jekyll and Hyde*, see Julian Wolfreys, *Deconstruction: Derrida* (Basingstoke: Palgrave Macmillan, 2006), pp. 73–5; and

Jodey Castricano, 'Much Ado about Handwriting: Countersigning with the Other Hand in Stevenson's *The Strange Case of Dr. Jekyll and Mr. Hyde*', *Romanticism on the Net*, 44 (2006), https://doi.org/10.7202/014001ar (last accessed 12 January 2023).
4. Jacques Derrida, *Specters of Marx: The State of the Debt, the Work of Mourning, and the New International*, trans. Peggy Kamuf (New York: Routledge, 1994).
5. Jacques Derrida, 'Foreword', in Nicolas Abraham and Maria Torok, *The Wolf Man's Magic Word: A Cryptonymy*, trans. Nicholas Rand (Minneapolis MN: University of Minnesota Press, 1986), p. xi.
6. Tilottama Rajan, 'Incorporations: The Gothic and Deconstruction', in J. E. Hogle and R. Miles (eds), *The Gothic and Theory: An Edinburgh Companion* (Edinburgh: Edinburgh University Press, 2020), p. 222. See also Carla Jodey Castricano, *Cryptomimesis: The Gothic and Jacques Derrida's Ghost Writing* (Montréal: McGill-Queen's University Press, 2001).
7. Stevenson, *Strange Case*, p. 76.
8. Adrian Parr (ed.), *The Deleuze Dictionary: Revised Edition* (Edinburgh: Edinburgh University Press, 2010), p. 181.
9. Stevenson, *Strange Case*, pp. 81–2, 89.
10. Stevenson, *Strange Case*, pp. 86, 89, 84.
11. Stevenson, *Strange Case*, pp. 36, 87.
12. Stevenson, *Strange Case*, p. 45.
13. Stevenson, *Strange Case*, p. 47.
14. Stevenson, *Strange Case*, p. 39.
15. Stevenson, *Strange Case*, pp. 33, 35.
16. Stevenson, *Strange Case*, pp. 60, 65, 67.
17. Stevenson, *Strange Case*, pp. 43, 75.
18. Stevenson, *Strange Case*, p. 46.
19. Stevenson, *Strange Case*, p. 82.
20. Stevenson, *Strange Case*, pp. 71, 89.
21. Stevenson, *Strange Case*, p. 89.
22. Stevenson, *Strange Case*, p. 74.
23. Stevenson, *Strange Case*, pp. 39, 40, 55.
24. Stevenson, *Strange Case*, p. 39.
25. Stevenson, *Strange Case*, p. 55.
26. Stevenson, *Strange Case*, p. 39.
27. Gilles Deleuze and Félix Guattari, *A Thousand Plateaus: Capitalism and Schizophrenia*, trans. Brian Massumi (Minneapolis MN: University of Minneapolis Press, 1987), p. 36.
28. Stevenson, *Strange Case*, p. 50.

29. Stevenson, *Strange Case*, p. 49.
30. Stevenson, *Strange Case*, p. 36.
31. Stevenson, *Strange Case*, p. 38.
32. Stevenson, *Strange Case*, p. 41.
33. Stevenson, *Strange Case*, p. 33.
34. Stevenson, *Strange Case*, p. 85.
35. Stevenson, *Strange Case*, p. 57.
36. Stevenson, *Strange Case*, p. 41.
37. Stevenson, *Strange Case*, p. 74.
38. Stevenson, *Strange Case*, p. 75.
39. Stevenson, *Strange Case*, p. 74.
40. Stevenson, *Strange Case*, p. 33.
41. Stevenson, *Strange Case*, p. 34.
42. Stevenson, *Strange Case*, p. 88.
43. Daphne Brooks, *Bodies in Dissent: Spectacular Performances of Race and Freedom, 1850–1910* (Durham NC: Duke University Press, 2006), p. 58.
44. Brooks, *Bodies in Dissent*, p. 57.
45. Brooks, *Bodies in Dissent*, p. 61.
46. Brooks, *Bodies in Dissent*, p. 61.
47. Brooks, *Bodies in Dissent*, p. 61.
48. As Mamoulian himself observes, 'Mr. Hyde is a replica of the Neanderthal man'. See Thomas R. Atkins, 'An Interview with Rouben Mamoulian', in H. M. Geduld (ed.), *The Definitive Dr. Jekyll and Mr. Hyde Companion* (New York: Garland, 1983), p. 176.
49. Stevenson, *Strange Case*, p. 79.
50. Robertson captures both sides of Carew, making him a version of Lord Henry Wotton who first tempts Jekyll into wrongdoing and then threatens to punish him for his misdeeds.
51. See Elaine Showalter, *Sexual Anarchy: Gender and Culture at the Fin de Siècle* (New York: Penguin Books, 1990), p. 111.
52. Stevenson, *Strange Case*, p. 89.
53. Stevenson, *Strange Case*, p. 41.
54. Ivan Thomas Evans, *Cultures of Violence: Lynching and Racial Killing in South Africa and the American South* (Manchester: Manchester University Press, 2009), p. 34. Italics in original.
55. Virginia Wright Wexman, 'Horrors of the Body: Hollywood's Discourse on Beauty and Rouben Mamoulian's *Dr. Jekyll and Mr. Hyde*', in W. Veeder and G. Hirsch (eds), *Dr. Jekyll and Mr. Hyde After One Hundred Years* (Chicago

IL: University of Chicago Press, 1988), p. 289. Wexman argues that Hyde's killing is a symbolic lynching for his attempted rape of Muriel.
56. See Robert E. Conot, *Rivers of Blood, Years of Darkness* (New York: Bantam Books, 1968); and Gerald Horne, *Fire This Time: The Watts Uprising and the 1960s* (Charlottesville VA: University Press of Virginia, 1995).
57. Josh Sides, *L.A. City Limits: African American Los Angeles from the Great Depression to the Present* (Berkeley CA: University of California Press, 2003), pp. 135, 137.
58. Max Felker-Kantor, *Policing Los Angeles: Race, Resistance, and the Rise of the LAPD* (Chapel Hill NC: University of North Carolina Press, 2018), p. 2.
59. *Violence in the City: An End or a Beginning? A Report* (Los Angeles: [n. pub.], 1965), p. 27.
60. Randall Collins, *Sociology of Marriage and the Family: Gender, Love, and Property*, 2nd edn (Chicago IL: Nelson-Hall, 1988), p. 191.
61. *The Negro Family: The Case for National Action* (Washington: US Government Printing Office, 1965), pp. n.p., 30, n.p.
62. Kenneth Bancroft Clark, *Dark Ghetto: Dilemmas of Social Power*, 2nd edn (Middletown CT: Wesleyan University Press, 1989), p. 70.
63. Clark, *Dark Ghetto*, p. 70.
64. The National Advisory Commission on Civil Disorders, *The Kerner Report*, 2016 edn, Julian E. Zelizer (ed.) (Princeton NJ: Princeton University Press, 2016), p. 14.
65. The National Advisory Commission on Civil Disorders, *The Kerner Report*, p. 17.
66. The National Advisory Commission on Civil Disorders, *The Kerner Report*, p. 1.
67. Richard L. Ernst and Donald E. Yett, *Physician Location and Specialty Choice* (Ann Arbor MI: Health Administration Press, 1985), p. 64.
68. See Theodore Caplow, Louis Hicks and Ben J. Wattenberg, *The First Measured Century: An Illustrated Guide to Trends in America, 1900–2000* (Washington DC: AEI Press, 2001), p. 43. See also James L. Curtis, *Blacks, Medical Schools, and Society* (Ann Arbor MI: University of Michigan Press, 1971), p. 33.
69. Daniel Widener, *Black Arts West: Culture and Struggle in Postwar Los Angeles* (Durham NC: Duke University Press, 2010), pp. 222–3.
70. Jeffrey Ogbonna Green Ogbar, *Black Power: Radical Politics and African American Identity* (Baltimore MD: Johns Hopkins University Press, 2019), p. 2.
71. Sides, *L.A. City Limits*, p. 192.

72. David M. Grant, Melvin L. Oliver and Angela D. James, 'African Americans: Social and Economic Bifurcation', in R. Waldinger and M. Bozorgmehr (eds), *Ethnic Los Angeles* (New York: Russell Sage Foundation, 1996), p. 380.
73. Stevenson, *Strange Case*, p. 75.
74. See John C. Deshaies, *Social and Health Indicators System, Los Angeles* (Washington, DC: US Department of Commerce, Social and Economic Statistics Administration, Bureau of the Census, 1973), p. 22.
75. R. B. Baird, 'Shelter from the storm: the Los Angeles Free Clinic, 1967–1975' (unpublished PhD thesis, Arizona State University, 2016), i.
76. Cécile Whiting, *Pop L.A.: Art and the City in the 1960s* (Berkeley CA: University of California Press, 2006), p. 158.
77. See Cynthia Marie Erb, *Tracking King Kong: A Hollywood Icon in World Culture*, 2nd edn (Detroit MI: Wayne State University Press, 2009), p. 207.
78. Stevenson, *Strange Case*, p. 63.
79. James H. Jones, *Bad Blood: The Tuskegee Syphilis Experiment*, new edn (New York: Free Press, 1993), p. 12.
80. Shamim M. Baker, Otis W. Brawley and Leonard S. Marks, 'Effects of Untreated Syphilis in the Negro Male, 1932 to 1972: A Closure Comes to the Tuskegee Study, 2004', *Urology*, 65/6 (2005), 1259–60. For the reactions of some Black physicians to the Tuskegee Study, see Wilbur H. Watson, *Against the Odds: Blacks in the Profession of Medicine in the United States* (New Brunswick NJ: Transaction Publishers, 1999), pp. 144–5.
81. Baker, Brawley and Marks, 'Effects of Untreated Syphilis in the Negro Male', p. 1261.
82. Jones, *Bad Blood*, pp. 12, 13.
83. *The Negro Family* describes how boys without fathers at home are especially disadvantaged in terms of education, and at greater risk for delinquency, than those in two-parent families. See pp. 34–8. Clark likewise notes that 'Negro boys [have] the additional problem of finding no strong male father figure upon which to model their own behavior'. See *Dark Ghetto*, p. 70.
84. *The Negro Family*, p. 5.
85. Campbell, *Marked Women*, pp. 371–2.
86. Sterling A. Brown, 'The American Race Problem as Reflected in American Literature', *The Journal of Negro Education*, 8/3 (1939), 275.
87. Clark, *Dark Ghetto*, p. 64.
88. Clark, *Dark Ghetto*, p. 64.
89. John Storey, *Cultural Theory and Popular Culture: An Introduction*, 7th edn (Abingdon: Routledge, 2015), p. 132.

90. In keeping with its focus on transformation and multiplicity, the film's title changed from *Dr. Black and Mr. White* to *Dr. Black, Mr. Hyde* and *The Watts Monster*. See Ric Meyers, *For One Week Only: The World of Exploitation Films* (Guilford: Emery Books, 1983), p. 147.
91. Erb, *Tracking King Kong*, p. 206.
92. Marvin Edward McAllister, *Whiting Up: Whiteface Minstrels and Stage Europeans in African American Performance* (Chapel Hill NC: The University of North Carolina Press, 2011), pp. 8–9, 10.
93. William Van Deburg, *Black Camelot: African-American Culture Heroes in Their Times, 1960–1980* (Chicago IL: University of Chicago Press, 1997), pp. 8–9, 10. Robin R. Means Coleman also discusses 'scared comic-Negro roles'. See *Horror Noire: Blacks in American Horror Films from the 1890s to Present* (New York and London: Routledge, 2011), pp. 66, 82–4.
94. Joseph M. Flora, Lucinda Hardwick MacKethan and Todd W. Taylor (eds), *The Companion to Southern Literature: Themes, Genres, Places, People, Movements, and Motifs* (Baton Rouge LA: Louisiana State University Press, 2002), p. 305.
95. Flora, Hardwick MacKethan and Taylor, *The Companion to Southern Literature*, p. 305.
96. Flora, Hardwick MacKethan and Taylor, *The Companion to Southern Literature*, p. 306.
97. Sigmund Freud, 'The Uncanny' (1919), in James Strachey (ed.), *The Standard Edition of the Complete Psychological Works of Sigmund Freud*, vol. 17 (London: Hogarth Press and the Institute of Psycho-Analysis, 1955 (1981)), pp. 241, 247.
98. Herman Melville, *Moby-Dick*, ed. Tony Tanner (Oxford: Oxford University Press, 2020), pp. 171, 175.
99. Stevenson, *Strange Case*, p. 78.
100. See Patricia MacCormack, 'Unnatural Alliances', in C. Nigianni and M. Storr (eds), *Deleuze and Queer Theory* (Edinburgh: Edinburgh University Press, 2009), p. 136.
101. Rosi Braidotti, *Nomadic Subjects: Embodiment and Sexual Difference in Contemporary Feminist Theory*, 2nd edn (New York: Columbia University Press, 2011), p. 216.
102. Charles Waddell Chesnutt, 'What Is a White Man?', in Joseph R. McElrath, Robert C. Leitz and Jesse S. Crisler (eds), *Charles W. Chesnutt: Essays and Speeches* (Stanford CA: Stanford University Press, 1999), p. 68.
103. Chesnutt, 'The Future American: What the Race Is Likely to Become in the Process of Time', *Charles W. Chesnutt*, p. 122.

104. Chesnutt, 'The Future American', *Charles W. Chesnutt*, p. 125.
105. Nikos Papastergiadis, 'Tracing Hybridity in Theory', in P. Werbner and T. Modood (eds), *Debating Cultural Hybridity: Multicultural Identities and the Politics of Anti-Racism* (London: Zed Books, 2015), p. 259.
106. In films, this link is drawn most directly in *Daughter of Dr. Jekyll* (Edgar G. Ulmer, 1957) and *Dr. Jekyll y el Hombre Lobo* (León Klimovsky, 1972). In the former, both Jekyll and his daughter appear to be werewolves. The latter blends a werewolf and Hyde into a hybrid monster.
107. Howard L. Malchow, *Gothic Images of Race in Nineteenth-Century Britain* (Stanford CA: Stanford University Press, 1996), p. 183.
108. See Thomas E. Wartenberg, 'Humanizing the Beast: *King Kong* and the Representation of Black Male Sexuality', in Daniel Bernardi (ed.), *Classic Hollywood, Classic Whiteness* (Minneapolis MN: University of Minnesota Press, 2001), pp. 157–77.
109. Joshua Bloom and Waldo E. Martin, *Black Against Empire: The History and Politics of the Black Panther Party* (Oakland CA: University of California Press, 2016), p. 13.
110. Curtis J. Austin and Elbert 'Big Man' Howard, *Up Against the Wall: Violence in the Making and Unmaking of the Black Panther Party* (Fayetteville AR: University of Arkansas Press, 2006), p. 57.
111. Austin and Howard, *Up Against the Wall*, p. 93.
112. Austin and Howard, *Up Against the Wall*, p. 61.
113. Austin and Howard, *Up Against the Wall*, p. 61.
114. It makes sense that Newcliffe, a ruthless capitalist, omits 'their black berets, donned in honor of the much loved Argentine revolutionary Che Guevara'. See Austin and Howard, *Up Against the Wall*, p. 61.
115. Stokely Carmichael, 'Black Power', in Richard W. Leeman and Bernard K. Duffy (eds), *The Will of a People: A Critical Anthology of Great African American Speeches* (Carbondale IL: Southern Illinois University Press, 2012), p. 317.
116. Ward Churchill and Jim Vander Wall, *Agents of Repression: The FBI's Secret Wars Against the Black Panther Party and the American Indian Movement*, 2nd edn (Cambridge MA: South End Press, 2002), p. 39.
117. Churchill and Vander Wall, *Agents of Repression*, p. 47.
118. For a discussion of werewolves and subjectivity, see Carys Crossen, *The Nature of the Beast: Transformations of the Werewolf from the 1970s to the Twenty-First Century* (Cardiff: University of Wales Press, 2019), pp. 17–52.

4 Body and Soul: The Zombie and the Evil Spirit

1. William Seabrook, *The Magic Island* (Mineola NY: Dover, 1929 (2016)), p. 93.
2. See Roger Luckhurst, *Zombies: A Cultural History* (London: Reaktion Books, 2015), pp. 56–67.
3. See Per Faxneld, *Satanic Feminism: Lucifer as the Liberator of Woman in Nineteenth-Century Culture* (New York: Oxford University Press, 2017), p. 148. For the original source, see Ann B. Tracy, *The Gothic Novel 1790–1830: Plot Summaries and Index to Motifs* (Lexington KY: University Press of Kentucky, 1981), p. 203.
4. George A. Romero, 'Introduction', in Seabrook, *The Magic Island*, p. xix.
5. Paul Christopher Johnson, 'Introduction: Spirits and Things in the Making of the Afro-Atlantic World', in P. C. Johnson (ed.), *Spirited Things: The Work of 'Possession' in Afro-Atlantic Religions* (Chicago IL: University of Chicago Press, 2014), p. 44.
6. Paul Christopher Johnson, 'Toward an Atlantic Genealogy of "Spirit Possession"', in Johnson (ed.), *Spirited Things*, p. 4.
7. *Vodou* is the spiritual tradition practised in Haiti and elsewhere. *Voodoo* refers to how this tradition has been imagined in western texts. Likewise, while *zombi* signifies a Haitian term for a person raised from the dead to perform labour, *zombie* is associated with popular representations of this being. For a discussion of these distinctions, see Christopher M. Moreman and Cory James Rushton, 'Introduction: Race, Colonialism, and the Evolution of the "Zombie"', in C. M. Moreman and C. J. Rushton (eds), *Race, Oppression and the Zombie: Essays on Cross-Cultural Appropriations of the Caribbean Tradition* (Jefferson NC: McFarland & Co., 2011), pp. 2–4.
8. See Benjamin Hebblethwaite, *A Transatlantic History of Haitian Vodou: Rasin Figuier, Rasin Bwa Kayiman, and the Rada and Gede Rites* (Jackson MS: University Press of Mississippi, 2021).
9. Sarah Juliet Lauro, *The Transatlantic Zombie: Slavery, Rebellion, and Living Death* (New Brunswick NJ: Rutgers University Press, 2015), p. 7.
10. Sigmund Freud, 'The Uncanny' (1919), in James Strachey (ed.), *The Standard Edition of the Complete Psychological Works of Sigmund Freud*, vol. 17 (London: Hogarth Press and the Institute of Psycho-Analysis, 1955 (1981)), p. 234.
11. Freud, 'The Uncanny', pp. 246, 241.
12. Freud, 'The Uncanny', p. 227.
13. Jean-François Lyotard, *The Postmodern Condition: A Report on Knowledge*, trans. Geoffrey Bennington and Brian Massumi (Minneapolis MN: University of Minnesota Press, 1984), pp. x, xii, xix.

14. Leslie Gérald Desmangles, *The Faces of the Gods: Vodou and Roman Catholicism in Haiti* (Chapel Hill NC: The University of North Carolina Press, 1992), p. 3.
15. Jan Lundius and Mats Lundahl, *Peasants and Religion: A Socioeconomic Study of Dios Olivorio and the Palma Sola Movement in the Dominican Republic* (London: Routledge, 2000), p. 357.
16. Lundius and Lundahl, *Peasants and Religion*, p. 357, n. 185.
17. Joseph A. Brown, *To Stand on the Rock: Meditations on Black Catholic Identity* (Maryknoll NY: Orbis Books, 1998), p. 24.
18. Seabrook, *The Magic Island*, p. 67.
19. Carole Boyce Davies, *Encyclopedia of the African Diaspora: Origins, Experiences, and Culture* (Santa Barbara CA: ABC-CLIO, 2008), p. 821.
20. Stephane Dunn, *'Baad Bitches' and Sassy Supermamas: Black Power Action Films* (Urbana IL: University of Illinois Press, 2008), p. 2.
21. See Audre Lorde, 'The Master's Tools Will Never Dismantle the Master's House', in C. Moraga and G. Anzaldúa (eds), *This Bridge Called My Back: Writings by Radical Women of Color*, 4th edn (Albany NY: State University of New York Press, 2015), pp. 94–7.
22. John Vervaeke, Christopher Mastropietro and Filip Miscevic, *Zombies in Western Culture: A Twenty-First Century Crisis* (Cambridge: Open Book Publishers, 2017), p. 16.
23. Sherrie Almes, 'African Goddesses and Creole Voodoo', in T. Greenfield (ed.), *The Goddess in America: The Divine Feminine in Cultural Context* (Alresford: Moon Books, 2016), p. 69.
24. Hans Peter Oswald, *Vodoo: Der Zauber Haitis* (N.p.: Books on Demand, 2008), p. 25.
25. As Chera Kee notes, 'Andrew is a bit of an enigma', given his unusual role as the mixed-race protagonist of a Blaxploitation film. See *Not Your Average Zombie: Rehumanizing the Undead from Voodoo to Zombie Walks* (Austin TX: University of Texas Press, 2017), pp. 123–4.
26. Harry M. Benshoff, 'Blaxploitation Horror Films: Generic Reappropriation or Reinscription?', *Cinema Journal* 39/2 (2000), 48–9, n. 35.
27. See Mikel J. Koven, *Blaxploitation Films* (Harpenden: Pocket Essentials, 2001), p. 77.
28. Christopher J. Olsen and Carrie Lynn D. Reinhard, *Possessed Women, Haunted States: Cultural Tensions in Exorcism Cinema* (Lanham MD: Lexington Books, 2017), pp. 53, 54.
29. Benshoff, 'Blaxploitation Horror Films', 49, n. 200, 42.

30. Mikhail Bakhtin, *Rabelais and His World*, trans. Hélène Iswolsky (Bloomington IN: Indiana University Press, 1965 (1984)), p. 38.
31. Emanuel Bolaji Idowu, *Olodumare: God in Yoruba Belief* (London: Longman, 1962), p. 56.
32. Samuel Erivwo, 'The Worship of Ọghẹnẹ', in E. A. A. Adegbọla (ed.), *Traditional Religion in West Africa* (Ibadan: Daystar Press, 1983), p. 363.
33. In using this phrase, I recognise that 'although there is no monolithic "Black Church"', the term is 'a way to acknowledge the importance of institutions of organized religion to African Americans'. See Henry Louis Gates, T*he Black Church: This Is Our Story, This Is Our Song* (New York: Penguin, 2021), p. 1.
34. Miguel 'Willie' Ramos, *Obí Agbón: Lukumí Divination with Coconut* (N.p.: Eleda.org Publications, 2012), p. 125.
35. C. Eric Lincoln and Lawrence H. Mamiya, *The Black Church in the African American Experience* (Durham NC: Duke University Press, 1990), p. 275.
36. Bettye Collier-Thomas, *Jesus, Jobs, and Justice: African American Women and Religion* (New York: Knopf, 2010), p. 467.
37. Dennis C. Dickerson, *The African Methodist Episcopal Church: A History* (Cambridge: Cambridge University Press, 2020), p. 15.
38. Dickerson, *The African Methodist Episcopal Church*, p. 15.
39. Dickerson, *The African Methodist Episcopal Church*, p. 448.
40. Matthew J. Cressler, *Authentically Black and Truly Catholic: The Rise of Black Catholicism in the Great Migration* (New York: New York University Press, 2018), pp. 120, 131.
41. For Black theology and the AME Church, see Dickerson, *The African Methodist Episcopal Church*, pp. 468–72. For Black theology and the Catholic Church, see Cressler, *Authentically Black and Truly Catholic*, pp. 163–4.
42. James H. Cone, *Black Theology and Black Power* (Maryknoll NY: Orbis Books, 1969 (2018)), p. 62.
43. Frank A. Salamone, 'A Yoruba Healer as Syncretic Specialist: Herbalism, Rosicrucianism and the Babalawo', in S. M. Greenfield and A. F. Droogers (eds), *Reinventing Religions: Syncretism and Transformation in Africa and the Americas* (Lanham MD: Rowman & Littlefield, 2001), p. 47.
44. Cressler, *Authentically Black and Truly Catholic*, pp. 147, 139.
45. Jacquelyn Grant, 'Black Theology and the Black Woman', in J. Bobo, C. Hudley, and C. Michel (eds), *The Black Studies Reader* (New York: Routledge, 2004), pp. 422, 425.
46. Olóyè Àìná Ọlọmọ, 'Ṣàngó beyond Male and Female', in J. E. Tishken, T. Falola and A. Akínyẹmí (eds), *Ṣàngó in Africa and the African Diaspora* (Bloomington IN: Indiana University Press, 2009), p. 316.

47. Robert Plant Armstrong, 'Oshe Shango and the Dynamic of Doubling', *African Arts*, 16/2 (1983), 32, 30.
48. See Ọlọmọ, 'Ṣàngó beyond Male and Female', p. 316.
49. Carol J. Adams, *The Sexual Politics of Meat: A Feminist-Vegetarian Critical Theory* (New York: Bloomsbury Academic, 1990 (2015)), pp. 20, 40.
50. See Kobena Mercer, 'Black Hair/Style Politics', *New Formations*, 1/3 (1987), 37–40, 45–9.
51. Willie J. Harrell Jr, 'Mardi Gras Costumes and Masks', in O. L. Dyson, J. L. Jeffries and K. L. Brooks (eds), *African American Culture: An Encyclopedia of People, Traditions, and Customs* (Santa Barbara CA: Greenwood-ABC-CLIO, 2020), p. 615.
52. Eve Kosofsky Sedgwick, *The Coherence of Gothic Conventions* (New York: Methuen, 1986), p. 143.
53. Robert Louis Stevenson, *Strange Case of Dr Jekyll and Mr Hyde*, ed. Martin A. Danahay, 3rd edn (Peterborough ON: Broadview Press, 2015), p. 33.
54. Sigmund Freud, 'Beyond the Pleasure Principle' (1920), in James Strachey (ed.), *The Standard Edition of the Complete Psychological Works of Sigmund Freud*, vol. 18 (London: Hogarth Press and the Institute of Psycho-Analysis, 1955 (1981)), p. 35.
55. Benita Roth, *Separate Roads to Feminism: Black, Chicana, and White Feminist Movements in America's Second Wave* (Cambridge: Cambridge University Press, 2004), p. 86.
56. Roderick A. Ferguson, *Aberrations in Black: Toward a Queer of Color Critique* (Minneapolis MN: University of Minnesota Press, 2004), p. 246.
57. Michele Wallace, *Black Macho and the Myth of the Superwoman* (London: Verso, 1999), p. 12.
58. Wallace, *Black Macho*, p. 12. Italics in original.
59. Fran Sanders, 'Dear Black Man', in T. C. Bambara (ed.), T*he Black Woman: An Anthology* (New York: New American Library, 1970), p. 79.
60. Jean Carey Bond and Patricia Peery, 'Is the Black Male Castrated?', in T. C. Bambara (ed.), *The Black Woman*, pp. 113–18.
61. Bond and Peery, 'Is the Black Male Castrated?', p. 117.
62. The 1930s blues singer William Bunch, known as Peetie Wheatstraw and the inspiration for *Petey Wheatstraw*, may have drawn the name from a trickster figure in Black folklore. See Steven C. Tracy, 'The Devil's Son-In-Law and Invisible Man', *MELUS*, 15/3 (1988), 53–4.
63. Robert E. Hemenway, *Zora Neale Hurston: A Literary Biography* (Urbana IL: University of Illinois Press, 1980), pp. 223–4.
64. Zora Neale Hurston, *Mules and Men* (New York: Harper Perennial, 2008), p. 3.

Conclusion: The Legacy of the Blaxploitation Horror Film

1. Ed Guerrero, *Framing Blackness: The African American Image in Film* (Philadelphia PA: Temple University Press, 1993), pp. 70, 105.
2. Novotny Lawrence, *Blaxploitation Films of the 1970s: Blackness and Genre* (New York: Routledge, 2008), p. 96.
3. Lawrence, *Blaxploitation Films of the 1970s*, pp. 96–7.
4. Robin R. Means Coleman, *Horror Noire: Blacks in American Horror Films from the 1890s to Present* (New York and London: Routledge, 2011), p. 12.
5. Means Coleman, *Horror Noire*, p. 12.
6. John Reid, *Black America in the 1980s* (Washington DC: Population Reference Bureau, 1982), p. 7.
7. Reid, *Black America in the 1980s*, p. 7.
8. Reid, *Black America in the 1980s*, p. 8.
9. Seeking to quantify this phenomenon, Mark H. Harris concludes that the 'mortality rate' of Black characters is 'about 45%', and that in the *Friday the 13th* films, 'an astounding 16 out of 19 black characters die'. See 'The Black Death: A Brief History of Black People Dying in Horror Movies', *Black Horror Movies*, www.blackhorrormovies.com/blackdeath/ (last accessed 15 June 2022). The notion that in horror films Black characters not only die at a higher rate than white ones but also die first has become commonplace. Robin Means Coleman titles a chapter devoted to horror films of the 1980s, 'We Always Die First'. See Means Coleman, *Horror Noire*, pp. 145–68. Jordan Peele claims that 'the black guy is the first to die in every horror movie'. See Caity Weaver, 'Jordan Peele on a Real Horror Story: Being Black in America', *GQ*, 3 February 2017, www.gq.com/story/jordan-peele-get-out-interview (last accessed 20 June 2022). Peele overstates the case and overlooks films such as *Deep Blue Sea* (Renny Harlin, 1999) and *House on Haunted Hill* (William Malone, 1999), which by deliberately subverting the cliché reinforce its potency.
10. Jane Caputi, *Goddesses and Monsters: Women, Myth, Power, and Popular Culture* (Madison WI: University of Wisconsin Press/Popular Press, 2004), p. 318.
11. Caputi, *Goddesses and Monsters*, p. 67.
12. Giselle Liza Anatol, 'Narratives of Race and Gender: Black Vampires in U.S. Film', in D. Brode and L. Deyneka (eds), *Dracula's Daughters: The Female Vampire on Film* (Lanham MD: The Scarecrow Press, 2013), p. 210.
13. In addition to *Scream Blacula Scream*, Grier starred in *Coffy* (Jack Hill, 1973), *Foxy Brown* (Jack Hill, 1974), *Friday Foster* (Arthur Marks, 1975), *Bucktown* (Arthur Marks, 1975) and *Sheba, Baby* (William Girdler, 1975).

14. Angelique Jackson, '"Blacula" Reboot in the Works From MGM, Bron and Hidden Empire Film Group', *Variety*, 17 June 2021, https://variety.com/2021/film/news/blacula-reboot-deon-taylor-1234999358/ (last accessed 30 December 2021).
15. Films featuring Frankenstein's Creature include *Frankenstein Unbound* (Roger Corman, 1990), *Mary Shelley's Frankenstein* (Kenneth Branagh, 1994), *Van Helsing* (Stephen Sommers, 2004), *I, Frankenstein* (Stuart Beattie, 2014), *Victor Frankenstein* (Paul McGuigan, 2015) and *Frankenstein* (Bernard Rose, 2015). Those featuring Jekyll/Hyde include *Edge of Sanity* (Gérard Kikoïne, 1989), *Mary Reilly* (Stephen Frears, 1996), *The League of Extraordinary Gentlemen* (Stephen Norrington, 2003) and *Jekyll* (Scott Zakarin, 2007). One might argue for *The Nutty Professor* (Tom Shadyac, 1996), starring Eddie Murphy, as either an extremely loose adaptation or an appropriation of *Jekyll and Hyde*. It adapts the 1963 Jerry Lewis film of the same title, which original was inspired by Stevenson's novella.
16. Among the most noteworthy films about werewolves are *The Howling* (Joe Dante, 1981), *An American Werewolf in London* (John Landis, 1981), *Teen Wolf* (Rod Daniel, 1985), *Silver Bullet* (Dan Attias, 1985), *Wolf* (Mike Nichols, 1994), *Ginger Snaps* (John Fawcett, 2000), *Dog Soldiers* (Neil Marshall, 2002), *Cursed* (Wes Craven, 2005), *The Wolfman* (Joe Johnston, 2010) and *Red Riding Hood* (Catherine Hardwicke, 2011).
17. Joseph Conrad, *Notes on Life and Letters* (Garden City NY: Doubleday, 1923), p. 46.
18. See Caity Weaver, 'Jordan Peele on a Real Horror Story: Being Black in America', *GQ*, 3 February 2017, www.gq.com/story/jordan-peele-get-out-interview (last accessed 20 June 2022). See also Adam Lowenstein, 'Jordan Peele and Ira Levin Go to the Movies: The Black/Jewish Genealogy of Modern Horror's Minority Vocabulary', in D. Keetley (ed.), *Jordan Peele's Get Out: Political Horror* (Columbus OH: The Ohio State University Press, 2020), pp. 101–13.
19. Mary Wollstonecraft Shelley, *Frankenstein; or, The Modern Prometheus*, eds D. L. Macdonald and Kathleen Scherf, 3rd edn (Peterborough ON: Broadview Press, 2012), p. 136.
20. See Robert Louis Stevenson, *Strange Case of Dr Jekyll and Mr Hyde*, ed. Martin A. Danahay, 3rd edn (Peterborough ON: Broadview Press, 2015), pp. 34, 52, 54, 62, 63, 67, 68, 69, 70, 77, 78, 80, 81, 82, 86, 87, 89.
21. Since the release of *Get Out* in 2017, a number of notable horror movies featuring African Americans have appeared in theatres and on streaming services in the United States. Among the most recent is *Nope* (Jordan Peele, 2022). Other films include *Ma* (Tate Taylor, 2019), *Sweetheart* (J. D. Dillard,

2019), *Antebellum* (Gerard Bush and Christopher Renz, 2020), *Black Box* (Emmanuel Osei-Kuffour Jr, 2020), *Bad Hair* (Justin Simien, 2020), *Spell* (Mark Tonderai, 2020), *The Boy Behind the Door* (David Charbonier and Justin Powell, 2021), *Candyman* (Nia DaCosta, 2021), *Black as Night* (Maritte Lee Go, 2021), *Horror Noire* (Zandashé Brown, Robin Givens and Rob Greenlea, 2021), *Master* (Mariama Diallo, 2022) and *Day Shift* (J. J. Perry, 2022). In addition, the documentary *Horror Noire: A History of Black Horror* (Xavier Burgin, 2019) is available on Shudder, and the television series *Lovecraft Country* (2020) on HBO and *Them* (2021) on Amazon Prime. Upcoming films include remakes of *Blacula* and *Blade*. For the former, see Jackson, '"Blacula" Reboot in the Works'. For the latter, see Cooper Hood, 'Everything We Know So Far About MCU *Blade*', *Screenrant*, 25 June 2022, https://screenrant.com/blade-mcu-movie-cast-story-release-date (last accessed 28 June 2022).

22. Jesse Algeron Rhines, *Black Film, White Money* (New Brunswick NJ: Rutgers University Press, 1996), p. 45.
23. Toni Morrison, *Playing in the Dark: Whiteness and the Literary Imagination* (Cambridge MA: Harvard University Press, 1992), p. 38.
24. See D. Keetley (ed.), *Jordan Peele's Get Out*; Aviva Briefel, 'Live Burial: The Deep Intertextuality of Jordan Peele's *Get Out*', *Narrative*, 29/3 (2021), 297–320; M. Keith Booker, and Isra Daraiseh, 'Lost in the Funhouse: Allegorical Horror and Cognitive Mapping in Jordan Peele's *Us*', *Horror Studies*, 12/1 (2021), 119–31; Alison Landsberg, 'Horror Vérité: Politics and History in Jordan Peele's *Get Out* (2017)', *Continuum*, 32/5 (2018), 629–42; Kevin Wynter, *Critical Race Theory and Jordan Peele's* Get Out (New York: Bloomsbury, 2022). In addition, the latest issue of *Black Camera* features essays on contemporary Black horror films. See *Black Camera: The New Series*, 14/2 (2023), 243–363, especially Delphine Letort, '*Get Out* from the Horrors of Slavery', 295–307; Catherine Zimmer, 'The Work of Horror after *Get Out*', 308–18; Lauren McLeod Cramer and Catherine Zimmer, 'Dossier: Spectacles of Anti-Black Violence and Contemporary Black Horror', 319–63. Finally, see Robin R. Means Coleman and Mark H. Harris, *The Black Guy Dies First: Black Horror Cinema from Fodder to Oscar* (New York: Saga Press, 2023).

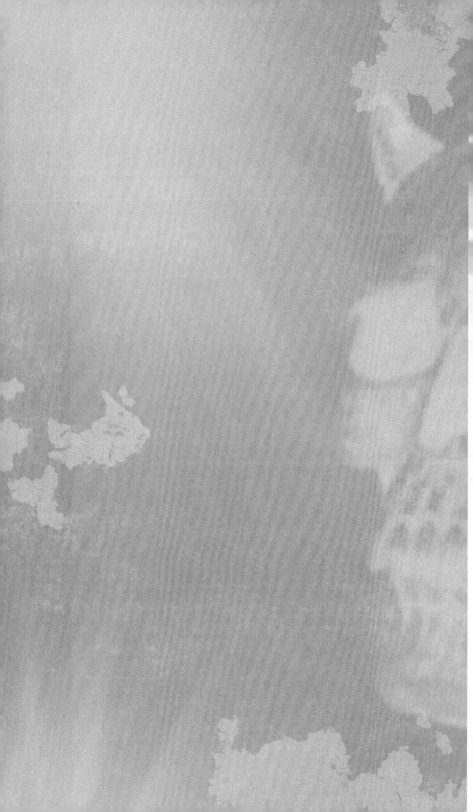

Bibliography

Adams, Carol J., *The Sexual Politics of Meat: A Feminist-Vegetarian Critical Theory* (New York: Bloomsbury Academic, 1990 (2015)).
Aldana Reyes, Xavier, *Gothic Cinema* (London and New York: Routledge, 2020).
Almes, Sherrie, 'African Goddesses and Creole Voodoo', in T. Greenfield (ed.), *The Goddess in America: The Divine Feminine in Cultural Context* (Alresford: Moon Books, 2016), pp. 65–72.
Anatol, Giselle Liza, 'Narratives of Race and Gender: Black Vampires in U.S. Film', in D. Brode and L. Deyneka (eds), *Dracula's Daughters: The Female Vampire on Film* (Lanham MD: The Scarecrow Press, 2013), pp. 195–218.
Arata, Stephen, *Fictions of Loss in the Victorian* Fin de Siècle (Cambridge: Cambridge University Press, 1996).
Arend, Orissa, *Showdown in Desire: The Black Panthers Take a Stand in New Orleans* (Fayetteville AR: University of Arkansas Press, 2009).
Armstrong, Robert Plant, 'Oshe Shango and the Dynamic of Doubling', *African Arts*, 16/2 (1983), 28–33.
Atkins, Thomas R., 'An Interview with Rouben Mamoulian', in H. M. Geduld (ed.), *The Definitive Dr. Jekyll and Mr. Hyde Companion* (New York: Garland, 1983), pp. 174–82.
Austin, Curtis J., and Elbert 'Big Man' Howard, *Up Against the Wall: Violence in the Making and Unmaking of the Black Panther Party* (Fayetteville AR: University of Arkansas Press, 2006).
Baird, R. B., 'Shelter from the storm: the Los Angeles Free Clinic, 1967–1975' (unpublished PhD thesis, Arizona State University, 2016).

Baker, Shamim M., Otis W. Brawley and Leonard S. Marks, 'Effects of Untreated Syphilis in the Negro Male, 1932 to 1972: A Closure Comes to the Tuskegee Study, 2004', *Urology*, 65/6 (2005), 1259–60.

Bakhtin, Mikhail, *The Dialogic Imagination: Four Essays*, ed. Michael Holquist, trans. Caryl Emerson and Michael Holquist (Austin TX: University of Texas Press, 1981 (2008)).

— *Rabelais and His World*, trans. Hélène Iswolsky (Bloomington IN: Indiana University Press, 1965 (1984)).

Bauder, David, 'AP says it will capitalize Black but not white', *AP News*, 20 July 2020, *https://apnews.com/article/entertainment-cultures-race-and-ethnicity-us-news-ap-top-news-7e36c00c5af0436abc09e051261fff1f* (last accessed 20 June 2022).

Benshoff, Harry M., 'Blaxploitation Horror Films: Generic Reappropriation or Reinscription?', *Cinema Journal*, 39/2 (2000), 31–50.

— *Monsters in the Closet: Homosexuality and the Horror Film* (Manchester: Manchester University Press, 1997).

Bernhart, Walter, and Werner Wolf, *Framing Borders in Literature and Other Media* (Amsterdam: Rodopi, 2006).

Bersani, Leo, 'Is the Rectum a Grave?', *October*, 43 (1987), 197–222.

The Bible: Authorized King James Version with Apocrypha, eds. R. Carroll and S. Prickett (Oxford: Oxford University Press, 1997).

Blinderman, Charles S., 'Vampurella: Darwin and Count Dracula', *The Massachusetts Review*, 21/2 (1980), 411–28.

Bloom, Harold, *The Anxiety of Influence: A Theory of Poetry* (Oxford: Oxford University Press, 1975).

Bloom, Joshua, and Waldo E. Martin, *Black Against Empire: The History and Politics of the Black Panther Party* (Oakland CA: University of California Press, 2016).

Bogle, Donald, *Toms, Coons, Mulattoes, Mammies, and Bucks: An Interpretive History of Blacks in American Films*, 4th edn (New York: Continuum, 2001).

Boisseron, Bénédicte, *Afro-Dog: Blackness and the Animal Question* (New York: Columbia University Press, 2018).

Bond, Jean Carey, and Patricia Peery, 'Is the Black Male Castrated?', in T. C. Bambara (ed.), *The Black Woman: An Anthology* (New York: New American Library, 1970), pp. 113–18.

Booker, M. Keith, and Isra Daraiseh, 'Lost in the Funhouse: Allegorical Horror and Cognitive Mapping in Jordan Peele's Us', *Horror Studies*, 12/1 (2021), 119–31.

Borus, Jonathan F., 'The Reentry Transition of the Vietnam Veteran', *Armed Forces and Society*, 2/1 (1975), 97–114.

Botting, Fred, *Gothic* (London and New York: Routledge, 1996).
Bourne, Peter G., 'The Viet Nam Veteran', in *The Vietnam Veteran in Contemporary Society: Collected Materials Pertaining to the Young Veterans* (Washington DC: US Government Printing Office, 1972), pp. 224–7.
Braidotti, Rosi, *Nomadic Subjects: Embodiment and Sexual Difference in Contemporary Feminist Theory*, 2nd edn (New York: Columbia University Press, 2011).
Briefel, Aviva, 'Live Burial: The Deep Intertextuality of Jordan Peele's *Get Out*', *Narrative*, 29/3 (2021), 297–320.
Brooks, Daphne, *Bodies in Dissent: Spectacular Performances of Race and Freedom, 1850–1910* (Durham NC: Duke University Press, 2006).
Brown, Joseph A., *To Stand on the Rock: Meditations on Black Catholic Identity* (Maryknoll NY: Orbis Books, 1998).
Brown, Sterling A., 'The American Race Problem as Reflected in American Literature', *The Journal of Negro Education*, 8/3 (1939), 275–90.
Bruce, Katherine McFarland, *Pride Parades: How a Parade Changed the World* (New York: New York University Press, 2016).
Caplow, Theodore, Louis Hicks and Ben J. Wattenberg, *The First Measured Century: An Illustrated Guide to Trends in America, 1900–2000* (Washington DC: AEI Press, 2001).
Caputi, Jane, *Goddesses and Monsters: Women, Myth, Power, and Popular Culture* (Madison WI: University of Wisconsin Press/Popular Press, 2004).
Carmichael, Stokely, 'Black Power', in Richard W. Leeman and Bernard K. Duffy (eds), *The Will of a People: A Critical Anthology of Great African American Speeches* (Carbondale IL: Southern Illinois University Press, 2012), pp. 304–19.
Carter, David, *Stonewall: The Riots That Sparked the Gay Revolution*, 2nd edn (New York: St Martin's Griffin, 2010).
Castricano, Jodey, *Cryptomimesis: The Gothic and Jacques Derrida's Ghost Writing* (Montréal: McGill-Queen's University Press, 2001).
— 'Much Ado about Handwriting: Countersigning with the Other Hand in Stevenson's *The Strange Case of Dr. Jekyll and Mr. Hyde*', *Romanticism on the Net*, 44 (2006), *https://doi.org/10.7202/014001ar* (last accessed 12 January 2023).
Chapman, Mark L., *Christianity on Trial: African-American Religious Thought Before and After Black Power* (Eugene OR: Wipf and Stock Publishers, 1996).
Chesnutt, Charles Waddell, 'The Future American: What the Race Is Likely to Become in the Process of Time', in Joseph R. McElrath, Robert C. Leitz and Jesse S. Crisler (eds), *Charles W. Chesnutt: Essays and Speeches* (Stanford CA: Stanford University Press, 1999), pp. 121–5.
— 'What Is a White Man?', *Charles W. Chesnutt*, pp. 68–73.

Churchill, Ward, and Jim Vander Wall, *Agents of Repression: The FBI's Secret Wars Against the Black Panther Party and the American Indian Movement*, 2nd edn (Cambridge MA: South End Press, 2002).

Clark, Kenneth Bancroft, *Dark Ghetto: Dilemmas of Social Power*, 2nd edn (Middletown CT: Wesleyan University Press, 1989).

Clarke, Cheryl, 'The Failure to Transform: Homophobia in the Black Community', in E. Brandt (ed.), *Dangerous Liaisons: Blacks, Gays, and the Struggle for Equality* (New York: The New Press, 1999), pp. 31–44.

Collier-Thomas, Bettye, *Jesus, Jobs, and Justice: African American Women and Religion* (New York: Knopf, 2010).

Collins, Randall, *Sociology of Marriage & the Family: Gender, Love, and Property*, 2nd edn (Chicago IL: Nelson-Hall, 1988).

Cone, James H., *Black Theology and Black Power* (Maryknoll NY: Orbis Books, 1969 (2018)).

Conot, Robert E., *Rivers of Blood, Years of Darkness* (New York: Bantam Books, 1968).

Conrad, Joseph, *Notes on Life and Letters* (Garden City NY: Doubleday, 1923).

Corrigan, Timothy, 'Defining Adaptation', in T. M. Leitch (ed.), *The Oxford Handbook of Adaptation Studies* (Oxford: Oxford University Press, 2017), pp. 23–35.

Craft, Christopher, '"Kiss Me with Those Red Lips": Gender and Inversion in Bram Stoker's *Dracula*', *Representations*, 8 (1984), 107–33.

Cramer, Lauren McLeod, and Catherine Zimmer, 'Dossier: Spectacles of Anti-Black Violence and Contemporary Black Horror', *Black Camera: The New Series*, 14/2 (2023), 319–63.

Cressler, Matthew J., *Authentically Black and Truly Catholic: The Rise of Black Catholicism in the Great Migration* (New York: New York University Press, 2018).

Crompton, Louis, *Byron and Greek Love: Homophobia in 19th-Century England* (Berkeley CA: University of California Press, 1985).

Crossen, Carys, *The Nature of the Beast: Transformations of the Werewolf from the 1970s to the Twenty-First Century* (Cardiff: University of Wales Press, 2019).

Crow, Charles L., *American Gothic* (Cardiff: University of Wales Press, 2009).

Curtis, James L., *Blacks, Medical Schools, and Society* (Ann Arbor MI: University of Michigan Press, 1971).

D'Arcy, Uriah Derick, *The Black Vampyre: A Legend of St. Domingo* (Edinburgh: Gothic World Literature Editions, 1819 (2020)).

Davies, Carole Boyce, *Encyclopedia of the African Diaspora: Origins, Experiences, and Culture* (Santa Barbara CA: ABC-CLIO, 2008).

Davies, Tom Adam, *Mainstreaming Black Power* (Oakland CA: University of California Press, 2017).

Deleuze, Gilles, and Félix Guattari, *A Thousand Plateaus: Capitalism and Schizophrenia*, trans. Brian Massumi (Minneapolis MN: University of Minneapolis Press, 1987).

D'Emilio, John, *Sexual Politics, Sexual Communities: The Making of a Homosexual Minority in the United States, 1940–1970*, 2nd edn (Chicago IL: University of Chicago Press, 1998).

Derrida, Jacques, 'Foreword', in Nicolas Abraham and Maria Torok, *The Wolf Man's Magic Word: A Cryptonymy*, trans. Nicholas Rand (Minneapolis MN: University of Minnesota Press, 1986), pp. xi–xlviii.

— *Specters of Marx: The State of the Debt, the Work of Mourning, and the New International*, trans. Peggy Kamuf (New York: Routledge, 1994).

Deshaies, John C., *Social and Health Indicators System, Los Angeles* (Washington DC: US Department of Commerce, Social and Economic Statistics Administration, Bureau of the Census, 1973).

Desmangles, Leslie Gérald, *The Faces of the Gods: Vodou and Roman Catholicism in Haiti* (Chapel Hill NC: University of North Carolina Press, 1992).

Diawara, Manthia, and Phyllis R. Klotman, '*Ganja and Hess*: Vampires, Sex, and Addictions', *Black American Literature Forum*, 25/2 (1991), 299–314.

Dickel, Simon, *Black/Gay: The Harlem Renaissance, the Protest Era, and Constructions of Black Gay Identity in the 1980s and 90s* (Münster: LIT Verlag, 2011).

Dickerson, Dennis C., *The African Methodist Episcopal Church: A History* (Cambridge: Cambridge University Press, 2020).

Donaldson, Stephen, and Wayne R. Dynes, *History of Homosexuality in Europe and America* (New York: Garland, 1992).

Dowland, Seth, *Family Values and the Rise of the Christian Right* (Philadelphia PA: University of Pennsylvania Press, 2015).

Downs, Jim, *Stand by Me: The Forgotten History of Gay Liberation* (New York: Basic Books, 2016).

Dunn, Stephane, *'Baad Bitches' and Sassy Supermamas: Black Power Action Films* (Urbana IL: University of Illinois Press, 2008).

Easthope, Anthony, *The Unconscious* (London: Routledge, 1999).

Edelman, Lee, *Homographesis: Essays in Gay Literary and Cultural Theory* (New York: Routledge, 1994).

Elliott, Kamilla, *Rethinking the Novel/Film Debate* (Cambridge: Cambridge University Press, 2003).

Epp, Charles R., *Making Rights Real: Activists, Bureaucrats, and the Creation of the Legalistic State* (Chicago IL: University of Chicago Press, 2010).

Erb, Cynthia Marie, *Tracking King Kong: A Hollywood Icon in World Culture*, 2nd edn (Detroit MI: Wayne State University Press, 2009).
Erivwo, Samuel, 'The Worship of Ọghẹnẹ', in E. A. A. Adegbọla (ed.), *Traditional Religion in West Africa* (Ibadan: Daystar Press, 1983), pp. 358–65.
Ernst, Richard L., and Donald E. Yett, *Physician Location and Specialty Choice* (Ann Arbor MI: Health Administration Press, 1985).
Evans, Ivan Thomas, *Cultures of Violence: Lynching and Racial Killing in South Africa and the American South* (Manchester: Manchester University Press, 2009).
Faderman, Lillian, and Stuart Timmons, *Gay L.A.: A History of Sexual Outlaws, Power Politics, and Lipstick Lesbians* (Berkeley CA: University of California Press, 2009).
Faxneld, Per, *Satanic Feminism: Lucifer as the Liberator of Woman in Nineteenth-Century Culture* (New York: Oxford University Press, 2017).
Felker-Kantor, Max, *Policing Los Angeles: Race, Resistance, and the Rise of the LAPD* (Chapel Hill NC: University of North Carolina Press, 2018).
Fendrich, James M., 'The Returning Black Vietnam-Era Veteran', *Social Service Review*, 46/1 (1972), 60–75.
Ferguson, Roderick A., *Aberrations in Black: Toward a Queer of Color Critique* (Minneapolis MN: University of Minnesota Press, 2004).
— *One-Dimensional Queer* (Cambridge: Polity Press, 2019).
Field, Allyson Nadia, Jan-Christopher Horak and Jacqueline Najuma Stewart, 'Introduction: Emancipating the Image: The L.A. Rebellion of Black Filmmakers', in A. N. Field, J. Horak and J. N. Stewart, *L.A. Rebellion: Creating a New Black Cinema* (Oakland CA: University of California Press, 2015), pp. 1–54.
Fincher, Max, *Queering Gothic in the Romantic Age: The Penetrating Eye* (Basingstoke: Palgrave Macmillan, 2007).
Flora, Joseph M., Lucinda Hardwick MacKethan and Todd W. Taylor (eds), *The Companion to Southern Literature: Themes, Genres, Places, People, Movements, and Motifs* (Baton Rouge LA: Louisiana State University Press, 2002).
Fontana, Ernest, 'Lombroso's Criminal Man and Stoker's *Dracula*', in Margaret L. Carter (ed.), *Dracula: The Vampire and the Critics* (Ann Arbor MI: UMI Research Press, 1988), pp. 159–65.
Forry, Steven Earl, *Hideous Progenies: Dramatizations of Frankenstein from Mary Shelley to the Present* (Philadelphia PA: University of Pennsylvania Press, 1990).
Foucault, Michel, *Power/Knowledge: Selected Interviews and Other Writings, 1972–1977*, ed. Colin Gordon, trans. Colin Gordon, Leo Marshall, John Mepham and Kate Soper (New York: Pantheon Books, 1980).

Freud, Sigmund, 'Beyond the Pleasure Principle' (1920), in J. Strachey (ed.), *The Standard Edition of the Complete Psychological Works of Sigmund Freud*, vol. 18 (London: Hogarth Press and the Institute of Psycho-Analysis, 1955 (1981)), pp. 35.
— 'Character and Anal Erotism' (1908), in J. Strachey (ed.), *The Standard Edition of the Complete Psychological Works of Sigmund Freud*, vol. 9 (London: Hogarth Press and the Institute of Psycho-Analysis, 1959 (1981)), pp. 167–76.
— *The Complete Letters of Sigmund Freud to Wilhelm Fliess, 1887–1904*, ed. J. Moussaief Masson (Cambridge MA: Belknap Press of Harvard University Press, 1985).
— 'The Interpretation of Dreams (First Part)' (1900), in J. Strachey (ed.), *The Standard Edition of the Complete Psychological Works of Sigmund Freud*, vol. 4 (London: Hogarth Press and the Institute of Psycho-Analysis, 1953 (1971)), pp. 1–338.
— 'Jokes and their Relation to the Unconscious' (1905), in J. Strachey (ed.), *The Standard Edition of the Complete Psychological Works of Sigmund Freud*, vol. 8 (London: Hogarth Press and the Institute of Psycho-Analysis, 1960 (1981)), pp. 9–236.
— 'Notes Upon a Case of Obsessional Neurosis' (1909), in J. Strachey (ed.), *The Standard Edition of the Complete Psychological Works of Sigmund Freud*, vol. 10 (London: Hogarth Press and the Institute of Psycho-Analysis, 1955 (1981)), pp. 155–249.
— 'Three Essays on the Theory of Sexuality' (1905), in J. Strachey (ed.), *The Standard Edition of the Complete Psychological Works of Sigmund Freud*, vol. 7 (London: Hogarth Press and the Institute of Psycho-Analysis, 1953 (1981)), pp. 135–243.
— 'The Uncanny' (1919), in J. Strachey (ed.), *The Standard Edition of the Complete Psychological Works of Sigmund Freud*, vol. 17 (London: Hogarth Press and the Institute of Psycho-Analysis, 1955 (1981)), pp. 219–52.
García Lorenzo, María M., 'The Unwhitening of Discourse: The Gothic in African-American Literature', in I. Soto and V. Showers, *Western Fictions, Black Realities: Meanings of Blackness and Modernities* (East Lansing MI: Michigan State University Press, 2012), pp. 47–60.
Garland, David, *Peculiar Institution: America's Death Penalty in an Age of Abolition* (Cambridge MA: Belknap Press of Harvard University Press, 2010).
Garrin, Ashley R., and Sara B. Marcketti, 'The Impact of Hair on African American Women's Collective Identity Formation', *Clothing and Textiles Research Journal*, 36/2 (2018), 104–18.

Gates, Henry Louis, *The Black Church: This Is Our Story, This Is Our Song* (New York: Penguin, 2021).
— *The Signifying Monkey: A Theory of Afro-American Literary Criticism* (New York: Oxford University Press, 1988).
Genette, Gérard, *Palimpsests: Literature in the Second Degree* (Lincoln NE: University of Nebraska Press, 1997).
George, Cesare, Luke G. Tedeschi and William G. Eckert, *Forensic Medicine: A Study in Trauma and Environmental Hazards* (Philadelphia PA: Saunders, 1977).
Gilbert, Sandra M., and Susan Gubar, *The Madwoman in the Attic: The Woman Writer and the Nineteenth-Century Literary Imagination* (New Haven CT: Yale University Press, 1979).
Glover, David, *Vampires, Mummies, and Liberals: Bram Stoker and the Politics of Popular Fiction* (Durham NC: Duke University Press, 1996).
Goddu, Teresa A., *Gothic America: Narrative, History, and Nation* (New York: Columbia University Press, 1997).
Goethe, Johann Wolfgang von, *Faust*, trans. Walter Kaufmann (New York: Anchor Books, 1961 (1990)).
Gordon, Suzanne, *The Battle for Veterans' Healthcare: Dispatches from the Frontlines of Policy Making and Patient Care* (Ithaca NY: Cornell Publishing, 2017).
— *Wounds of War: How the VA Delivers Health, Healing, and Hope to the Nation's Veterans* (Ithaca NY: ILR Press, 2018).
Graham III, Herman, *The Brothers' Vietnam War: Black Power, Manhood, and the Military Experience* (Gainesville FL: University Press of Florida, 2003).
Grant, David M., Melvin L. Oliver and Angela D. James, 'African Americans: Social and Economic Bifurcation', in R. Waldinger and M. Bozorgmehr (eds), *Ethnic Los Angeles* (New York: Russell Sage Foundation, 1996), pp. 379–412.
Grant, Jacquelyn, 'Black Theology and the Black Woman', in J. Bobo, C. Hudley and C. Michel (eds), *The Black Studies Reader* (New York: Routledge, 2004), pp. 421–33.
Greenslade, William M., *Degeneration, Culture, and the Novel, 1880–1940* (Cambridge: Cambridge University Press, 1994).
Griffin, Junius, 'Black Movie Boom – Good or Bad?', *The New York Times*, 17 December 1972, *www.proquest.com/historical-newspapers/article-1-no-title/docview/119532594/se-2?accountid=12073* (last accessed 18 June 2022).
Guerrero, Ed, *Framing Blackness: The African American Image in Film* (Philadelphia PA: Temple University Press, 1993).
Haefele-Thomas, Ardel, Thatcher Combs and Cameron Rains, *Introduction to Transgender Studies* (New York: Harrington Park Press, 2019).

Haggerty, George, *Men in Love: Masculinity and Sexuality in the Eighteenth Century* (New York: Columbia University Press, 1999).

Hanson, Ellis, 'Undead', in D. Fuss (ed.), *Inside/Out: Lesbian Theories, Gay Theories* (New York: Routledge, 1991), pp. 324–40.

Harrell Jr, Willie J., 'Mardi Gras Costumes and Masks', in O. L. Dyson, J. L. Jeffries and K. L. Brooks (eds), *African American Culture: An Encyclopedia of People, Traditions, and Customs* (Santa Barbara CA: Greenwood-ABC-CLIO, 2020), pp. 614–15.

Harris, Keith M., *Boys, Boyz, Bois: An Ethics of Black Masculinity in Film and Popular Media* (New York: Routledge, 2006).

Harris, Mark H., 'The Black Death: A Brief History of Black People Dying in Horror Movies', *Black Horror Movies*, *www.blackhorrormovies.com/blackdeath/* (last accessed 15 June 2022).

Hebblethwaite, Benjamin, *A Transatlantic History of Haitian Vodou: Rasin Figuier, Rasin Bwa Kayiman, and the Rada and Gede Rites* (Jackson MI: University Press of Mississippi, 2021).

Hefner, Brooks E., 'Rethinking *Blacula*: Ideological Critique at the Intersection of Genres', *The Journal of Popular Film and Television*, 40/2 (2012), 62–74.

Hemenway, Robert E., *Zora Neale Hurston: A Literary Biography* (Urbana IL: University of Illinois Press, 1980).

Higgins, Scarlett, *Collage and Literature: The Persistence of Vision* (New York: Routledge, 2019).

Hitchcock, Susan Tyler, *Frankenstein: A Cultural History* (New York and London: W. W. Norton, 2007).

Hood, Cooper, 'Everything We Know So Far About MCU Blade', *Screenrant*, 25 June 2022, *https://screenrant.com/blade-mcu-movie-cast-story-release-date* (last accessed 28 June 2022).

Horak, Jan-Christopher, 'Tough Enough: Blaxploitation and the L.A. Rebellion', in A. N. Field, J. Horak and J. N. Stewart, *L.A. Rebellion*, pp. 119–55.

Hornblum, Allen M., *Acres of Skin: Human Experiments at Holmesburg Prison: A Story of Abuse and Exploitation in the Name of Medical Science* (New York: Routledge, 1998).

Horne, Gerald, *Fire This Time: The Watts Uprising and the 1960s* (Charlottesville VA: University Press of Virginia, 1995).

HoSang, Daniel, and Joseph E. Lowndes, *Producers, Parasites, Patriots: Race and the New Right-Wing Politics of Precarity* (Minneapolis MN: The University of Minnesota Press, 2019).

Hughes, William, and Andrew Smith, 'Introduction: Queering the Gothic', in W. Hughes and A. Smith (eds), *Queering the Gothic* (Manchester: Manchester University Press, 2009), pp. 1–10.

Hurston, Zora Neale, *Mules and Men* (New York: Harper Perennial, 2008).
Hutcheon, Linda, *A Theory of Adaptation*, 2nd edn (London and New York: Routledge, 2013).
Hutchings, Peter, *The Horror Film* (London and New York: Routledge, 2004).
Idowu, Emanuel Bolaji, *Olodumare: God in Yoruba Belief* (London: Longman, 1962).
Jackson, Angelique, '"Blacula" Reboot in the Works From MGM, Bron and Hidden Empire Film Group', *Variety*, 17 June 2021, *https://variety.com/2021/film/news/blacula-reboot-deon-taylor-1234999358/* (last accessed 30 December 2021).
Johnson, Paul Christopher, 'Introduction: Spirits and Things in the Making of the Afro-Atlantic World', in P. C. Johnson (ed.), *Spirited Things: The Work of 'Possession' in Afro-Atlantic Religions* (Chicago IL: University of Chicago Press, 2014), pp. 1–22.
— 'Toward an Atlantic Genealogy of "Spirit Possession"', in P. C. Johnson (ed.), *Spirited Things*, pp. 23–46.
Jones, James H., *Bad Blood: The Tuskegee Syphilis Experiment*, new edn (New York: Free Press, 1993).
Joslin, Lyndon W., *Count Dracula Goes to the Movies: Stoker's Novel Adapted*, 3rd edn (Jefferson NC: McFarland & Co., 2017).
Kee, Chera, *Not Your Average Zombie: Rehumanizing the Undead from Voodoo to Zombie Walks* (Austin TX: University of Texas Press, 2017).
Keetley, Dawn (ed.), *Jordan Peele's Get Out: Political Horror* (Columbus OH: Ohio State University Press, 2020).
Ketterer, David, 'Thematic Anatomy: Intrinsic Structures', in H. Bloom (ed.), *Frankenstein* (Philadelphia PA: Chelsea House, 2004), pp. 33–54.
Kirkland, Ewan, *Videogames and the Gothic* (London and New York: Routledge, 2021).
Klarman, Michael J., *From Jim Crow to Civil Rights: The Supreme Court and the Struggle for Racial Equality* (New York: Oxford University Press, 2004).
Koven, Mikel J., *Blaxploitation Films* (Harpenden: Pocket Essentials, 2001).
Kovic, Ron, *Born on the Fourth of July: A True Story of Innocence Lost and Courage Found* (New York: Pocket Books, 1977).
Kramer, Eithne, and Peter Krämer, 'Blaxploitation', in M. Hammond and L. R. Williams (eds), *Contemporary American Cinema* (Maidenhead: Open University Press, 2006), pp. 184–98.
Kristeva, Julia, *Desire in Language: A Semiotic Approach to Literature and Art* (New York: Columbia University Press, 1980).
— *Powers of Horror: An Essay on Abjection*, trans. Leon S. Roudiez (New York:

Columbia University Press, 1982).
— 'Word, Dialog and Novel', in Toril Moi (ed.), *The Kristeva Reader* (New York: Columbia University Press, 1986), pp. 34–61.
Landsberg, Alison, 'Horror Vérité: Politics and History in Jordan Peele's *Get Out* (2017)', *Continuum*, 32/5 (2018), 629–42.
Lankester, E. Ray, *Degeneration: A Chapter in Darwinism* (London: Macmillan, 1880).
Lapin, Daniel, *The Vampire, Dracula and Incest* (San Francisco CA: Gargoyle Press, 1995).
Lauro, Sarah Juliet, *The Transatlantic Zombie: Slavery, Rebellion, and Living Death* (New Brunswick NJ: Rutgers University Press, 2015).
Lawrence, Novotny, *Blaxploitation Films of the 1970s: Blackness and Genre* (New York: Routledge, 2008).
— 'Fear of a Blaxploitation Monster: Blackness as Generic Revision in AIP's *Blacula*', *Film International*, 7/3 (2009), 14–27.
Leal, Amy, 'Unnameable Desires in Le Fanu's *Carmilla*', *Names*, 55/1 (2007), 37–52.
Le Fanu, Joseph Sheridan, *Carmilla: A Critical Edition*, ed. Kathleen Costello-Sullivan (Syracuse NY: Syracuse University Press, 2013).
Lehman, Paul R., and John Edgar Browning, 'The *Dracula* and the *Blacula* (1972) Cultural Revolution', in J. E. Browning and C. J. Picart (eds), *Draculas, Vampires, and Other Undead Forms: Essays on Gender, Race, and Culture* (Lanham MD: Scarecrow Press, 2009), pp. 19–36.
Lenhardt, Corinna, *Savage Horrors: The Intrinsic Raciality of the American Gothic* (Bielefeld: Transcript, 2020).
Letort, Delphine, 'Get Out from the Horrors of Slavery', *Black Camera: The New Series*, 14/2 (2023), 295–307.
Lincoln, C. Eric, and Lawrence H. Mamiya, *The Black Church in the African American Experience* (Durham NC: Duke University Press, 1990).
Lombroso, Cesare, *Criminal Man*, trans. Mary Gibson and Nicole Hahn Rafter (Durham NC: Duke University Press, 2006).
Long, Kathleen P., *Gender and Scientific Discourse in Early Modern Culture* (Farnham: Ashgate, 2010).
Lorde, Audre, 'The Master's Tools Will Never Dismantle the Master's House', in C. Moraga and G. Anzaldúa (eds), *This Bridge Called My Back: Writings by Radical Women of Color*, 4th edn (Albany NY: State University of New York Press, 2015), pp. 94–7.
Lowenstein, Adam, 'Jordan Peele and Ira Levin Go to the Movies: The Black/Jewish Genealogy of Modern Horror's Minority Vocabulary', in D. Keetley (ed.),

Jordan Peele's Get Out: Political Horror (Columbus OH: Ohio State University Press, 2020), pp. 101–13.

Luckhurst, Roger, *Zombies: A Cultural History* (London: Reaktion Books, 2015).

Lundius, Jan, and Mats Lundahl, *Peasants and Religion: A Socioeconomic Study of Dios Olivorio and the Palma Sola Movement in the Dominican Republic* (London: Routledge, 2000).

Lvovsky, Anna, 'Cruising in Plain View: Clandestine Surveillance and the Unique Insights of Antihomosexual Policing', *Journal of Urban History*, 46/5 (2020), 980–1001.

Lyotard, Jean-François, *The Postmodern Condition: A Report on Knowledge*, trans. Geoffrey Bennington and Brian Massumi (Minneapolis MN: University of Minnesota Press, 1984).

MacCarthy, Fiona, *Byron: Life and Legend* (New York: Farrar, Straus and Giroux, 2002).

MacCormack, Patricia, 'Unnatural Alliances', in C. Nigianni and M. Storr (eds), *Deleuze and Queer Theory* (Edinburgh: Edinburgh University Press, 2009).

Macdonald, D. L., *Poor Polidori: A Critical Biography of the Author of* The Vampyre (Toronto: University of Toronto Press, 2016).

Major, Adrienne Antrim, 'Other Love: Le Fanu's Carmilla as Lesbian Gothic', in R. Bienstock Anolik (ed.), *Horrifying Sex: Essays on Sexual Difference in Gothic Literature* (Jefferson NC: McFarland & Co., 2007), pp. 151–66.

Malchow, Howard L., *Gothic Images of Race in Nineteenth-Century Britain* (Stanford CA: Stanford University Press, 1996).

Mank, Gregory W., *The Very Witching Time of Night: Dark Alleys of Classic Horror Cinema* (Jefferson NC: McFarland & Company, 2014).

Marshall, Tim, *Murdering to Dissect: Grave-robbing, Frankenstein and the Anatomy Literature* (Manchester: Manchester University Press, 1995).

Martinez, Gerald, *Diana Martinez and Andres Chavez, What It Is ... What It Was! The Black Film Explosion of the '70s in Words and Pictures* (New York: Hyperion, 1998).

Massood, Paula J., *Black City Cinema: African American Urban Experiences in Film* (Philadelphia PA: Temple University Press, 2003).

McAllister, Marvin Edward, *Whiting Up: Whiteface Minstrels and Stage Europeans in African American Performance* (Chapel Hill NC: The University of North Carolina Press, 2011).

Means Coleman, Robin R., and Mark H. Harris, *The Black Guy Dies First: Black Horror Cinema from Fodder to Oscar* (New York: Saga Press, 2023).

— *Horror Noire: Blacks in American Horror Films from the 1890s to Present* (New York and London: Routledge, 2011).

Medovoi, Leerom, 'Theorizing Historicity, or the Many Meanings of *Blacula*', *Screen*, 39/1 (1998), 1–21.
Melville, Herman, *Moby-Dick*, ed. Tony Tanner (Oxford: Oxford University Press, 2020).
Mercer, Kobena, 'Black Hair/Style Politics', *New Formations*, 1/3 (1987), 33–54.
Meyers, Ric, *For One Week Only: The World of Exploitation Films* (Guilford: Emery Books, 1983).
Miles, Robert, 'Ann Radcliffe and Matthew Lewis', in D. Punter (ed.), *A New Companion to the Gothic* (Hoboken: Wiley-Blackwell, 2011), pp. 93–109.
Moreman, Christopher M., and Cory James Rushton, 'Introduction: Race, Colonialism, and the Evolution of the "Zombie"', in C. M. Moreman and C. J. Rushton (eds), *Race, Oppression and the Zombie: Essays on Cross-Cultural Appropriations of the Caribbean Tradition* (Jefferson NC: McFarland & Co., 2011), pp. 1–12.
Morrison, Toni, *Playing in the Dark: Whiteness and the Literary Imagination* (Cambridge MA: Harvard University Press, 1992).
Mumford, Kevin J., *Not Straight, Not White: Black Gay Men from the March on Washington to the AIDS Crisis* (Chapel Hill NC: The University of North Carolina Press, 2016).
Munby, Jonathan, 'Signifyin' Cinema: Rudy Ray Moore and the Quality of Badness', *Journal for Cultural Research*, 11/3 (2007), 203–19.
Murray, Simone, *The Adaptation Industry: The Cultural Economy of Contemporary Literary Adaptation* (New York: Routledge, 2012).
The National Advisory Commission on Civil Disorders, *The Kerner Report*, 2016 edn, ed. Julian E. Zelizer (Princeton NJ: Princeton University Press, 2016).
The Negro Family: The Case for National Action (Washington DC: US Government Printing Office, 1965).
Nelson, Jennifer, *Women of Color and the Reproductive Rights Movement* (New York: New York University Press, 2003).
Newton, Huey P., 'The Women's Liberation and Gay Liberation Movements: August 15, 1970', in D. Hilliard and D. Weise (eds), *The Huey P. Newton Reader* (New York: Seven Stories Press, 2002), pp. 157–9.
Nordau, Max, *Degeneration* (Lincoln NE: University of Nebraska Press, 1895 (1993)).
Ogbar, Jeffrey Ogbonna Green, *Black Power: Radical Politics and African American Identity* (Baltimore MD: Johns Hopkins University Press, 2019).
Ọlọmọ, Olóyè Àìná, 'Ṣàngó beyond Male and Female', in J. E. Tishken, T. Falola, and A. Akínyẹmí (eds), *Ṣàngó in Africa and the African Diaspora* (Bloomington IN: Indiana University Press, 2009), pp. 311–22.

Olson, Christopher J., and CarrieLynn D. Reinhard, *Possessed Women, Haunted States: Cultural Tensions in Exorcism Cinema* (Lanham MD: Lexington Books, 2017).

Ongiri, Amy Abugo, *Spectacular Blackness: The Cultural Politics of the Black Power Movement and the Search for a Black Aesthetic* (Charlottesville VA: University of Virginia Press, 2010).

Oswald, Hans Peter, *Vodoo: Der Zauber Haitis* (N.p.: Books on Demand, 2008).

Papastergiadis, Nikos, 'Tracing Hybridity in Theory', in P. Werbner and T. Modood (eds), *Debating Cultural Hybridity: Multicultural Identities and the Politics of Anti-Racism* (London: Zed Books, 2015), pp. 257–82.

Parker, Paula Jai, 'Paula Jai Parker and William Crain', *Horror Noire*: Uncut Podcast, 2020 *www.shudder.com/play/7bb2480e5670cdbd* (last accessed 30 June 2022).

Parr, Adrian (ed.), *The Deleuze Dictionary: Revised Edition* (Edinburgh: Edinburgh University Press, 2010).

Perry, Dennis R., 'The Recombinant Mystery of Frankenstein: Experiments in Film Adaptation', in T. M. Leitch (ed.), *The Oxford Handbook of Adaptation Studies* (Oxford: Oxford University Press, 2017), pp. 137–53.

Pick, Daniel, '"Terrors of the night": *Dracula* and "Degeneration" in the Late Nineteenth Century', *Critical Quarterly*, 30/4 (1988), 71–87.

Pincheon, Bill Stanford, 'Mask Maker, Mask Maker: The Black Gay Subject in 1970s Popular Culture', *Sexuality & Culture*, 5/1 (2001), 49–78.

Polidori, John William, *The Vampyre*, in R. Morrison and C. Baldick (eds), The Vampyre *and Other Tales of the Macabre* (Oxford: Oxford University Press, 2008), pp. 3–23.

Ponder, Justin, '"We Are Joined Together Temporarily": The Tragic Mulatto, Fusion Monster in Lee Frost's *The Thing with Two Heads*', *Ethnic Studies Review*, 34/1 (2011), 135–55.

Putnam, George P. (ed.), *Hand-book of Chronology and History: The World's Progress, a Dictionary of Dates: With Tabular Views of General History, and a Historical Chart*, 6th edn (New York: George P. Putnam, 1852).

Quinn, Eithne, *A Piece of the Action: Race and Labor in Post-Civil Rights Hollywood* (New York: Columbia University Press, 2019).

Rachlin, Harvey, *Scandals, Vandals, and da Vincis: A Gallery of Remarkable Art Tales* (New York: Penguin, 2007).

Raboteau, Albert J., *African-American Religion* (New York: Oxford University Press, 1999).

Radelet, Michael L., Hugo Adam Bedau and Constance E. Putnam, *In Spite of Innocence: Erroneous Convictions in Capital Cases* (Boston MA: Northeastern University Press, 1992).

Rajan, Tilottama, 'Incorporations: The Gothic and Deconstruction', in J. E. Hogle and R. Miles (eds), *The Gothic and Theory: An Edinburgh Companion* (Edinburgh: Edinburgh University Press, 2020), pp. 220–39.

Ramos, Miguel 'Willie', *Obí Agbón: Lukumí Divination with Coconut* (N.p.: Eleda. org Publications, 2012).

Reid, John, *Black America in the 1980s* (Washington DC: Population Reference Bureau, 1982).

Reverby, Susan, *Examining Tuskegee: The Infamous Syphilis Study and its Legacy* (Chapel Hill NC: University of North Carolina Press, 2009).

Rhines, Jesse Algeron, *Black Film, White Money* (New Brunswick NJ: Rutgers University Press, 1996).

Rohy, Valerie, *Lost Causes: Narrative, Etiology, and Queer Theory* (New York: Oxford University Press, 2015).

Romero, George A., 'Introduction', in William Seabrook, *The Magic Island* (Mineola NY: Dover, 1929 (2016)), pp. xv–xxiii.

Roth, Benita, *Separate Roads to Feminism: Black, Chicana, and White Feminist Movements in America's Second Wave* (Cambridge: Cambridge University Press, 2004).

Roth, Phyllis, 'Suddenly Sexual Women in Bram Stoker's *Dracula*', *Literature and Psychology*, 27 (1977), 113–21.

Rutledge, Leigh W., *The Gay Decades: From Stonewall to the Present: The People and Events That Shaped Gay Lives* (New York: Plume, 1992).

Salamone, Frank A., 'A Yoruba Healer as Syncretic Specialist: Herbalism, Rosicrucianism and the Babalawo', in S. M. Greenfield and A. F. Droogers (eds), *Reinventing Religions: Syncretism and Transformation in Africa and the Americas* (Lanham MD: Rowman & Littlefield, 2001), pp. 43–53.

Sanders, Fran, 'Dear Black Man', in T. C. Bambara (ed.), *The Black Woman: An Anthology* (New York: New American Library, 1970), pp. 73–9.

Sanders, Julie, *Adaptation and Appropriation* (London: Routledge, 2006).

Schneider, Steven Jay, 'Mixed Blood Couples: Monsters and Miscegenation in U. S. Horror Cinema', in R. B. Anolik and D. L. Howard (eds), *The Gothic Other: Racial and Social Constructions in the Literary Imagination* (Jefferson NC: McFarland & Co., 2004), pp. 72–89.

— 'Possessed By Soul: Generic (Dis)Continuity in the Blaxploitation Horror Film', in X. Mendik (ed.), *Necronomicon Presents Shocking Cinema of the Seventies* (Hereford: Noir Publishing, 2002), pp. 106–20.

Seabrook, William, *The Magic Island* (Mineola NY: Dover, 1929 (2016)).

Sedgwick, Eve Kosofsky, *Between Men: English Literature and Male Homosocial Desire* (New York: Columbia University Press, 2015).

—— *The Coherence of Gothic Conventions* (New York: Methuen, 1986).

Senf, Carol A., *The Vampire in Nineteenth-Century English Literature* (Bowling Green OH: Bowling Green State University Popular Press, 1988).

Scivally, Bruce, *Dracula FAQ: All That's Left to Know About the Count from Transylvania* (Milwaukee WI: Backbeat Books, 2015).

Shakespeare, William, *Richard III*, ed. Barbara A. Mowat and Paul Werstine (New York: Washington Square Press, 1996).

Shelley, Mary Wollstonecraft, *Frankenstein; or, The Modern Prometheus*, eds D. L. Macdonald and Kathleen Scherf, 3rd edn (Peterborough ON: Broadview Press, 2012).

Showalter, Elaine, *Sexual Anarchy: Gender and Culture at the* Fin de Siècle (New York: Penguin Books, 1990).

Sides, Josh, *L.A. City Limits: African American Los Angeles from the Great Depression to the Present* (Berkeley CA: University of California Press, 2003).

Sims, Yvonne D., *Women of Blaxploitation: How the Black Action Film Heroine Changed American Popular Culture* (Jefferson NC: McFarland & Co., 2006).

Skal, David J., *Hollywood Gothic: The Tangled Web of Dracula from Novel to Stage to Screen*, rev. edn (New York: Faber and Faber, 2004).

Small, Christopher, *Mary Shelley's Frankenstein: Tracing the Myth* (Pittsburgh PA: University of Pittsburgh Press, 1973).

Sontag, Susan, 'Notes on "Camp"', in *A Susan Sontag Reader* (New York: Farrar, Straus, Giroux, 1982), pp. 105–20.

Spencer, Kathleen L., 'Purity and Danger: *Dracula*, the Urban Gothic, and the Late Victorian Degeneracy Crisis', *ELH*, 59/1 (1992), 197–225.

Stein, Marc, *Rethinking the Gay and Lesbian Movement* (New York: Routledge, 2012).

Stevenson, Robert Louis, *Strange Case of Dr Jekyll and Mr Hyde*, ed. Martin A. Danahay, 3rd edn (Peterborough ON: Broadview Press, 2015).

Stewart, Chuck, *Lesbian, Gay, Bisexual, and Transgender Americans at Risk: Problems and Solutions* (Santa Barbara CA: Praeger, 2018).

Stewart-Winter, Timothy, 'Queer Law and Order: Sex, Criminality, and Policing in the Late Twentieth-Century United States', *The Journal of American History*, 102/1 (2015), 61–72.

Stoker, Bram, *Dracula*, ed. Roger Luckhurst (Oxford: Oxford University Press, 2020).

Stollznow, Karen, *On the Offensive: Prejudice in Language Past and Present* (Cambridge: Cambridge University Press, 2020).

Storey, John, *Cultural Theory and Popular Culture: An Introduction*, 7th edn (Abingdon: Routledge, 2015).

Tarlow, Sarah, and Emma Battell Lowman, *Harnessing the Power of the Criminal Corpse* (Basingstoke: Palgrave Macmillan, 2018), *https://doi.org/10.1007/978-3-319-77908-9_3* (last accessed 12 January 2023).

Thomas, Ardel, *Queer Others in Victorian Gothic: Transgressing Monstrosity* (Cardiff: University of Wales Press, 2012).

Towlson, Jon, *The Turn to Gruesomeness in American Horror Films, 1931–1936* (Jefferson NC: McFarland & Co., 2016).

Tracy, Ann B., *The Gothic Novel 1790–1830: Plot Summaries and Index to Motifs* (Lexington KY: University Press of Kentucky, 1981).

Tracy, Steven C., 'The Devil's Son-In-Law and Invisible Man', *MELUS*, 15/3 (1988), 47–64.

Van Deburg, William, *Black Camelot: African-American Culture Heroes in Their Times, 1960–1980* (Chicago IL: University of Chicago Press, 1997).

Veeder, William, 'Carmilla: The Arts of Repression', *Texas Studies in Literature and Language*, 22/2 (1980), 197–223.

Vervaeke, John, Christopher Mastropietro, and Filip Miscevic, *Zombies in Western Culture: A Twenty-First Century Crisis* (Cambridge: Open Book Publishers, 2017).

'Veteran-Related Job Programs Detailed', *Commanders Digest*, 12/24 (1972), 14.

Violence in the City: An End or a Beginning? A Report (Los Angeles: [n. pub.], 1965).

Wallace, Michele, *Black Macho and the Myth of the Superwoman* (London: Verso, 1999).

Walpole, Horace, *The Castle of Otranto: A Gothic Story*, ed. Nick Groom (Oxford: Oxford University Press, 2014).

Wartenberg, Thomas E., 'Humanizing the Beast: King Kong and the Representation of Black Male Sexuality', in Daniel Bernardi (ed.), *Classic Hollywood, Classic Whiteness* (Minneapolis MN: University of Minnesota Press, 2001), pp. 157–77.

Washington, Harriet A., *Medical Apartheid: The Dark History of Medical Experimentation on Black Americans from Colonial Times to the Present* (New York: Anchor Books, 2008).

Watson, Wilbur H., *Against the Odds: Blacks in the Profession of Medicine in the United States* (New Brunswick NJ: Transaction Publishers, 1999).

Weaver, Caity, 'Jordan Peele on a Real Horror Story: Being Black in America', *GQ*, 3 February 2017, *www.gq.com/story/jordan-peele-get-out-interview* (last accessed 20 June 2022).

Wester, Maisha, *African American Gothic: Screams from Shadowed Places* (New York: Palgrave Macmillan, 2012).

— 'Black Diasporic Gothic', in M. Wester and X. Aldana Reyes (eds), *Twenty-First-Century Gothic: An Edinburgh Companion* (Edinburgh: Edinburgh University Press, 2019), pp. 289–303.
— 'The Gothic in and as Race Theory', in J. E. Hogle and R. Miles (eds), *The Gothic and Theory: An Edinburgh Companion* (Edinburgh: Edinburgh University Press, 2019), pp. 53–70.
— 'Re-Scripting Blaxploitation Horror: *Ganja and Hess* and the Gothic Mode', in J. Edwards and J. Höglund (eds), *B-Movie Gothic* (Edinburgh: Edinburgh University Press, 2017), pp. 32–49.
Westheider, James E., *Fighting on Two Fronts: African Americans and the Vietnam War* (New York: New York University Press, 1997).
Wexman, Virginia Wright, 'Horrors of the Body: Hollywood's Discourse on Beauty and Rouben Mamoulian's *Dr. Jekyll and Mr. Hyde*', in W. Veeder and G. Hirsch (eds), *Dr. Jekyll and Mr. Hyde After One Hundred Years* (Chicago IL: University of Chicago Press, 1988), pp. 283–307.
Whiting, Cécile, *Pop L.A.: Art and the City in the 1960s* (Berkeley CA: University of California Press, 2006).
Widener, Daniel, *Black Arts West: Culture and Struggle in Postwar Los Angeles* (Durham NC: Duke University Press, 2010).
Wlodarz, Joe, 'Beyond the Black Macho: Queer Blaxploitation', *The Velvet Light Trap*, 53 (2004), 10–25.
Wolfreys, Julian, *Deconstruction: Derrida* (Basingstoke: Palgrave Macmillan, 2006).
Wood, Robin, *Hollywood from Vietnam to Reagan ... and Beyond*, rev. edn (New York: Columbia University Press, 2003).
Woods, Jordan Blair, 'The Birth of Modern Criminology and Gendered Constructions of Homosexual Criminal Identity', *Journal of Homosexuality*, 62/2 (2015), 131–66.
Woolsey, Morgan, 'Hearing and Feeling the Black Vampire: Queer Affects in the Film Soundtrack', *Current Musicology*, 106 (2020), 9–26.
Yearwood, Gladstone Lloyd, *Black Film as a Signifying Practice: Cinema, Narration and the African American Aesthetic Tradition* (Trenton: Africa World Press, 2000).
Young, Elizabeth, *Black Frankenstein: The Making of an American Metaphor* (New York: New York University Press, 2008).
Young, Whitney, 'When the Negroes in Vietnam Come Home', *Harper's Magazine*, 234 (1967), 63–9.
Zimmer, Catherine, 'The Work of Horror after *Get Out*', *Black Camera: The New Series*, 14/2 (2023), 308–18.

Filmography

Abby, dir. William Girdler (United States, 1974).
The Alchemist Cookbook, dir. Joel Potrykus (United States, 2016).
An American Werewolf in London, dir. John Landis (United Kingdom, United States, 1981).
Antebellum, dir. Gerard Bush and Christopher Renz (United States, 2020).
Bad Hair, dir. Justin Simien (United States, 2020).
The Beast Must Die, dir. Paul Annett (United Kingdom, 1974).
Bedazzled, dir. Stanley Donen (United Kingdom, 1967).
The Birth of a Nation, dir. D. W. Griffith (United States, 1915).
Black as Night, dir. Maritte Lee Go (United States, 2021).
Black Box, dir. Emmanuel Osei-Kuffour Jr (United States, 2020).
Black Devil Doll from Hell, dir. Chester Novell Turner (United States, 1984).
Black Panther, dir. Ryan Coogler (United States, 2018).
Blackenstein, dir. William A. Levey (United States, 1973).
Blacula, dir. William Crain (United States, 1972).
Blade, dir. Stephen Norrington (United States, 1998).
Blade II, dir. Guillermo del Toro (United States, 2002).
Blade: Trinity, dir. David S. Goyer (United States, 2004).
Bloodz vs. Wolvez, dir. John Bacchus (United States, 2006).
Bones, dir. Ernest Dickerson (United States, 2001).
The Bride of Frankenstein, dir. James Whale (United States, 1935).
Bucktown, dir. Arthur Marks (United States, 1975).
Candyman, dir. Nia DaCosta (United States, 2021).

Candyman, dir. Bernard Rose (United States, 1992).
Candyman: Day of the Dead, dir. Turi Meyer (United States, 1999).
Candyman: Farewell to the Flesh, dir. Bill Condon (United States, 1995).
Change of Mind, dir. Robert Stevens (United States, 1969).
Coffy, dir. Jack Hill (United States, 1973)
Cotton Comes to Harlem, dir. Ossie Davis (United States, 1970).
Cryptz, dir. Danny Draven (United States, 2002).
The Curse of Frankenstein, dir. Terence Fisher (United Kingdom, 1957).
The Curse of the Werewolf, dir. Terence Fisher (United Kingdom, 1961).
Cursed, dir. Wes Craven, (Germany, United States, 2005).
Da Sweet Blood of Jesus, dir. Spike Lee (United States, 2014).
Damn Yankees, dir. George Abbott and Stanley Donen (United States, 1958).
Daughter of Dr. Jekyll, dir. Edgar G. Ulmer (United States, 1957).
Day Shift, dir. J. J. Perry (United States, 2022).
Deathly Realities, dir. S. Torriano Berry (United States, 1985).
Def by Temptation, dir. James Bond III (United States, 1990).
Deep Blue Sea, dir. Renny Harlin (United States, 1999).
The Devil, dir. D. W. Griffith (United States, 1908).
The Devil Rides Out, dir. Terence Fisher (United Kingdom, 1968).
The Devil's Daughter, dir. Arthur H. Leonard (United States, 1939).
Dog Day Afternoon, dir. Sidney Lumet (United States, 1975).
Dog Soldiers, dir. Neil Marshall (United Kingdom, Luxembourg, 2002).
Dr. Black, Mr. Hyde, dir. William Crain (United States, 1976).
Dr. Jekyll and Mr. Hyde, dir. John S. Robertson (United States, 1920).
Dr. Jekyll and Mr. Hyde, dir. Rouben Mamoulian (United States, 1931).
Dr. Jekyll and Mr. Hyde, dir. Victor Fleming (United States, 1941).
Dr. Jekyll y el Hombre Lobo, dir. León Klimovsky (Spain, 1972).
Dracula, dir. Tod Browning (United States, 1931).
Edge of Sanity, dir. Gérard Kikoïne (United Kingdom, Hungary, 1989).
The Exorcist, dir. William Friedkin (United States, 1973).
Fallen, dir. Gregory Hoblit (United States, 1998).
Faust, dir. F. W. Murnau (Germany, 1926).
Foxy Brown, dir. Jack Hill (United States, 1974).
Frankenstein, dir. Bernard Rose (United States, Germany, 2015).
Frankenstein, dir. James Whale (United States, 1931).
Frankenstein Unbound, dir. Roger Corman (United States, 1990).
Friday Foster, dir. Arthur Marks (United States, 1975).
Friday the 13th, dir. Sean S. Cunningham (United States, 1980).
Ganja & Hess, dir. Bill Gunn (United States, 1973).

Get Out, dir. Jordan Peele (United States, 2017).
The Ghost Breakers, dir. George Marshall (United States, 1940).
The Ghost of Frankenstein, dir. Erle C. Kenton (United States, 1942).
Ginger Snaps, dir. John Fawcett (Canada, United States, 2000).
Halloween, dir. John Carpenter (United States, 1978).
A Haunted House, dir. Michael Tiddes (United States, 2013).
The Haunted Mansion, dir. Rob Minkoff (United States, 2003).
Hidden Figures, dir. Theodore Melfi (United States, 2016).
Hood of Horror, dir. Stacy Title (United States, 2006).
Hood of the Living Dead, dir. Eduardo Quiroz and Jose Quiroz (United States, 2005).
Horror Noire, dir. Zandashé Brown, Robin Givens and Rob Greenlea (United States, 2021).
Horror Noire: A History of Black Horror, dir. Xavier Burgin (United States, 2019).
Horror of Dracula, dir. Terence Fisher (United Kingdom, 1958).
The House Next Door: Meet the Blacks 2, dir. Deon Taylor (United States, 2021).
House on Haunted Hill, dir. William Malone (United States, 1999).
The House on Skull Mountain, dir. Ron Honthaner (United States, 1974).
The Howling, dir. Joe Dante (United States, 1981).
I Am Legend, dir. Francis Lawrence (United States, 2007).
I, Frankenstein, dir. Stuart Beattie (United States, Australia, 2014).
I Walked with a Zombie, dir. Jacques Tourneur (United States, 1943).
Jaws, dir. Steven Spielberg (United States, 1975).
J. D.'s Revenge, dir. Arthur Marks (United States, 1976).
Jekyll, dir. Scott Zakarin (United States, 2007).
King Kong (United States, 1932).
King of the Zombies, dir. Jean Yarbrough (United States, 1941).
The Last Man on Earth, dir. Ubaldo Ragona and Sidney Salkow (Italy, United States, 1964).
Le Manoir du Diable, dir. Georges Méliès (France, 1896).
The League of Extraordinary Gentlemen, dir. Stephen Norrington (United States, Germany, Czech Republic, United Kingdom, 2003).
Leaves from Satan's Book, dir. Carl Theodor Dreyer (Denmark, 1920).
Lord Shango, dir. Ray Marsh (United States, 1975).
Ma, dir. Tate Taylor (Japan, United States, 2019).
Mary Reilly, dir. Stephen Frears (United States, United Kingdom, 1996).
Mary Shelley's Frankenstein, dir. Kenneth Branagh (United States, Japan, United Kingdom, 1994).
Master, dir. Mariama Diallo (United States, 2022).

Mean Streets, dir. Martin Scorsese (United States, 1973).
Night of the Living Dead, dir. George A. Romero (United States, 1968).
A Nightmare on Elm Street, dir. Wes Craven (United States, 1984).
Nope, dir. Jordan Peele (United States, 2022).
Nosferatu, dir. F. W. Murnau (Germany, 1922).
The Nutty Professor, dir. Tom Shadyac (United States, 1996).
Obeah, dir. Hugh A. Robertson (United States, 1987).
The Omega Man, dir. Boris Sagal (United States, 1971).
Ouanga, dir. George Terwilliger (United States, 1936).
Petey Wheatstraw, dir. Cliff Roquemore (United States, 1977).
Red Riding Hood, dir. Catherine Hardwicke (United States, Canada, 2011).
Revolt of the Zombies, dir. Victor Halperin (United States, 1936).
Rocky, dir. John G. Avildsen (United States, 1976).
Rosemary's Baby, dir. Roman Polanski (United States, 1968).
RuPaul's Trilogy of Terror, dir. John Witherspoon (United States, 1984).
Satanas, dir. F. W. Murnau (Germany, 1920).
Saturday Night Fever, dir. John Badham (United States, 1977).
Scary Movie, dir. Keenen Ivory Wayans (United States, 2000).
Scream Blacula Scream, dir. Bob Kelljan (United States, 1973).
Shaft, dir. Gordon Parks (United States, 1971).
Sheba, Baby, dir. William Girdler (United States, 1975).
Silent Death, dir. Vaughn Christion (United States, 1983).
Silver Bullet, dir. Dan Attias (United States, 1985).
Son of Frankenstein, dir. Rowland V. Lee (United States, 1939).
The Sorrows of Satan, dir. D. W. Griffith (United States, 1926).
Spell, dir. Mark Tonderai (United States, 2020).
Star Wars, dir. George Lucas (United States, 1977).
The Stepford Wives, dir. Bryan Forbes (United States, 1975).
Sugar Hill, dir. Paul Maslansky (United States, 1974).
Super Fly, dir. Gordon Parks Jr (United States, 1972).
*Sweet Sweetback's Baadasssss Son*g, dir. Melvin Van Peebles (United States, 1971).
Sweetheart, dir. J. D. Dillard (United States, 2019).
Tales from the Hood, dir. Rusty Cundieff (United States, 1995).
Tales from the Hood 2, dir. Rusty Cundieff and Darin Scot (United States, 2018).
Tales from the Hood 3, dir. Rusty Cundieff and Darin Scot (United States, 2020).
Tales from the QuadeaD Zone, dir. Chester Novell Turner (United States, 1987).
Taxi Driver, dir. Martin Scorsese (United States, 1976).
Teen Wolf, dir. Rod Daniel (United States, 1985).
The Thing with Two Heads, dir. Lee Frost (United States, 1972).

Transfiguration, dir. Michael O'Shea (United States, 2016).
Underworld, dir. Len Wiseman (United States, 2003).
Us, dir. Jordan Peele (United States, 2019).
Vamp, dir. Richard Wenk (United States, 1986).
A Vampire in Brooklyn, dir. Wes Craven (United States, 1995).
Vampires vs. The Bronx, dir. Oz Rodriguez (United States, 2020).
Vampiyaz, dir. John Bacchus (United States, 2004).
Van Helsing, dir. Stephen Sommers (United States, 2004).
Victor Frankenstein, dir. Paul McGuigan (United Kingdom, Canada, United States, 2015).
Voodoo Dawn, dir. Steven Fierberg (United States, 1990).
Welcome Home Brother Charles, dir. Jamaa Fanaka (United States, 1975).
Werewolf of London, dir. Stuart Walker (United States, 1935).
White Zombie, dir. Victor Halperin (United States, 1932).
Wolf, dir. Mike Nichols (United States, 1994).
The Wolf Man, dir. George Waggner (United States, 1941).
The Wolfman, dir. Joe Johnston, (United States, 2010).
Zombie Island Massacre, dir. John Carter (United States, 1984).
Zombies on Broadway, dir. Gordon Douglas (United States, 1945).
Zombiez, dir. John Bacchus (United States, 2005).

Index

A
Abby (1974) 5, 126, 137–44
the abject 24
   see also Kristeva, Julia
adaptation 6, 7, 12
Afro 84, 132, 153
   see also hairstyles
The Alchemist Cookbook (2016) 168
alchemy 23–4, 26
the AME Church (African Methodist Episcopal Church) 142, 143
   see also religion
anal eroticism and anality 23–5, 30
appropriation 7, 8, 12
aristocracy and aristocrats 18, 33–4
   see also class

B
Bacchus, John 169
Bakhtin, Mikhail 16, 138
   see also carnivalesque
Bassett, Angela 167
The Beast Must Die (1974) 5, 10, 11, 116–23, 169

Bedazzled (1967) 126
Benshoff, Harry M. 5, 7, 9, 43, 137
The Birth of a Nation (1915) 89
Black as Night (2021) 168
Black Devil Doll from Hell (1984) 166, 168
the Black Gothic 8–11
   see also the Gothic
Black nationalism and nationalists 50, 57, 82, 156
Black Panther (2018) 11
The Black Panthers 35, 36, 44, 47, 120–1
Black Power 3, 12, 17, 34–6, 42, 58, 87, 103, 120, 143, 144
Black theology 58, 59, 60, 143, 144
   see also religion
Blackenstein (1973) 5, 11, 12, 55, 68, 82–9, 106, 171
Blackness and blackness 2, 5, 8, 10, 11, 93, 97, 98, 111–15
   see also whiteness
Blacula (1972) 4, 5, 7, 10, 11, 15, 16, 17, 34–50, 55, 56, 61, 168

Blade (film franchise) 168
    Blade (1998) 167
    Blade II (2002) 167
    Blade: Trinity (2004) 167
Blaxploitation 1–3
Blaxploitation horror films 3–13
Bloodz vs. Wolvez (2006) 169
Bogle, Donald 2, 3
Bond III, James 167
Bones (2001) 167–8
Born on the Fourth of July (memoir) 84
The Bride of Frankenstein (1935) 73, 77, 89, 171
Bryant, Anita 49

C

Caleb Williams (novel) 64
camp 38, 39, 47
Candyman (1992) 167, 168
Candyman: Day of the Dead (1999) 167
Candyman: Farewell to the Flesh (1995) 167
cannibalism 84, 87, 88, 117, 126
capital crime and punishment 72, 77, 79, 122
Carmichael, Stokely 82, 121
Carmilla (novella) 16, 17, 20–2, 26, 31, 61
carnivalesque 138
    see also Bakhtin, Mikhail
the Catholic Church and Catholicism 134, 137, 143, 144
    see also religion
Change of Mind (1969) 170–1
Chesnutt, Charles Waddell 115
Christianity and Christians 56, 57, 58, 60, 61, 129, 135, 137, 138, 143, 149, 157
    see also religion

civil rights movement 1, 12, 17, 43, 50, 82, 87, 165
Clark, Kenneth B. 110
    Dark Ghetto 102, 111
class 18, 26, 33, 82, 97, 98, 104
    see also aristocracy and aristocrats
Cleage, Albert 58
Coalition Against Blaxploitation 2
COINTELPRO (Counterintelligence Program) 121
collage 12, 64, 65, 66, 67, 68, 69, 71, 73, 74, 75, 83, 89, 169–70
Cone, James 58, 143
Conrad, Joseph 169
conk 153
    see also hairstyles
Corrigan, Timothy 7
Cotton Comes to Harlem (1970) 1, 2
Crain, William 4, 5
Cryptz (2002) 168
Cundieff, Rusty 167
The Curse of Frankenstein (1957) 68, 73–6, 89
The Curse of the Werewolf (1961) 120

D

Da Sweet Blood of Jesus (2014) 168
Damn Yankees (1958) 126
Deathly Realities (1985) 166
Def by Temptation (1990) 167, 168
degeneration 32–3, 71, 93, 106
Deleuze, Gilles 92, 94
    see also multiplicity
Derrida, Jacques 92
The Devil (1908) 126
'The Devil and Daniel Webster' (story) 159
The Devil Rides Out (1968) 126
The Devil's Daughter (1939) 126

Dog Day Afternoon (1975) 3
doppelgänger 12, 59, 65, 81, 86, 98, 108, 114, 128, 131, 146–9, 153, 155, 159–60, 171–2
    see also the uncanny
Dr. Black, Mr. Hyde (1976) 4, 5, 11, 12, 55, 92, 100–16, 122, 123, 171, 172
Dr. Jekyll and Mr. Hyde (1920) 96–100
Dr. Jekyll and Mr. Hyde (1931) 96–100
Dr. Jekyll and Mr. Hyde (1941) 96, 98–100
Dr. Jekyll and Mr. Hyde (play) 96, 97
Dracula (1931) 17, 27, 33–4
Dracula (novel) 15, 16, 17, 22–6, 27, 28, 29, 30, 32, 37, 55, 61, 67
Dracula (play) 27
duality 92, 103, 116, 137
    see also multiplicity

E

Elijah Muhammad 57
the evil spirit 12, 125, 149, 163, 168
    see also monsters and monstrosity
exorcism 139, 140, 141, 142, 143, 144, 158
The Exorcist (1973) 126, 137, 141
The Exorcist (novel) 126
experimentation and experiments 73, 77, 81, 88, 91, 94, 100, 105, 107, 108, 110, 114

F

Fallen (1998) 167, 168
Faust (1926) 126
Faust (play) 64
Frankenstein (1931) 68–73, 79, 83, 84, 86, 88
Frankenstein (novel) 63–8, 69, 70, 72, 73, 74, 81, 84, 88, 89, 170, 171
Frankenstein (play) 69, 83
Frankenstein's Creature 8, 12, 125, 169, 170, 171
    see also monsters and monstrosity
Freud, Sigmund 21, 24, 25, 114, 127, 139, 155
    'Character and Anal Erotism' 23
    'The Uncanny' 86
    see also the Oedipus Complex; the uncanny
Friday the 13th (1980) 166
Furman v. Georgia 77, 79

G

Galton, Francis 33
Ganja & Hess (1973) 4, 5, 10, 17, 49, 56–61, 168
Gates, Henry Louis
    The Signifying Monkey 7–8
    see also signifying
gay rights movement 3, 12, 17, 34–6, 47, 48
Genette, Gérard 16
    see also intertextuality
Get Out (2017) 170, 171
The Ghost Breakers (1940) 126
The Ghost of Frankenstein (1942) 171
Girard, René 19
    see also triangular relationships
the Gothic 6–7, 12, 92, 137, 162, 169
    see also the Black Gothic
Gothic fiction 18, 29, 38, 71, 125, 127, 154
Gothic framing 15, 27, 28, 38, 57, 65, 70
the Gothic veil 154
    see also Sedgwick, Eve Kosofsky

Grier, Pam 168
Griffin, Junius 1
Grosz, Karoly 71
Guattari, Félix 94
  see also multiplicity
Guerrero, Ed 165
Gunn, Bill 4, 5, 10, 57, 58, 167

H
hairstyles 84, 132, 153
  see also Afro; conk
Halloween (1978) 166
Hammer Film Productions 8
A Haunted House (2013) 168
The Haunted Mansion (2003) 167
Heller, Jean 80
Hidden Figures (2016) 11
homoeroticism 19, 31, 43, 51, 52, 59
homophobia 18, 36, 42, 43
homosexual panic 29
  see also Sedgwick, Eve Kosofsky
homosexuality 18, 29, 31, 33, 35, 36, 42, 43, 49, 51, 52, 59
  see also queerness
homosexuals 23, 35, 36, 48, 49
Hood of Horror (2006) 169
Hood of the Living Dead (2005) 169
Horror of Dracula (1958) 17, 27, 28, 31–2
The House Next Door: Meet the Blacks 2 (2021) 168
The House on Skull Mountain (1974) 5, 126, 133–7, 163
The Hues Corporation 46
Hurston, Zora Neale 159
Hutcheon, Linda 6
Hutchings, Peter 11
hybrids and hybridity 12, 93, 103, 115–16, 122, 134, 168, 170

I
I Am Legend (2007) 167
integration 65, 74, 82, 83, 86–7, 89, 105, 171
intertextuality 6, 16–17, 70, 83
  see also Genette, Gérard; Kristeva, Julia
I Walked with a Zombie (1943) 126

J
Jaws (1975) 165
J.D.'s Revenge (1976) 5, 126, 150–8, 163, 167
Jekyll/Hyde 12, 91, 92, 99, 104, 110, 114, 116, 122, 125, 169, 171
  see also monsters and monstrosity
Jones, Grace 166
justice 12, 41, 66–8, 70, 72, 73, 76, 79, 87, 129, 130, 156, 158, 169, 170, 171

K
Karloff, Boris 84, 86
Kelly-Jordan Enterprises 4
King, Martin Luther, Jr 126
King Kong 106
King Kong (1932) 132
King of the Zombies (1941) 126
Kligman, Albert 80
Koven, Mikel J. 3
Kristeva, Julia 16, 17, 24
  see also the abject; intertextuality

L
LA Rebellion 4
Laemmle, Carl 69, 70
Laemmle, Carl, Jr 70, 86

LAPD (Los Angeles Police Department) 37, 50, 55, 77, 79, 100, 102, 105, 106
see also police and policing
The Last Man on Earth (1964) 167
Lawrence, Novotny 1, 165
Le Manoir du Diable (1896) 126
Leaves from Satan's Book (1920) 126
Lee, Spike 167, 168
Lee, Wilbert 79
Lombroso, Cesare 32, 33
Lord Shango (1975) 5, 126, 144–50, 163

M

The Magic Island (travelogue) 125, 126, 132
Malcolm X 35
'The Mark of the Beast' (story) 97
Marshall, William 37–8, 42
masochism 43, 155
see also sadism
Mean Streets (1973) 3
Means Coleman, Robin R.
Horror Noire (2011) 5, 165–6
Moby-Dick (novel) 114
The Monk (novel) 125
monsters and monstrosity 9, 10, 12, 27, 43, 56, 64, 65, 67, 70–1, 75, 79, 81, 84, 88, 89, 112, 123, 137, 160, 168, 169
see also the evil spirit; Frankenstein's Creature; Jekyll/Hyde; the vampire; the werewolf; the zombie
Morrison, Toni 172
the Moynihan Report 102, 156, 157
see also *The Negro Family*

multiplicity 12, 92–3, 94, 96, 97, 103, 115, 116, 120, 122, 171
see also Deleuze, Gilles; duality; Guattari, Félix
The Murder Act 72, 79
Murphy, Eddie 167

N

The Nation of Islam 57
NAACP (The National Association for the Advancement of Colored People) 1, 2, 110
The Negro Family (report) 102, 108, 156
see also the Moynihan Report
Newton, Huey 36
Night of the Living Dead (1968) 89, 126
A Nightmare on Elm Street (1984) 166
Nordau, Max 32, 33
Nosferatu (1922) 17, 27–8, 28–31, 45, 61

O

Obeah (1987) 166
the Oedipus Complex 108, 109, 110, 139–40, 162
see also Freud, Sigmund
The Omega Man (1971) 167
oral eroticism and orality 25, 30
Ouanga (1936) 126

P

Paradise Lost (poem) 64, 70, 74
patriarchs and patriarchy 21, 57, 70, 72 73, 98, 99, 107, 110, 133, 137, 140, 141, 160
Peele, Jordan 167, 170, 171
Petey Wheatstraw (1977) 4, 126, 158–63, 165

pimps 54–5, 56, 60, 100, 105, 112, 157
Pitts, Freddie 79
Plutarch's Lives (biography) 64
police and policing 3, 6, 35, 36, 37, 47, 48, 50, 68, 77, 79, 80, 81, 89, 91, 92, 95, 96, 98, 99, 100, 102, 103, 105, 106, 120, 128, 129, 157, 169, 171, 172
see also LAPD
possession 12, 41, 126–7, 134, 135, 138, 142, 149, 151, 153, 154, 155, 156, 168, 170
The Private Memoirs and Confessions of a Justified Sinner (novel) 125
prostitutes and prostitution 55, 100, 104, 105, 108, 109–10, 116

Q

queerness 12, 17, 18–19, 20, 21, 23, 24, 26, 27, 28–9, 30, 31, 32, 33, 34, 38, 39, 41–3, 46, 47–8, 49, 51, 54, 56, 59, 61, 138
see also homosexuality

R

race 9–10, 12, 39, 41, 48, 59, 68, 79, 81, 88, 93, 97, 115, 118, 122, 143, 168
race relations 82, 117, 123
racism 3, 36, 48, 81, 82, 100, 111, 156, 167, 170
religion 3, 11, 13, 56, 57, 61, 127, 129, 130, 137, 138, 140, 142, 143, 144, 148, 149, 163
see also the AME Church; Black theology; the Catholic Church and Catholicism; Christianity; syncretism; Vodou; the Yoruba religion

Report of the National Advisory Commission on Civil Disorders 102
repression 8, 17, 19, 26, 30, 32, 95, 110, 114, 137, 154, 155, 172
the return of the repressed 8, 9, 43, 93, 129, 140, 156, 168
Revolt of the Zombies (1936) 126
Rhines, Jesse Algeron 172
The Rime of the Ancient Mariner (poem) 64
Rocky (1976) 3
Roquemore, Cliff 4–5
Rosemary's Baby (1968) 126, 170
Rosemary's Baby (novel) 125
RuPaul's Trilogy of Terror (1984) 166

S

sadism 24, 43, 71
see also masochism
Sanders, Julie 7
Satanas (1920) 126
Saturday Night Fever (1977) 165
Scary Movie (2000) 169
Schneider, Steven Jay 5, 10, 11
Scot, Darin 167
Scream Blacula Scream (1973) 5, 11, 17, 36, 48, 49, 50–6, 168
Sedgwick, Eve Kosofsky 18, 19, 29, 154
see also the Gothic veil; homosexual panic; triangular relationships
segregation 82, 86, 97, 142
Shaft (1971) 1, 2
signifying 7–8
see also Gates, Henry Louis, *The Signifying Monkey*

Silent Death (1983) 166
slaves and slavery 25, 36, 37, 38, 41, 55, 58, 97, 113–14, 125, 127, 130, 131, 142, 143
Smith, Will 167
Snipes, Wesley 167
Snoop Dogg 167
Son of Frankenstein (1939) 171
The Sorrows of Satan (1926) 126
The Sorrows of Young Werther (novel) 64
Star Wars (1977) 165
The Stepford Wives (1975) 170
Strange Case of Dr Jekyll and Mr Hyde (novella) 5, 67, 91–6, 97, 103, 104, 105, 106, 112, 115, 122, 172
subjectivity 9, 92, 93, 122, 171
Sugar Hill (1974) 5, 126, 128–33, 163
Super Fly (1972) 1, 2
Sweet Sweetback's Baadasssss Song (1971) 1, 2
syncretism 129, 130, 134, 136, 144
see also religion

T

Tales from the Hood (1995) 167, 168, 169
Tales from the Hood 2 (2018) 167
Tales from the Hood 3 (2020) 167
Tales from the QuadeaD Zone (1987) 166
Taxi Driver (1976) 3
Taylor, Deon 168
'There Shall Be No Darkness' (story)
The Thing with Two Heads (1972) 5, 10, 12, 68, 76–82, 89, 170, 171
Transfiguration (2016) 168

triangular relationships 19, 29–32, 52, 54, 61
see also Girard, René; Sedgwick, Eve Kosofsky
tricksters 137, 159, 162
Tunbridge Walks (play) 18
The Tuskegee Syphilis Study 80, 81, 100, 107–8

U

the uncanny 12, 81, 86, 88, 114, 127, 128–9, 133–4, 136, 137–9, 146, 153–4, 159, 162, 163
see also doppelgänger; Freud, Sigmund
Underworld (2003) 169
Universal Pictures 8, 69
Us (2019) 171–2

V

Vamp (1986) 166–7
the vampire 12, 16, 18, 22, 32, 125, 168
see also monsters and monstrosity
A Vampire in Brooklyn (1995) 167, 168
Vampires vs. The Bronx (2020) 168
Vampiyaz (2004) 169
The Vampyre (novella) 16, 17–19, 20, 22, 26, 29
Van Sloan, Edward 68, 69, 70, 74
Vathek (novel) 125
Vietnam veterans 83, 84, 86, 87, 89
the Vietnam War 80, 83, 84, 86, 87
Vodou 127, 128, 132, 166
see also religion
voodoo 50, 51, 55, 128, 129, 130, 132, 133, 134, 135, 136
Voodoo Dawn (1990) 169

W

Washington, Denzel 167
Watts 2, 100, 102, 104, 105, 106, 113, 114
the Watts Health Center 104
the Watts riots 100, 102, 106
the Watts Towers 100, 103, 106
Wester, Maisha 9–10, 11
the werewolf 169
   see also monsters and monstrosity
Werewolf of London (1935) 120
White Zombie (1932) 126
whiteface 113, 114, 166
whiteness 9, 41, 93, 97, 106, 110–15
   see also Blackness and blackness

The Wolf Man (1941) 120
Wood, Robin 8

Y

Yoruba religion 137, 138, 140, 142, 143, 144, 148, 149, 150
   see also religion

Z

Zofloya (novel) 125
Zombie Island Massacre (1984) 166
the zombie 13, 88, 126–7, 128, 130, 131, 136, 169
   see also monsters and monstrosity
Zombies on Broadway (1945) 126
Zombiez (2005) 169

also in series

Lindsey Decker, *Transnationalism and Genre Hybridity in New British Horror Cinema* (2021)

Stacey Abbott and Lorna Jowett (eds), *Global TV Horror* (2021)

Michael J. Blouin, *Stephen King and American Politics* (2021)

Eddie Falvey, Joe Hickinbottom and Jonathan Wroot (eds), *New Blood: Critical Approaches to Contemporary Horror* (2020)

Darren Elliott-Smith and John Edgar Browning (eds), *New Queer Horror Film and Television* (2020)

Jonathan Newell, *A Century of Weird Fiction, 1832–1937* (2020)

Alexandra Heller-Nicholas, *Masks in Horror Cinema: Eyes Without Faces* (2019)

Eleanor Beal and Jonathan Greenaway (eds), *Horror and Religion: New literary approaches to Theology, Race and Sexuality* (2019)

Dawn Stobbart, *Videogames and Horror: From Amnesia to Zombies, Run!* (2019)

David Annwn Jones, *Re-envisaging the First Age of Cinematic Horror, 1896–1934: Quanta of Fear* (2018)